# THE

# Milkman's

# SON

*A Memoir of Family History.*
*A DNA Mystery. A Story of Paternal Love.*

RANDY LINDSAY

SHADOW
MOUNTAIN

To learn more about this book
and to see photos of Randy and his family,
visit MilkmansSonBook.com

Library of Congress Cataloging-in-Publication Data

Names: Lindsay, Randy, 1959– author.
Title: The milkman's son : a memoir of family history, a DNA mystery, and paternal love / Randy
    Lindsay.
Description: Salt Lake City : Shadow Mountain, [2020] | Summary: "This memoir traces one
    man's journey through his family history when a DNA test reveals that his dad was not his
    biological father"— Provided by publisher.
Identifiers: LCCN 2019044950 | ISBN 9781629727387 (hardback)
Subjects: LCSH: Lindsay, Randy, 1959—Family. | Fathers and sons—Biography. | DNA finger-
    printing—Popular works. | Birthfathers—Biography. | LCGFT: Autobiographies.
Classification: LCC HQ755.85 L564 2020 | DDC 306.874/2—dc23
LC record available at https://lccn.loc.gov/2019044950

Printed in the United States of America
Publishers Printing, Salt Lake City, UT
10    9    8    7    6    5    4    3    2    1

# CONTENTS

# AUTHOR'S NOTE

It turns out that if you tell people your dad is not your biological father, you've officially invited them to play twenty questions. Although the order in which they're asked varies from person to person, the first few questions are always the same

"How did you find out?"

"Have you met your real/biological father?"

"How did your siblings react to the news?"

And . . .

"What did your mom say when you found out you have a different father?"

My mother did a wonderful job of raising me. I had an intimate relationship with Misfortune, and Mom remained calm during my frequent childhood trips to the hospital. Like the time one of the neighbor kids pushed my face into the mud, and my eyes were so covered with dirt I couldn't find my way home. Mom followed my cries until she found me, and nearly started crying herself when she discovered why I hadn't come to her when she called. Then she drove me to the hospital. Despite my mother's urgings to break off my relationship with the God of Incidents and Accidents, he and I had regular dates until I was well into my twenties.

Mom tolerated my emotional teens and all the minutia-induced drama that comes with that stage of life. No matter how far down the ladder of self-doubt I traveled, she shone a spotlight on my positive traits and convinced me that I mattered as a person.

I was one of the original nerds—back before being nerdy was popular—a weird kid who liked Godzilla, dinosaurs, and space aliens. To my mother, however, I was a creative kid, one who was unafraid of exploring new frontiers where the rest of the family dared not venture.

If a life-sized poster of unconditional love exists in the halls of human achievement, then it has my mom's picture at the center—short, smiling, and beautiful.

But this isn't a story about my mother.

This is a story about me and my two dads. I share this portion of my life with the world because it is a tale that will become more common as technology continues to improve. All anyone needs to know about my mother is that she loves me and I love her.

# CHAPTER 1

# GHOSTS OF FAMILY PAST

The dastardly thing about a life-changing event is that it can disguise itself as a normal day. Months, or even years, later you discover that what looked and felt like an ordinary Monday was the first step on the road to what-happened-to-my-normal-life?

At the far-from-youthful age of fifty-seven, I found out that my dad, the man who had been a vital part of my life since the moment I arrived in the world, was not my father. Most people I tell about my situation find it . . . surprising. While to others the event is an amusing anecdote, for me it represents the sudden destruction of my sheltering concept of family.

—— ——

I load the four youngest children into my minivan. It isn't even 10:00 a.m., but the temperature is over a hundred. The inside of the van feels like an oven, but my kids are troopers and don't complain when the air conditioning fails to reach the back seats. Only my oldest daughter, riding in the front seat, endures the drive with any sense of comfort.

The trip to the far side of Phoenix to visit my dad takes almost two hours—most of it freeway. I bring the children with me because Dad loves to see them. They don't have a chance to see one another very often.

I turn down the dirt road that leads to his trailer home in the desert. Even though the windows are up, I can smell the dust. Gravel and stone crunch under the tires as I pull into my dad's personal five-acre slice of desert. In addition to the mobile home, his mini cowboy kingdom has a barn, a horse in a pen, and a roping corral complete with a donkey to rope. The familiar stockyard smell of my youth sneaks past the closed windows.

As soon as the van stops, the kids bail out of the vehicle. I yell to them to watch for rattlesnakes, but they're too busy petting my dad's horse to pay attention to me. These are suburbanite kids—members of the YouTube generation—who know nothing about rattlers. Or lizards. Or scorpions, for that matter. When I was their age, I scoured the sand and scrub for snakes and lizards. I knew the difference between the harmless and the poisonous varieties of wildlife living among the desert shrubs and usually had the sense to stay away from the dangerous ones.

The plywood floor of the back porch sags dangerously as I walk across it, making me wonder whether my next step is going to smash a hole through the ancient building material. Various bits of tack and harness hang from the walls of the enclosed patio. Cardboard boxes clutter the dusty floor. I slide open the glass door to Dad's trailer and shout, "We're here!"

Dad struggles to push himself out of his easy chair and then hobbles over to give me a hug. With his Tom Selleck mustache, a tan cap advertising the local grain-and-feed store, and his long-sleeved western shirt, he looks every bit the cowboy. "Good to see you, son. Where are the kids? I made sure we stocked up on Popsicles."

Popsicles. Dad feeds them to the kids until they can't eat any more. I tried a couple of times in the past to stop them after eating two, but Dad just points out he's my father, this is his house, and the grandchildren can have as many Popsicles as they want.

My dad mentions Popsicles, and the children, as if guided by some mystic sugar radar, file in through the back door. Within minutes the kids are lounging around the living room with rainbow-colored lips.

Dad and I visit for a few minutes before his attention is drawn away from me and to the television like the Millennium Falcon was dragged aboard the Death Star. My dad is riveted to the bright colors and loud screeching sounds of *SpongeBob SquarePants*. Not that it makes a difference. Our conversations follow the same pattern every time we meet.

"What's new, Dad?"

"Same as always. Nothing ever changes around here."

And for the most part, that's true. His life consists of reading Louis L'Amour books, watching the national rodeo finals on television, and driving down to the local steer-roping event to compete with men half his age. He has his second wife, a dog, and the livestock to keep him company. On Thanksgiving and Christmas, he drives to one of his children's homes for the holiday and is the first to leave because he needs to get back home and feed the livestock.

My siblings and I tease him that he loves his animals more than his own children. There's a strange sense of comfort in the ritual. That's the way Dad has always been, and if he acted any different, we'd worry something was wrong.

But Dad doesn't return to watching cartoons with the children. Instead, he turns and stares at me with his good eye. The blue one. The green one watches me too, but it hasn't worked properly since he almost lost it in a BB gun fight as a kid. Dad tilts his head to favor his undamaged eye. He rubs his hands together. I can tell he has something to say and is working it out in his mind before he opens his mouth.

"I've been having dreams," he tells me.

A chill creeps along my arms and down my back. Dad tells stories about his youth in Long Beach or his time in the marines, but he doesn't talk about his dreams. Why would he? They aren't part of his regular world. He deals only in reality.

Dad's as tough and stable as they come. I can't imagine any dream has the power or imagery to bother him, but obviously, this one has.

"I see ghosts," he says.

Now I'm worried. Ghosts, like dreams, are not a part of my dad's world. A spooky tale for him involves the billing department of the divorce lawyer he used when he and Mom split. He might even go as far as describing the interactions with his doctor as nightmarish, but his mind places anything from the realm of the supernatural into the category of children's fiction.

"Most every night when I go to sleep," Dad continues, "I close my eyes and see all these faces in my mind. I don't know any of them, but some of them look alike. They resemble my dead relatives."

The theme music from *The Twilight Zone* plays in my head. For a moment, I feel as if I am standing outside of time, wondering what I should make of Dad's ghost story. I know he isn't insane or losing his mind. The Lindsays may not always make the best decisions, but there's no history of dementia or mental illness. And I don't place much stock in stories by average people who claim to have had revelatory visions.

My natural sense of disbelief for ghost stories wavers, though, when it comes to encounters with family members who have passed on. That is something my dad could possibly experience.

"What do they say to you?" I ask.

"None of them speak." Dad pauses and rolls a cigarette. His hands shake, and I can't tell if that's from his age or because of his dreams. "They float above me and look down."

He lights the cigarette, draws a couple of puffs, and then continues. "I keep having the same dream. The faces of my ancestors look down at me while I sleep. When I wake up, I know they want me to do their family history."

I lean back and rub my face. Despite my reluctance to believe in ghosts or dream visions, my dad's telling of the dream sounds reasonable. At least the motivation behind this sort of encounter with the supernatural makes sense. If the spirits of dead family members had the ability to contact the living, they might want to have their genealogical work done.

Then again, it might be nothing more than my dad's subconscious compelling him to put together a lovely, filled-out family tree. Print it. Frame it. Place it on the wall.

Either way, the conversation leaves me feeling off-balance. Why can't he stick to talking about who's in the bull-riding finals this year? My gut instinct tells me to change the subject, but instead, I ask him if he plans to start researching the family history.

"Nah." Dad shakes his head and then flicks his ashes into a porcelain bowl one of the grandchildren made for him during art class. "I'm going to have you do it."

# CHAPTER 2

# WHERE'S WILLIAM?

Dad and my stepmom have a "computer" in the house . . . at least that's what they call it. My new smartphone has more computing power than the antique box of electronics gathering dust in my stepmom's office. Not that it matters. Dad has never operated a computer; and with so much of the current genealogy work being done online, he'd be lost as to how to find the ancestors visiting him in his dreams. But he knows I can do it.

As the oldest child, it feels like my responsibility to help my dad do what he is unable to do himself. I can bring our family together—the living and the dead occupying the same glorious pedigree chart! A thrill passes through me at the prospect of tracking down family members. I'll be like a high-tech Indiana Jones, exploring the dusty catacombs of data storage for the names of unknown ancestors from distant lands. The excitement is only slightly tinged by a dread sense of having agreed to a Herculean task better suited to a team of historians or research specialists.

"Here you go," says Dad. As if that's all he needs to tell me. He officially passes me the torch with only those three words. The man can spend hours telling the most amazing stories . . . when he's in the mood. But when it comes to giving instructions, he tends to stay on the sparse end of the conversational scale.

Dad hands me the few documents he gathered years ago, during his own attempt at family research. The information fits into a nearly pristine manila folder and contains copies of birth and death certificates for Dad's parents and grandparents, a couple of baptism certificates, his parents' marriage license, and an affidavit attesting to the birth of my great-grandfather as given by his older sister, along with a few other documents. These documents represent my only link to family members long-since dead. The contents of the folder are likely to be the only help I can expect in my search.

At least Dad doesn't expect me to conduct the research here. On my stepmother's electronic antique. I can take the files with me and work from home.

Later, I herd the kids outside and load them into the van. Dad waves goodbye from inside the back porch, then turns around and carefully ambles inside. A couple of questions burn in my mind. Who are the Lindsays? And why do they want their genealogy done so badly that they would visit Dad in a dream-haunting?

━ ━

It takes the better part of a week to open an Ancestory.com account, search the internet for the right family history software to record my findings, and prepare my mind to dive into the work. Dad has already provided me the names, dates, and places for my grandparents' and great-grandparents' births, marriages, and deaths. The dates on the documents are years old and had to have been assembled the old-fashioned way—by writing letters and visiting courthouses in person.

But this is 2005. Tons of data is available online. I can search the internet from the comfort of home, never leaving my chair or abandoning the cool beverage strategically positioned within easy reach. And thanks to Dad, I have a pair of names for family members four generations before me. My great-great-grandparents: John Crawford Lindsay and Minerva Leedom.

Crawford?

Crawford strikes me as an unusual middle name. I like it, though. The name has character. Immediately, there's a connection between me and John Crawford Lindsay. I want to find out more about him. Then I pause and wonder if he, wherever he is, knows about me. I imagine him gazing down from the heavens, urging me to work faster.

The great Lindsay mystery lies before me, waiting to be unraveled. Each name is a piece of a grand jigsaw puzzle. Every family has its own unique shape that makes it stand out against all the other Lindsay, Williams, and Jones families in the Missouri/Arkansas area. A picture starts to form, becoming clearer with each name that is added to the family record. My parents, grandparents, and great-grandparents form only a small section of that family portrait, but it is beautiful.

I fill in the family tree with the more detailed information my dad collected. Then I type in my great-great-grandfather's name on Ancestry.com and hit the search function. Let the treasure hunt begin.

There are no entries for John Crawford Lindsay.

I look through the documents again to make sure my information is correct. The birth certificate for my great-grandfather lists his father as J. C. Lindsey. With an *e* . . . not an *a* like my family spells it. After another pass through the documents, I find that the marriage license for my great-grandfather displays his last name as Lindsey. Both of these records scream of a clerical error.

At least I hope it's only a misspelling.

My family believes the *a* in our name means we come from Scotland; an *e* would make us English. While there's nothing wrong with England, my family embraces a Scottish ancestry. My brother wears a tie made with the Lindsay tartan pattern. He gave "Lindsay with an *a*" ties to Dad and me for Christmas one year. The collective family mind firmly believes we hail from the land of fighting clans and kilted pipers.

Finally, I find that one of the documents in the folder is a petition to have my great-grandfather's name changed because of a mistake in recording the original birth certificate. It lists my great-grandfather as a Lindsay—with an *a*—and identifies his father as John Crawford Lindsay.

I breathe a sigh of relief. My Scottish tartan tie is safe. I can continue to listen to my favorite pipe-and-drum CD with the same sense of national pride as always. But the number of records I have to consider in my electronic search has now more than doubled. Because of a clerical error—or even outright carelessness—the John Crawford Lindsay that is my great-great-grandfather could be listed as John C. Lindsey, or John Lynsey, or any similar-sounding variation of the name.

This is turning out to be a bigger challenge than I originally thought; but rather than discourage me, the added difficulty makes it even more of an adventure.

The task feels like an electronic version of hacking my way through the jungle with a machete as I search for the lost crypts of my family. Sure, I'll get there . . . eventually, but the process is exhausting. At least there aren't any tarantulas or vipers lurking in the dense foliage, waiting to ambush me.

Ancestry.com allows me to filter my searches. I approximate John's age in 1870 based on his son's birth and death dates and look for results limited to Ohio, where his son—my great-grandfather—was born. That returns eighteen matches in the 1870 census. Only one of them lives in Portsmouth, the same town I believe my great-grandfather was born in. This has to be it!

I rub my hands together and then crack my knuckles. A double click on the result opens the census entry. There they are. John C. Lindsey and his wife, Minerva, were living in Portsmouth with their two-year-old daughter in 1870. My pulse quickens as a rush of adrenaline pumps through my body. I shout, "Yes!"

Oops. My wife is sleeping in the next room. I wait to see if she comes out to investigate the noise. Then, when the wrath of Hon fails to appear, I pump my fist in the air and whisper another, "Yes!"

Who would've thought family history could be so exciting? It's supposed to be a hobby for grandparents who want to sit around their mothball-smelling homes and show old, black-and-white pictures to anyone trapped by their elderly wiles. Instead, my mind is already racing to uncover the next family mystery.

The next step is to search further back and find John's parents. But first I realize that John would have been a young man during Civil War times, and I wonder if he fought in that horrible conflict. Since he lived in Ohio, he most likely would've joined the Union army. Curiosity pulls my mind in that direction, but I decide to save that search for later. I need to find his parents first.

The census results are like footprints in time. With them I can track my family in reverse, discovering where they went and what they did. Each step along the way gives me clues as to where to look next. I'm hoping they take me back to a time when John lived with his parents. If they do, I will have found the next older generation in our family tree.

I check the 1860 census, but I can't find John in Portsmouth for that census year. In fact, the census doesn't show Lindsays of any kind in Portsmouth. No Lindsays with an *a*, or an *e*, or even Lynseys with a *y*. I expand my search to include all of Ohio and spend hours searching for variant after variant of the name.

My search uncovers nine possible matches. Any of them could be my ancestor. Or none of them. I need more than an approximate birth year to connect one of the results to my John Lindsay.

I check my watch and discover it's two in the morning. Can that be right? Even though my eyes burn from looking at the computer screen all night, it doesn't feel that late. I struggle with the decision of whether I should go to bed or check one more name.

Even though I have the luxury of working from home as a writer, I'm still the primary caretaker for the children. The kids are still going to need me in the morning. My love for them outweighs my passion for the quest. I sigh, sign out of the program, and trudge off to sleep.

Different spellings of my name bounce around inside my head as I lie in bed. They give way to doubts about my method. Have I missed searching for any reasonable variation of my name? Should I not worry about the census results and look through Civil War records to see if I can find him there? Either way, the family history bug has bitten me . . . and I love it.

The alarm clock goes off, and I roll out of bed. My eyes burn, and I stumble through the morning routine. Cold cereal for breakfast. Money for the older children so I don't have to make lunches. I hug the kids heading off for school and mumble something that resembles "I love you." Then I turn on the television to occupy the two still at home.

Teletubbies! I hate them. But not as much as I hate that goofy purple dinosaur they like to watch. Sometimes it comes down to the lesser of two evils, and today the weird fluffy things with televisions in their bellies win the battle of who annoys me the least.

I pass by the computer on my way back to the kitchen. The great Lindsay mystery taunts me like a half-watched movie where I think I know who killed the no-good, cheating husband but I want to see it play out. I have to know where my Lindsays came from, and the only way to find that out is to locate John's parents.

My two youngest children laugh at the Teletubbies' antics. I decide they'll be fine if I spend an hour on the computer. The search might keep me from thinking about how tired I am, and if I focus hard enough, I can tune out the morning lineup of mind-numbing children's programming.

It seems as if the further back I go, the less information census results provide. I switch directions and look through more recent census records.

The strategy works. A John C. Lindsay appears in the 1880 census, along with his wife, his daughter, and a son with the same name and approximate age as my great-grandfather. The family is in Portsmouth.

13

Better yet, the 1880 census lists where each person's parents were born, and John's folks are both listed as having been born in Ohio.

Burning eyes, lack of sleep, and ear-grating educational shows for children are all forgotten as I plunge forward with the search. The 1890 census was almost entirely destroyed by a fire at the Commerce Center in Washington, DC, so I search the 1900 census records. John's there! At least I think it's him. The month and year he was born are listed. But this entry states that his father was from Ireland—not Ohio, as was entered in the 1880 census.

From what I've learned, I determine that John died in 1906, so there will be no record in the 1910 census listing his father's place of birth. I'm guessing—and hoping—that it's Ohio and the Irish listing was just a mistake. That leaves more room for Scottish heritage. But there is no way to find out without returning to earlier censuses for clues about his father.

I start with the 1850 census and attempt to track any viable matches down through the rest of the records. I eliminate one John Lindsay after another based on location and other minor details. By comparing the names of parents and siblings in each family, I finally narrow the choice to just three. If I could just—

"Daddy, I'm hungry."

I jump at the sound of a voice at my side. Lucy, my tiny, blonde, three-year-old daughter, looks up at me, her hair strung out in every direction because I haven't taken the time to brush it this morning. I look at my watch and realize it's well after lunch. No wonder the poor girl is hungry. And so am I, having missed breakfast in this quest-absorbed haze.

But my mind starts to drift back to the computer. Only three more families to track before I discover which of the John Lindsays in the 1850 census belongs to me. Which should only take an hour. Then I can search for the next previous generation . . . who are probably—

"When are we going to eat?" my daughter asks.

"Right now, Pumpkin," I tell her and push away from the computer desk.

I set out a glorious feast of peanut butter and jelly sandwiches with a side of barbecue chips and a glass of milk. My daughter talks about the shows she watched in the morning. My son eats quickly and bolts back to the television. I sit with my daughter, smile, and nod my head, throwing in an occasional "Uh-huh."

Laundry, grocery shopping, and baths occupy my time for the rest of the afternoon. I have a flexible schedule, but that doesn't mean I can spend all day playing ancestral sleuth. It takes a long, anxious week before I can return to the family hunt.

After a quick scan of my research on John Crawford Lindsay, I decide to take another look at the manila folder with the documents Dad gave me. The same record that gave me John's middle name also lists his place of birth: West Union, Ohio.

How did I miss this?

A quick look at Google Maps shows me that West Union is in Adams County. I remember seeing a Lindsay family living there and dismissing them because I assumed the location was incorrect. My fingers tremble as I log in to Ancestry and, for the hundredth time, type in search parameters for John Lindsay, this time with Adams County as a location instead of Scioto County (where Portsmouth is and where I'd been searching based on the location of my great-grandfather's birth).

For more than a very tense hour, I search through 1860 and 1850 census records, squirming in my seat each time I think I've landed on the right family. Worrying that I've missed an important detail, I decide to look at actual census images instead of electronic transcriptions of the indexes, starting with images from the town of Sprigg, in Adams County.

Boom, baby!

The electronic transcription lists the name I'm staring at as Jno

Lendsey, but the entry in the image it refers to looks a lot more like "Jon Lindsay" to me. The age is also correct, based on what I've learned. And Jno—or Jon—is listed as a blacksmith, a detail consistent with later censuses in which he appears. I do a little more searching and find who I believe to be John's parents. Parents who came to the United States from Ireland. And who spell Lindsey with an *e*.

My tartan tie is once again in danger.

John's father turns out to be William Lindsey. After several more days scouring through the marginally helpful pre-1850 census records, I determine that William arrived in Ohio sometime before 1830 and stayed in the township of Sprigg until after the Civil War.

Ohio represented the wild frontier in 1830. Records are scarce, almost nonexistent. There are no birth or death certificates for William. No marriage license. No immigration record. The only pre-1850 records that exist for him and his family are the census results, which are cryptically vague.

The 1830 census tells me that William Lindsey lived in Adams County that year, in a residence that included one male aged 30 to 40, three males under age 5, a female aged 30 to 40, and a female aged 10 to 15. As far as early census records go, this one is fairly easy to decipher. The only male over age 18 has to be William. The female of roughly his age is most likely his wife. The three males under 5 should be his sons. But the female aged 10 to 15 could be a daughter, a sister, a niece, or even a servant.

It's like I'm staring into a big, dark void, yelling, "William, where are you?"

The data trail has gone cold. I scour through the information, hoping to find a clue that will tell me where to look next. No matter how many times I sit in my chair and stare at the census results, no matter how many times I enter a new search parameter, I remain at the end of the trail. My legs bounce with nervous energy as my family history passion urges me to move forward and find the next generation . . . and then the generation after that.

I want names to investigate!

In order to find out where William was born, I have to leave the official records search behind. A few historical books mention predominant settlers to the area, but weeks of searching through every mention of the Lindsay/Lindsey name reveals that he isn't one of Ohio's early celebrities.

My next best option is to find a family Bible that contains some mention of William "The Immigrant" Lindsey. One of the better Clan Lindsay websites has a collection of family Bibles online. Months of reading through the transcripts leave me without a single hint that any of them are connected to my family.

I switch to Google searches, using combinations of names, dates, and places in the hope of stumbling across a news item stored in one of the endless electronic data vaults available on the internet. The process is slow and horrifically tedious, but the hours fly by as I concentrate on the task. I wade through dozens of searches, attempting to filter out information that doesn't apply to my family. My persistence pays off.

A match takes me to a family history site for the Crawfords.

The name clicks into place. My heart beats faster. John Crawford Lindsay. He has his mother's maiden name—a common practice in many families. I slap my forehead. Why hadn't I considered this possibility earlier? I doubt it would've helped me reach this point any sooner, but I feel stupid for not thinking of it.

I discover a genealogy titled *Crawfords of Adams County, Ohio*. The publication date is 1943. Whoever put the book together may have interviewed someone who knew William Lindsey. I order the book, giddy over the the treasure trove of information it might contain.

I feel that I'm on the cusp of a major discovery; excitement courses through my veins. I call my brother and tell him excitedly, "We come from Fintona, Ireland. At least, I'm pretty sure we do."

"That's great," my brother says. He doesn't sound excited.

"Okay, I just thought you would want to know."

Not much of a reaction. After all the work I've done to unearth this information, I expect a little more excitement from him. I hang up and call my dad. "It looks like the Lindsays emigrated from Fintona, Ireland."

"Good work," says Dad. The television is playing in the background. Past experience has taught me that as long he has eyes on the idiot box, he isn't going to remember anything I tell him. We can talk about my findings the next time I drive out to his place.

"Love you. Bye."

I decide to switch tactics and rush out to the kitchen. Maybe I'll have better luck talking with someone live and in person. My wife is preparing dinner. The aroma of grilled steak and vegetables fills the room. "I found out where the Lindsays lived in Ireland."

My wife smiles at me. "That's nice, dear."

Ah, forget it.

This is the second marriage for both LuAnn and me. The children in the house are a blend of hers, mine, and ours. I married LuAnn because she is beautiful, intelligent, and calm. Unfortunately, the whole "calm" thing means she's almost never as excited about an event or discovery as I am. Everything seems to excite me.

I shamble out of the kitchen and return to my office.

The book eventually arrives in the mail. It indicates that William Lindsay immigrated to the United States, lived in New York for a brief period, and then moved to Ohio. His wife, Nancy Crawford, died in 1842. Four sons are listed: James, Robert, John, and William.

There are no personal stories about William. The scant details have a sterile, distant feel to them. I think about William's short stay in New York. Everything must have been strange and unfamiliar to him and Nancy. The tall buildings, the odd way people dressed in America, and the melting pot of languages and cultures they experienced.

But I have found my immigrant ancestor! Although the book's information about William is limited, it lists that his wife, Nancy, was born in

Fintona, Ireland. A sigh of relief escapes me. The rest of my quest should be easy. All I need to do is check the records in Ireland and connect William to one of the Lindsey families there.

Fintona turns out to be a small town in Northern Ireland and is part of the area settled by the Scottish in the early seventeenth century. Although they lived in Ireland, the Scots-Irish continued to identify themselves as Scottish.

William turns out to be harder to find than expected. A week of searching provides me with no further information about him. Only a fragment of Irish church records is online, and the small town of Fintona is not mentioned among them.

I have gone as far as I can on the Great Lindsay Quest. Dozens of passes through the information I've collected fails to magically reveal any new leads. I consider quitting the search, but so many of my ancestors still remain unfound. I have an obligation to them as well. They deserve an equal amount of my time.

I dive back into the work. My passion to find immigrants from my other ancestral lines becomes nearly as powerful as my desire to find William in Ireland. I add name after name to the family tree. Occasionally I find an interesting bit of information that breathes life into the dry data about a family member.

John Crawford Lindsay—listed as John C. Lindsey in the National Park Service's Civil War database of soldiers—did fight in the Civil War. He served as a private in the 24th Regiment, Ohio Infantry, Companies D and F. The unit fought in the battles of Shiloh, Perryville, Chickamauga, Chattanooga, and Missionary Ridge. At some point during that terrible conflict, John was wounded. He drew a pension for his injury after the war, but the wound didn't stop him from working as a blacksmith and later as a mechanic.

I learned about another ancestor—Chester William. Chester's mother died when he was just a baby, and his cousins, Robert and Mary, adopted him. Chester was the only child Robert and Mary had. There isn't a diary around to tell me about Robert and Mary's history, but in my mind, I picture a couple who badly wanted children and couldn't have any of their own. The tragedy of Chester's mother passing away became an answer to their prayers.

Did it happen that way?

Maybe.

The ghosts of Robert and Mary don't visit me in my dreams. None of my ancestors have visited me—in my dreams or in my waking hours. The closest thing I have to Dad's experience is a strong sense that John Crawford Lindsay knows about my efforts to uncover the family links binding all of us together and he is pleased with those efforts.

It takes more than a decade to research each branch of my family history as far back as the records will allow me to go. I've connected more than five thousand names to the family tree, but John's father, William "The Immigrant" Lindsey, still eludes me.

At this point, in 2016, the only way I can connect William to one of the families in Ireland is to take a DNA test. The genetic markers in my DNA will firmly establish which branch of the Lindsay clan is ours. Then, hopefully, I can use that connection to find the information I need to link William to the Lindsays of Ireland.

I access my Ancestry.com account and open the DNA tab. They offer three different tests: the paternal Y-chromosome DNA, the maternal mitochondrial DNA, and the autosomal DNA. I read through the descriptions of each test and decide on the Y-chromosome test because it follows the male lineage. Then I pay for the test and hit the submit button.

The kit arrives a week later. I rip open the box and look through the contents. I carefully read the instructions. It seems simple enough. I read the instructions again, not wanting to make a mistake.

Open tube.

Spit into tube.

Seal tube.

Place tube in the return envelope.

Mail the envelope.

I unscrew the cap on the tube. The instructions want me to spit into the tube, but I'm more of a drool-on-command sort of guy. It takes a few minutes to transfer the required amount of spit to the inside of the container. The cap goes back on. Then I put the tube in the envelope and send it off.

The instructions give an estimated wait time of six to eight weeks before receiving the results, but they don't mention the anguish I'm already feeling. These tests should include a warning label like pharmaceutical manufacturers do when they list the side effects of taking their medication.

Still, how bad can it be? The Great Lindsay Quest has already taken twelve years. Another "six to eight weeks" should pass like a fleeting moment in time . . . right?

# CHAPTER 3

# THE DNA RESULTS

I know better than to expect my test results any sooner than eight weeks, but I check my Ancestry account every day after the six-week mark. Week eight arrives; Ancestry announces an unusually high demand for the service and extends the delivery date by another two weeks.

Frustration over the slow response time gnaws at the last of my patience. Two can play at this game. I take their added wait time and raise them two more weeks for the typical things-always-take-longer-than-expected adjustment. I vow not to check my account again for another month, two weeks more than necessary—just to show Ancestry, my ancestors, and family history in general who the real boss is in this situation.

Who's too cool for school now?

I almost make it the full month. A few days short of my targeted boycott termination, I slip into my office and sit at the computer. It's late at night, and the house is silent. The world outside my window is black. I log in to Ancestry.com and find that my DNA test results are back. In the next few moments, I will discover what secrets are contained within my spit.

A fluttering sensation passes through my stomach. I feel like a kid on Christmas Day, getting ready to open the biggest, most colorfully wrapped present under the tree. Scenes flash through my mind of what it will be like to finish the Great Lindsay Quest. I even picture a Holy Grail kind of ending where I place my foot on a conveniently placed stone and dramatically raise a shiny sword in the air, proclaiming the search to be over at last.

The DNA section of the website opens to a brightly colored pie chart depicting my ethnic components. A map sits next to the chart, the colors of my ethnic backgrounds marking the portions of Europe where my ancestors originated. Great Britain is the main ingredient in my genetic soup. The drab-yellow shade representing Britannia accounts for 64 percent of my heritage and covers England, Wales, Scotland—I knew I was Scottish—and a small part of Northern Ireland where the Scotch-Irish settled.

I lean closer to the computer screen and examine the yellow blob on the map. In addition to Britain, yellow covers portions of Belgium, the Netherlands, and France. A larger green blob extends up from Germany and overlaps Great Britain's sphere of influence on my historic past. No surprises there. My mother's side of the family is mostly from England and Germany. But based on the family history work I've done for both Mom and Dad, I expected a larger percentage of English heritage.

As I look at Great Britain's boring yellow hue, I become distracted for a moment. Western Europe is teal. Eastern Europe is represented by a lovely shade of grass green. Ireland and Scotland are light blue, Scandinavia is dark blue, and Finland and Western Russia are purple. That makes sense, I think. Finland is cold; and purple is the color of people's lips after they've taken a dip in a frozen lake. But shouldn't Ireland be green?

Ireland is known as the Emerald Island. It's the land of leprechauns who hide their pots of gold at the end of the rainbow and chase children who try to steal their Lucky Charms . . .

I realize my mind has wandered off at the same time I'm silently declaring that Ireland should be green, just like people who spend all day in the hot sun should be . . . red.

And then it hits me that the colors aren't indicative of a region's landscape or climate—they represent what percentage of your heritage comes from each particular region. The higher the percentage, the "hotter" the color. It's sort of like a grown-up version of the hot-or-cold game.

"Am I Russian?" I ask.

"No," says Ancestry.com. "You're ice cold."

"Am I . . . Irish?"

"You're getting warmer," Ancestry taunts.

My eyes roam over the map, placing family names on the countries where I know they originated. England . . . Scotland . . . Germany . . . Denmark . . . France . . . Poland.

Poland?

I don't have family from Poland. My research goes back to 1800 for most of my lines. All the branches have names that fit the countries where the family originated. There are no Romonovs, Bartollonis, or Kowalskis in my family tree. Not that there is anything wrong with those names or heritages, I just happen to know who is in the family and who isn't.

A forbidden romance with a member of a gypsy tribe might account for a tiny amount of Eastern European blood to register on my chart, but I have more ancestry there than in Western Europe, according to this map. That can't be right. Maybe I have a different idea of which countries belong in Eastern Europe than Ancestry does. I study the grass-green blob on the map.

Western Poland, Czechia, Austria, and the eastern portion of Germany all fall into the overlap area between my Western Europe and Eastern Europe heritage. It has to be my German ancestry that's causing the surprise result, but the manner in which the grass-green blob extends all the way to the eastern edge of the Ukraine concerns me. Could some of my family come from areas located more in the center of that blob?

The DNA testing seems to have created another mystery rather than solving the one.

Any new puzzles will have to wait for another day. I want answers, and so I move on to the DNA Matches tab. That is where the real magic will happen. Distant relatives who have succeeded in finding their ancestors in Ireland will have family trees already filled out. With any luck, some of my cousins in Ireland will have contracted the genealogy bug too and searched the church records in Fintona. All I need to do is skip through the forest of names until I find one I recognize. Easy-peasy.

The first family tree on the list indicates that the DNA donor is a close relative, possibly a first cousin. My heart rate soars. I can hardly wait to find out how this person is related to me. The discovery of relatives who share my enthusiasm for family history is a real game changer. We can share notes about our research, hunt the missing branches of our tree together, and swap exciting stories about our discoveries over a double-cheese-and-pepperoni pizza. I should have taken the DNA test years ago.

I open the family tree and see that my cousin's name is Petrauschke. P - E - T - R - A - U - S - C - H - K - E.

This isn't right. I don't know anyone name Petra . . . Petrauski. I mean . . . Petraushe. However it's pronounced, I don't have any relatives with that name. I'm not even sure I have any relatives who could pronounce the name.

I close the family tree and look at the relationship again. The information hasn't changed. "Close family—1st cousin," it claims. My family isn't that large. I know all of my cousins, and this person isn't one of them.

The DNA testing lab must have mixed up the samples, like hospitals switch babies at birth. I've waited three months for the results. And the wrong ones were sent to me. I mumble a few derogatory remarks about the DNA lab and stomp out of the office.

"Going for a walk?" asks my wife as I pass through the living room. She's busy knitting, or crocheting, or something she does with yarn and a couple of big needles.

"Can you believe it? They mixed up my DNA results with a person named Pet-something. How can they do that? The two names don't look anything alike."

LuAnn shakes her head and offers me a sympathy tsk. "Those things happen."

"I'll be back in a little bit," I tell her as I march out the door.

Walking helps me think. It also gives the neighbors an opportunity to watch the crazy man talk to himself. Twice around the block and I have the beginnings of a carefully worded email rattling around inside my head. LuAnn is already in bed by the time I return. I head straight into my office and contact Ancestry, telling them about their mistake and demanding they remedy the situation.

That should do it, I tell myself.

At the back of my mind, my inner voice responds with, Are you kidding? A big company like this is never going to admit they made a mistake.

— —

I don't bother to watch for Ancestry's response. Disappointment weighs too heavily on me. Even if they admit to a mistake, it will be another three or four months before I receive the correct results. And if they deny any error on their part, I can't afford a second test. In my current mood, this game of electronic hide-and-seek has become a symbol of failure.

Thanksgiving is just a week away. My frustrations are temporarily pushed aside with dreams about mountains of smoked turkey, buttery mashed-potato craters filled with lakes of gravy, marshmallow-topped sweet-potato casserole, pumpkin pie buried under fluffy whipped-cream clouds, and yummy-yummy deviled eggs.

Ah, the promised land!

An email notification tells me that someone—besides Ancestry—has left me a message. Several distant cousins have exchanged family history information with me in the past. The possibility of one contacting me with a new piece of my family history puzzle is enough to lure me back on to the website.

. Turns out it isn't one of my genealogy buddies.

The name looks familiar, but I know it's not one of the surnames from my family tree. Although polite, the stranger basically asks, "Who are you?"

Frankly, the question irks me. No matter how nicely worded it is, the message still comes across as a bit arrogant. What makes this person so special that he can flounce around the Ancestry site asking people who they are? I half expect him to pull out his electronic credentials identifying him as a member of a secret DNA police agency.

"Who are you?" I ask as I scowl at the monitor. Two can play at this game.

John Lodge tells me my DNA profile is showing up in his results but he doesn't recognize any of the names in my family. The data indicates that we're second or third cousins, and he'd like to work together to find the connection between our family trees.

Maybe he doesn't belong to some subversive genetics cult after all. I let him know the only two possibilities: "Someone in his family had an affair that no one has admitted to, or there's been a mistake in the DNA testing. My money is on the latter."

Wait a minute . . . An affair?

The idea comes out of nowhere as I type my response. That would change everything. I send off the message and open my DNA results.

A quick look at several of these Petrauschke ancestors reveals they've planted roots in New Jersey. And based on the information I see, it seems none of them has ever strayed far from the area. No one from my family lines has lived in that part of the country—ever, I think. A DNA testing error seems even more likely, but I continue. One of the biggest things I've learned about family history research is that you have to follow any and all leads all the way through.

My six closest "matches" all include the same person in their family tree. If there's a connection between our two families, it has to be through her.

Born in New Jersey. Died in New Jersey.

It doesn't look good for Ancestry.

Married in Arizona.

There's a connection after all.

I check the dates. She lived in Phoenix when my both of my parents' families moved here. An affair resulting in a first-cousin match for me has to mean one of my grandparents was involved. I eliminate the grandmothers. There would have been no way for them to conceal a pregnancy from the rest of the family. My maternal grandfather died before I was born and never stepped foot inside Arizona. That leaves Grandad.

If the DNA test results are correct . . . Dad has a brother no one knows about.

Several reactions clash with one another inside me. Concern rises and takes center stage as I worry about how this will affect my dad and whether I should tell him. Curiosity ignores Concern and jumps around like an excited puppy, eager to meet the new members of the family. The Spirit of Adventure dons his investigator hat, ready to seek out the truth about who these people are and how the events unfolded that led us here. And in one tiny corner of my mind, a dark specter giggles at the thought of scandal within the family.

I rush out to the living room to tell my wife. She's working on making baby toys out of yarn. "Dad has a secret brother no one knows about."

"Isn't that exciting," she says with as much enthusiasm as she uses to announce that Sunday dinner is ready. It's taken years of marriage for me to get used to her calm demeanor. Most of the time, it isn't a matter of my wife not caring about what I tell her. She just doesn't feel the need to jump around, scream and shout, or exhibit any of the other unnecessary emotional outbursts.

"Right?" I say as I point at her and nod. Then I retreat back to my office.

Even though I'm busting at the seams to call Dad and tell him about my suspicions, I wait until Thanksgiving so I can talk to him in person. There doesn't seem to be a right approach to breaking this kind of news to someone you love. I can't just walk up and say, "Dad, you have a brother you never knew about."

I try several lines out loud, hoping one of them will sound supportive.

"Hi, Dad. Do remember what a rascal Grandad was?"

Nope.

"Dad, how were your parents getting along when they moved to Phoenix?"

Not any better.

"Dad, how do you feel about surprises?"

My lines are getting worse. I decide to wing it. Maybe something in our conversation will give me a good starting point for the delicate discussion.

Dad arrives early. My stepmom gives me a hug and then continues into the kitchen to talk with my wife, my mom, and the rest of the ladies there. The football game is about to start, but I mute the sound to make sure I have Dad's attention.

"I took a DNA test. The results came back with matches to a family I don't know. Do the last names of Bennet, Collins, or Petrauschke sound familiar to you?"

"Nope." Dad's attention drifts back to the television screen. The beer commercial that's on depicts a room full of impossibly perfect people sitting around a poker table, toasting one another.

Ten seconds and I'm already in danger of losing him. "The results show I'm connected to these families through a first cousin. Which means one of my grandparents had a child the rest of us don't know about."

"Uh-huh." Even without the sound, the television is winning the battle to keep Dad's interest. I move in front of him and block his view. He looks up at me.

"Grandad is the most obvious candidate for having another child. I think you might have another brother. One you've never met." I watch to see how reacts.

Dad laughs. "Wouldn't surprise me."

It isn't the reaction I expected. The news hasn't shattered his world. If anything, it feels as if Dad is accepting this as one of the grand jokes life plays on each of us from time to time.

"Dad was a character, all right." He nods and smiles. "There might even be more."

I sit on the couch, unsure what to say. All that worry about hurting Dad's feelings and instead he gives me, "Wouldn't surprise me." His lack of emotion leaves me too mind-numbed to speak.

Dad saves me the trouble. He points to the television. "The game's started. Can you turn up the sound and find out when dinner will be ready?"

— • —

A week after Thanksgiving, Ancestry notifies me of another message. I waste no time retrieving it. Dad may not be interested in finding out more about his secret brother, or sister, but I'm eager to get as many details about what happened as I can. In his last message, John promised to contact me if he discovered anything new during his research.

This new message isn't from John.

Another researcher from John's family asks me, "Who are you?"

I roll my eyes. Not another one of these guys. He introduces himself as John's brother. I resist the urge to go through the whole "Who are you?" routine again. I tell him the theory about my grandfather having an affair.

Terry replies, "My grandfather seems to have had a child with her as well. He was a widower at the time, and the story of how they met and why they never married is lost to the ages. My granddad remarried and that is who I remember as my grandmom."

That confirms my theory—at least in my mind. All the evidence points to my grandfather having an affair with this woman while she lived in Phoenix. I call my dad and tell him the name of the person I suspect is his half brother. Dad thanks me again but shows no interest in finding out any more. He isn't interested in meeting or even contacting his newly discovered brother.

I don't get it. How can Dad be so cavalier about the news?

It seems strange that a man who was visited by his dead ancestors is not interested in meeting a live sibling. I don't press the matter. The question of why Dad isn't interested in reaching out to his brother creeps around inside my head for days.

I call my brother and youngest sister and ask, "What's up with Dad?"

They both give me the verbal equivalent of a shrug and quickly move on to other topics. Neither of them is interested in the discovery of a new family member. My sister suggests I drop the matter and tells me what time I'm supposed to arrive at her house on Christmas Day. We say good-bye, and I let loose a long, deep sigh.

I log back in to Ancestry and look through the list of DNA matches. John and his brother both show up as being my first to second cousins. Another result suggests an even closer relationship. I realize that if this isn't a big mistake on Ancestry's part, my long-lost uncle is John's parent. It might be better for everyone involved if a DNA mix-up is the case. Unable to leave the matter alone, I compose a message and send it off to Tammy. She's the person who owns the Ancestry account for the closest DNA match and is likely the mother, sister, or daughter of the person who took the actual test.

The message states, "I just got the results of my DNA test, and it shows a first cousin connection to a person listed in your family tree. That doesn't seem likely, but I would like to discuss the matter with you if possible."

She responds a couple of days later. Her brother provided the DNA sample for the test. They live in New Jersey . . . although her dad lived in Phoenix from 1947 until about 1956. She is using the DNA test to establish a link between her dad and his biological father.

I struggle to make the information fit my theory. Tammy's dad is old enough to be my uncle, but he wasn't born in Phoenix. As far as I know, my grandfather never set foot inside New Jersey. This doesn't exclude the possibility that Tammy's grandmother may have been in the same place as my grandfather at the time of Mr. Petrauschke's conception.

But it doesn't seem likely. I'm missing something.

I decide to switch gears and focus on preparations for Christmas. The Great Lindsay Quest can wait until after the holidays. Or even longer.

My wife is in charge of most of the decorating. If it were up to me, I'd cut a three-foot branch from one of the pine trees in the neighborhood, tack a wooden stand to it, and let the kids go crazy hanging tinsel and bulbs. If it's good enough for Charlie Brown, it's good enough for me. The same thing goes for holiday cooking. Ask me to prepare the Christmas feast and I'm happy to fill the table with heaping bowls of microwave popcorn, platters of toast slathered with butter, and jars of red and green jelly beans.

Fortunately, for the kids, I married well.

As family tradition dictates, we spend most of Christmas Day at my sister's house. Jana is running around the kitchen like a spastic Chihuahua because she stayed up all night cooking and cleaning. My brother, Mark, shows up late. And the oldest of the sisters, Carol, shows up even later.

Christmas is usually the only time I see Carol. The two of us lead different lives and are content with exchanging a few posts on Facebook. I love Carol. She loves me. And I think we love each other best from a distance.

Once everyone has eaten and the presents have been opened, I sit at the dining table with my siblings and Mom.

This is always my absolute favorite part of the entire year. Me and the sibs talk about anything and everything . . . and sometimes, like Seinfeld, about nothing at all. The conversation flows like a lazy river twisting through the beautiful countryside. I lean back in my chair and enjoy the comforting eddies of a discussion that isn't in a hurry to reach a conclusion.

I soak up as much of the family water as I can, needing it to sustain me during the long drought between our visits. When I'm here, I don't want to be anywhere else. I feel loved. And I know that I am loved. The frustrating confusion of my ancestral quest is forgotten . . . for the moment.

— • —

Frost covers the now-dormant, yellow yard. The heater kicks on to fight the February cold and fills my office with a smell that makes me think of toasted mittens. I wrap a blanket around me and sit at my desk.

An email notice advises me I have a message waiting for me on Ancestry.

It's from Tammy. She writes, "I can't tell you how many times I've tried to write this message to you."

I stop reading. Why would a stranger have a hard time writing me a message? A prickling sensation runs down my spine. I can already tell I'm not going to like whatever message follows the ominous opening sentence. Part of me screams to close the program and not read any farther. Deep inside, a premonition whispers that beyond this point lies the horrible, uncomfortable tendrils of change.

The rational portion of my mind rejects the idea of me having any ability to sense a pivotal moment in my life before it happens. Something that happened when my grandfather was young certainly doesn't have the power to shatter my life. Those kinds of things only happen in the movies.

Tammy continues. "So many things are rolling around in my head about what to say, but nothing sounds right. After receiving the message from John, I went back and checked my brother's DNA test. There's a symbol of a lowercase *i* on the result and it tells how much DNA is shared. It took a couple of weeks for the information to sink in. I am still confused and was not sure you really wanted to hear from me. Not sure where things will go from here, but if you have any questions please let me know."

What is she talking about?

I reach for the mouse. My hand hovers over the top of it. Do I really want to know?

It was better when everyone was asking me, "Who are you?" I push away from the desk and wander into the kitchen. The sink is full of dishes. Some of the groceries from the morning shopping trip are still on the counter. There's plenty to do. I don't need to be paying attention to some crazy lady.

Of course, I don't really know if she's crazy until I take a look at the DNA information.

My pacing around the kitchen counter turns into a slow, ambling march toward my home office. Her message is still displayed on the computer screen. All I have to do is click the DNA tab and it will take me to the same information that put Tammy in an obviously agitated state. Why does she have to be so vague about what she discovered? Why doesn't she just come out and tell me what she found?

I read through the message again to make sure I understand her instructions and then switch to the DNA results. Under her profile it lists our connection as "Close family—1st cousins."

Is that what it said before? I don't remember any mention of close family?

A white question mark inside a black circle sits next to the relationship tag. My cursor hovers over the question mark for a brief moment. Then I click on it and bring up a chart that explains how statistical variation makes it impossible to identify the exact relationship between DNA subjects. Ancestry believes Tammy and I are close family and could be as *distantly related* as first cousins. Somehow, I had missed that important detail the first time I studied the results. Only the part about being first cousins had caught my attention before.

Ancestry bases its estimate of family relations on the amount of DNA two people share. The higher the number, the closer the relationship. Tammy's brother and I share more than 1,700 centiMorgans of DNA.

A "What does this mean?" option on the information box opens another chart. I study the chart to understand what 1,700 centiMorgans means for Tammy and me. The amount is lower than the DNA shared between parent and child, and it's lower than the amount shared between full siblings. But the amount lands right in the middle of how much DNA I might share with a grandparent, an aunt or uncle, or . . . a half-sibling.

A half-sibling.

Based on the information from Tammy's family tree, I run the numbers and figure out her brother is close to my age. Maybe even younger. This rules out the possibility of him being my grandfather. It also makes it unlikely for him to be my uncle. That leaves only one alternative.

My dad doesn't have a long-lost, secret brother. I do.

A chilling sensation washes down my back. My head snaps back, and my body stiffens. I stare at the computer screen without seeing it. My mind moves slowly from one thought to the next as I slog through a mental bog of discovery. None of the unwelcomed revelations brings me joy.

If Tammy and her brother are my siblings . . . then Dad is not really my dad.

I shake my head in defiance of the unwelcome thoughts. I try taking a deep breath, but that does nothing to soothe my agitated mind. Because, if Dad is not my biological father . . . then my brother and sisters are only my half-siblings.

And if Dad isn't my biological father . . . that means I have a father I don't know.

No! Absolutely not.

It can't be true. It has to be a mistake. Tears well up in my eyes. I don't want it to be true. I want to go back in time and refuse to read Tammy's message. Then, even if all of this is true, I will be blissfully unaware of the facts.

No! No! No!

I love my family. They are the foundation of my life. I don't want everything to change. Why did I have to take that stupid DNA test? Stupid! Stupid! Stupid! I let the tears flow. The light in my office dims from bright sunlight to gray dusk. All I can think about is how I don't want this to be true.

What do I do now?

# CHAPTER 4

# I'M NOT IN EGYPT, SO THIS CAN'T BE DENIAL

An emotional lake builds inside me, held back by a weakening dam of denial. I return to the idea that this whole thing is merely a DNA testing error. It isn't a matter of simply wanting to believe that—I have to believe it. The alternative will leave me stranded in a strange familial landscape.

I go to bed and try to sleep but toss and turn most of the night. One disturbing scenario after another plays out in my head. My active imagination, which I regularly rely on to create fantastic tales of adventure, works against me. In my mind's eye, I see Dad staring down his nose at a six-year-old version of me, his lips curled back in disgust. "You aren't my son. Get out of here."

The image fades. In its place, I see a massive dead tree, its branches groaning and swaying in the wind, near the front of a creepy house. Curls of paint adorn the house's outside walls, showing years of neglect. The front door creaks open, but it's too dark inside to see what awaits me. I follow a dirt path carved between tall, brown weeds and step up to the front porch. My new family.

A sinister voice cackles from inside, "Hello, Randy. We're so glad to finally meet you."

— —

Sunshine pours through my bedroom window to announce a new day. I drag myself out of bed, kiss my wife goodbye, and then move through the morning routine like a hungover zombie. Pack the kids. Hug the lunches goodbye. I forget to tell them to have a nice day, which is probably for the best. Who knows what I would have actually said or if they would have even been able to understand my mumbling.

A hot shower wakes me up. A breakfast of peanut-butter toast stops the rumbling in my stomach. I trudge to my office and sit at the computer. The monitor is dark, and I wonder if I dare wake it. The infernal piece of technology has already thrown my emotions into turmoil. What's to prevent it from sending another zinger my way?

The bed calls to me from the other room. My eyes burn, and I know if I close them I'll be out cold within seconds. I could sleep most of the day and avoid facing any more shocking revelations, but the one I already know about will be waiting for me when I wake. I hit the power button on my computer. Something in the pit of my gut flutters as I watch the screen light up.

There's another message from Tammy. A jolt of energy courses through my chest.

Maybe I should go back to bed. I definitely need the sleep. Whatever life-disrupting message the crazy lady has for me can wait until later. I shut down the program and then spin my chair around so I can stand up.

But the notice nags at me. I know that no matter how tired I am, I won't be able to sleep. My mind will focus on the message waiting to be opened. I will imagine one bad scenario after another until it drives me back to the computer to find out what Tammy wrote. I shake my head and turn to the keyboard. A few keystrokes are all it takes to open the note.

She's sent pictures of her family.

Among the pictures is her dad's senior portrait from high school. Icy droplets of dread drizzle down my back. I slump in my seat. An undeniable resemblance exists between the young man in the picture . . . and me.

Undeniable!

I move to the next picture, hoping the resemblance is a fluke, perhaps something to do with the lighting used on picture day. The second picture is of Tammy's mom and dad standing together. They look to be in their forties. Her mother is tiny. Her dad, I decide, doesn't look that much like me after all. The tension in my shoulders lessens as I sigh in relief.

There's another picture of her father; he's standing in front of a door decked out with Christmas decorations. There might be a bit of similarity in the eyes and around the mouth. I quickly move on.

I look at a picture of Tammy. My shoulders slump. This is how I would look if I were female, I imagine. Or close enough, anyway. I study the picture for a moment and decide she looks like a nice person, the kind of person I'd like to meet.

The next photo confirms what I'm already thinking. A strong family resemblance exists between me and Tammy's brothers. My brothers.

Tammy. Joe. Bill. Mr. Petrauschke. No matter how many times I cycle through the pictures, my resemblance to them doesn't change. For years, the brother and sisters I grew up with have teased me about not looking anything like them. Before my hair took an early trip to the grayside, it was dark. My siblings are blond. They are trimly built, and I have the barrel chest that is common on my mother's side of the family. For years, my siblings have frequently called me the milkman's son. And it appears they are right. I am the milkman's son.

Do they already know I'm only their half brother? Have they known all along? A conspiracy to keep me in the dark about my origins seems out of place for my family. But it doesn't matter if my family knew about this. The damage is done. Their taunts that I'm the milkman's son echo in my head, stabbing me through the heart because they're true.

"It's not funny," I tell the specters of my siblings.

My wife isn't due home from work for several more hours. It's no use trying to write. The creative muse is silent whenever I'm upset. I decide to work on researching agents and publishers for my next novel. It's busy, repetitive work that keeps my mind from dwelling on the disastrous family news.

Eventually, I hear the garage door open. My wife is home. I rush into the kitchen to greet her. "Honey, um . . . I found out that Dad isn't my dad."

"Wow," says my wife.

I wait for her to say something else, but she just gives me a hug.

"The DNA matched me with a half brother in New Jersey," I tell her.

"Cool," says my wife with a smile.

"What?" It appears that Tammy isn't the only crazy lady running around.

LuAnn puts her lunch bag away and then turns to face me. "You can't make this stuff up. Not even you. This is better than one of your fictional stories."

"Sort of like the whole life-is-stranger-than-fiction thing," I say.

"Exactly." She wraps her arms around me. "I like when a story has a twist. I think it's great that your real-life story has the best twist of all."

"But . . . my life isn't a story." This must be what it feels like to be a character in one of my books. I silently vow to take it easier on my protagonists from now on. "And what's so great about my situation anyways?"

"I think it's kind of neat that you have more family."

I stare at her, unsure about what to say.

"Enjoy the new diversity of your family." LuAnn kisses me. "Family is good."

➤ ◄

Late the next morning, the door at the front of the house opens and closes. A few seconds later, my oldest son strolls into my office. "What's up, Pop?"

Roger is from my first marriage. He's over thirty and has a barrel chest like me, but he sports a full beard I could never hope to grow. His eyes are an icy blue, and his hair is already turning gray even though he's only in his midthirties.

"Do you remember me telling you about the crazy lady on Ancestry who thought we were siblings?" I motion him over and point to the picture of Mr. Petrauschke. Even though I know it's useless, my mind strains to find a way to deny the evidence. Maybe my son won't think the picture looks anything like me.

Roger peeks over my shoulder at the old black-and-white photo. Barely a second passes before he laughs and says, "There's the proof."

"Why are you laughing?"

"Because he looks just like you. The lips are the giveaway. You have his lips. Lucy and I have your lips. The lips don't lie. I guess the DNA test wasn't wrong."

"You're not being any help," I say.

"Why? Because I'm not upset about this?"

"No," I grumble. "Because you're not supposed to think he looks like me."

Roger laughs again. "Don't worry, Pop. I'm here for you."

I feel better hearing that I have someone who loves me and is willing to support me as I flounder through this experience. At least that hasn't changed. Roger claps me on the shoulder and then heads out to the kitchen to nuke whatever leftovers are in the fridge.

In a desperate attempt to avoid the truth, I call a friend who lives in the neighborhood. "Alan, can you come over . . . like now? I have something I want to show you."

"What is it?" he asks.

"You sort of have to see it. I'm sure you'll find it amusing."

"In that case, I'll be right over."

He ends the call. Fifteen minutes—that feel like an hour—pass before he knocks on the door. I open the door and invite him inside. Alan is in his usual outfit: slacks, a button-up shirt, and a newsboy cap. The hat fits with his neatly trimmed circle beard. "Remember the DNA test I sent in?"

"Yeah, the one they messed up?"

"That's the one. Someone sent me a picture, and I want you to take a look at it." I pull up the high school photo of Mr. Petrauschke.

Alan cuts loose with a gale of laughter. "That's funny."

"What's so funny about it?" I ask for the second time today.

"Oh yeah. That definitely looks like you. It must be your dad."

"I'm failing to see the humor in that."

"You've been running around complaining about a mistake with the DNA test. Then someone sends you this picture and—BOOM! Goodbye mistake. Hello, Daddy."

"I can tell you what's not funny," I say. "You're not funny. Go home."

"All right, see you Saturday for game night." Alan walks out of the house with a grin on his face. My anger fades as he drives off. I suppose it isn't his fault I look like my biological father.

I close my eyes and release the last remaining dregs of denial. The desperate motes of hope drift across the room and out the door. I have to accept the truth and face whatever problems are attached to the situation. Immediately, one springs to the forefront of my thoughts.

How am I going to tell my dad that he isn't my dad? I can't just walk up to him and say, "I came across a funny fact during my family history search—we're not actually related." Dad finds humor in a lot of situations that fail to amuse me, but I'm not sure he'll find this particular bit of news all that funny.

Do I even want to tell him?

# CHAPTER 5

# FORGET THE DUKE; MEET MY DAD

I don't know who I am anymore. Flailing about in an emotional free fall, I throw my arms around and cling to memories of the person who has influenced every aspect of who I am. If I focus my thoughts on Dad, maybe that will lead to an epiphany where my life makes sense once again.

A picture of John Wayne hangs in my office because it reminds me of Dad. Mr. Wayne portrayed some of the most memorable cowboys and marines in cinematic history. He and my dad even look vaguely similar. The difference is John Wayne shuffled off to his trailer between takes. He didn't live the experiences that audiences cherish on the screen. The "Duke" didn't actually have to cope with the obstacles and troubles his movie characters faced.

Dad, on the other hand, rode horses and herded cattle for a living. He went to high school during the day and ran mule trains in the evenings and summers to help support his siblings. He boxed in the marines, served as an MP (military police), and achieved the rank of sergeant. John Wayne movies rule, but Dad is the real deal.

He is a figure who stands solid and rock steady in my life. Suddenly, the strength and comfort I draw from Dad's gutsy, stalwart personality remind me of what I am not.

I spin around in my office chair, putting the picture of John Wayne behind me. But no matter where I look in my office, there are reminders of my dad. The boxed set of small blue reference books he gave me for Christmas the year he found out I wanted to be a writer. A poster for my first published book. The yellow cowboy-boot cup I saved from child-hood. The sight of these items sends me back on the life trail Dad and I have shared.

My oldest memory involves Dad and a train. I must have been about three years old at the time and was fascinated with the rail line that ran across the back of our property. My memory doesn't retain the exact words Dad said but includes a struggle to obey his warning to stay away from the tracks. I was still twenty feet away from the tracks when I heard a mechanical clacking noise to my right.

A train rumbled toward me. The ground vibrated beneath my feet. The thundering blast of the train's horn sent me running to Dad.

My feet pounded against the ground, keeping rhythm with my heart as it slammed against my chest. There might as well have been a T. rex chasing me across that field. Fear and adrenaline flooded my tiny body.

Tall, stiff weeds grabbed at my feet as I ran. I fell and started crying. The train was going to get me. Again and again I stood, I ran, and I fell. Another roar from the train's horn sounded from right behind me. My cries turned to screams.

Then Dad picked me up. I was safe. Nothing could harm me with Dad as my protector. . . . The memory fades.

My world stabilizes—ever so slightly—at the thought of Dad's con-tinued guardianship over me. He kept the monsters at bay when I was a child and has offered a protective wall of advice and support for me as an adult. But I don't know if he will remain a haven of fatherly comfort once he finds out I'm not his son.

My mother tells another story about me at the age of three. Our family would attend local roping events on the weekends. Dad would rope, Mom would watch him, and I would play in the dirt, piling rocks together to form miniature forts. If I hadn't seen Dad for a while, I would stand up and wander around the outer edge of the corral, yelling, "Honey. Where are you, Honey?"

Since that's what my mother called him, it seemed natural for me to do the same. Dad wasn't a big fan of his son addressing him as Honey in front of all his rugged cowboy friends. He'd usually duck his head, pull his Stetson down to cover as much of his face as possible, and then ride off in the opposite direction. (As a side note: Dad has recently taken to calling me Honey—a strange development for a man who was once so bothered by the name.)

The cowboy lifestyle shaped a good portion of my early years. I went with Dad whenever he had a horseshoeing job. The trips were usually to the fringes of civilization. While Dad shoed the horse and then drank a couple of beers with the owner, I would scour the desert for adventure.

I'd trek through grayish-green and yellow scrubs on a safari to capture anything that moved. Lizards, snakes, scorpions, and centipedes all made fine trophies to pay tribute to my hunting prowess. I avoided rattlesnakes, even though I was confident in my ability to catch them without being bitten. Neither Mom nor Dad were thrilled about the bountiful number of poisonous insects I bagged on my hunts, so bringing home a rattler would have put them over the edge.

Dad signed me up for junior rodeo when I turned twelve. He made sure I had all the gear I needed for calf riding. Sturdy jeans, cowboy hat, chaps, gloves, and a bull rope—complete with a cow bell. He stood taller and talked louder as we marched across a dirt field to register me for my first rodeo.

I was barely able to keep up with him. My trembling knees threatened to give way with every step. A large, dry lump had lodged itself in my throat. I didn't want to ride calves. I had never loved riding Dad's horse, who didn't have any sinister intentions of bucking me off and stomping me into the dust like the calves would, but I wanted Dad to be proud of me, so I kept quiet.

My stomach churned as I waited for my turn to ride. The announcer called my name, and I fought against the urge to run in the other direction. Dread over disappointing Dad forced my feet to march toward the calf pens. I tried to swallow, but my throat was too dry.

Several cowboys had already corralled a calf in the chute and were waiting for me. I climbed the rusted iron bars of the fence and looked down. The gate was pushed in against the calf to prevent it from thrashing about and hurting either me or itself.

Dad helped lower me onto the calf's back. The calf slammed its head against the gate in an effort to escape. The bars of the gate rattled, and the calf bawled, sounding as frightened as I felt.

One of the gate attendants fitted the thick, rough bull rope around the calf. I gripped the nearest iron bar with my left hand as the cowboy wrapped the rope around my right. I could feel the coarseness of the rope through the glove I wore. I sat and listened to the instructions both Dad and the gate attendant gave me about riding the calf.

It sounded easy enough. Watch the calf's head; wherever the head goes, that's the direction the calf's going. Then lean that way to keep my balance.

As soon as I signaled the cowboy, he would open the gate. The smell of dust and manure filled the air. Even though it wasn't particularly hot, sweat trickled down the side of my face. My heart pounded against my chest like a tribal war drum.

I looked at the gate attendant and gave a nod.

Then the world blurred. The calf bolted out of the chute. I clung to the bull rope with one hand and held the other high above my head. My legs squeezed against the calf's body as hard as I could manage, but it wasn't enough. I slid down the side of the calf in slow-motion.

I didn't watch the calf's head. I didn't try to adjust my balance. My mind froze, not able to focus on anything other than clinging to the beast with my legs. If it weren't for my grip on the rope, the calf would've tossed me with his initial leap.

It took a couple of seconds to realize the ride was over. In my mind, I was still sliding down the side of the calf, but in reality, I was sprawled out on the dusty arena floor. Someone helped me stand and then handed me my hat.

I limped over to the fence. My leg hurt. I wasn't sure whether I'd hit the ground hard or the calf had stepped on me. Then, suddenly, I forgot all about the pain. There was Dad! He stood waiting for me, his shoulders back, his chin high, and a huge grin on his face.

He placed a hand on my shoulder and walked me over to the snack truck. In small arenas like the one hosting junior rodeo events, the snack truck was a pickup with a camper shell and a couple of beverage coolers inside. If we were lucky, the concessions person also stocked a few boxes of beef sticks, candy bars, and hot pickles.

I ordered a root beer. Victory had never tasted better.

The routine repeated itself through the fall and the first half of the next year. Fear would mount in anticipation of the next event. Each time I straddled a calf in the chute, my mind would go blank. The chutes would open, the calf would buck, and I'd desperately cling to my bull rope, ultimately sliding off the beast.

Dad built a low-tech mechanical bull in our backyard to help me improve my calf-riding skills. He sank four six-by-eight posts into the ground, then attached a green fifty-gallon barrel to the posts with thick rope. A bull rope went around the barrel just like it went around the calves at the rodeo. I sat on the barrel, Dad strapped me in with the bull rope, and then he pulled on the ropes.

Somehow I always performed better on the fake cow, even though

Dad tossed me higher in the air than the calves ever did and it hurt more to land on the grassy lawn in our backyard than on the soft dirt of the arena. Despite the greater difficulty in riding Dad's rodeo Frankenstein, I wasn't afraid of the mechanical bull.

My friends enjoyed riding the bull more than I did. I preferred to pull the ropes, doing my best to buck them off the barrel. As word got out about our backyard attraction, more and more of the neighbor kids came over after school to give it a try. Dad wasn't big on playing catch with me, but he spent plenty of time bouncing me around with his homemade mechanical bull.

When summer vacation arrived, my favorite cousin came to stay for a few weeks. We planned to spend the next three months cruising the neighborhood on our bikes, without any concerns about homework. The first two or three days went according to plan, but then I started having problems walking when I'd get up in the morning. My right leg hurt. I'd hobble around the house until the pain subsided, then take off with my cousin for some outdoor fun.

This worked for a while, but then it began to take longer to warm-up the leg before I could easily put full pressure on it and join my cousin outside. Soon I couldn't put any pressure on it and had to get around by hopping on one foot. Mom made a doctor's appointment. By the time the appointment came around, I had resorted to crawling on my hands and one leg.

The doctor examined me and found an infection that had most likely been caused by a calf stepping on me after one of my falls at the rodeo. I hadn't noticed any signs of a rip or tear in my blue jeans, but apparently that didn't mean a raucous calf couldn't leave its mark on *my* calf.

Two small incisions released the built-up pus in my leg. The doctor filled the cavity with what looked like a thin strip of ticker tape, bandaged the wound, and sent me home. With instructions to stay off my feet for two entire weeks. It nearly killed me.

In my mind, the injury had ruined what should have been an

amazing summer. My cousin and I could still have some good times building models, watching television, and talking about whatever twelve-year-old boys talked about, but I was more than just a little upset. I decided to tell Dad I didn't want to ride calves anymore.

I waited for Dad to come home from work. Even though I was resolved to tell him I wanted to quit, I would have rather been in a chute, sitting on a calf, ready to ride. At least the calf wouldn't stare at me with a steely glare of disappointment.

Dad walked into the house and then grabbed a snack from the fridge. A glass of milk, stuffed full of bread. I didn't understand the appeal of soggy bread, but he liked it. Milk dripped from his mustache as he asked me how my leg was doing.

"I'm fine," I said as I followed him into the living room. "The injury has made me think about the whole rodeo thing. I want to stop riding calves."

"You can't let a minor injury stop you from doing something you love," Dad said.

My legs trembled, and a sick feeling festered in the bottom of my stomach. I took a deep breath and worked up the courage to tell him. "I don't love calf riding. In fact, it scares me."

Despite the summer heat, a chill encased my limbs as I stood before him. Dad studied me for a moment, a trace of disappointment on his face. "Then why have you been riding all this time?"

"Because I thought you wanted me to," I told him. "I wanted to make you happy."

"It takes a lot of guts to keep doing something that scares you." Dad nodded his head. "I'm proud of you for having the courage to face your fear every time you rode a calf. I respect you for telling me that you don't want to ride anymore."

"Thanks, Dad." The tension flowed out of me like water. I'd expected him to be mad at me.

"Everyone marches to the beat of a different drummer," Dad told me.

"You don't have to cowboy to make me happy. What I want is for you to follow your own path. Do whatever it is that makes you happy. If you do that, then I'll be happy too."

Dad frequently used the different-drummer speech on all of us kids. That day, for the first time in my life, it sank in that he really meant it. And not in that abstract way where you toss out the phrase to explain the strange behavior of people you see in the news. He understood that each of us is different and those diverse qualities are what makes the world function the way it should.

He also taught me to think for myself—not blindly follow everyone else. Dad said, "Don't listen to what people say, watch what they do." That in turn led me to spend a lot of time watching what people did and then wondering why they did it.

After high school, I worked construction with my dad's brothers. They started me out as a laborer and, because I represented the Lindsay family, I was expected to work harder and faster than anyone else on the jobsite. It wasn't enough for me to carry lumber from one spot to another, I was expected to run with it. If there were any other laborers on the job, I was expected to run faster with three sheets of plywood on my shoulder than they did with two.

My status as the owners' nephew marked me as the favorite target for jokes. Because I liked science-fiction movies, whenever I passed by the full-fledged carpenters, they shouted, "Pew. Pew-pew." All anyone needed to do to find me on the construction site was to follow the sounds of mock laser fire. It felt like running the trench at the end of the original *Star Wars* movie.

Dad worked construction as well, but not for his younger brothers. On days when I felt less than enthused about hauling lumber in the scorching 115-degree heat, he counseled me, "You start a day, you finish the day." Dad expected me to give everything my best effort. Without him saying a word, I knew his advice applied to all aspects of my life. You

start a job, you finish the job. You start a marriage, you finish the marriage.

After about a year, I graduated from laborer to carpenter-in-training.
I was given the jobs that required knowing only how to swing a hammer.
And I excelled at that skill. I reached a point where the other carpenters
had me compete with the new hires on their first day. Two of us would
race to hammer a line of sixpenny nails into the roof. I would set each
nail with my upward swing and then sink it with a single blow. Tap-pow.
Tap-pow. Tap-pow. The only thing that slowed me down was having to
pull more nails from my nail bag. If the new guys couldn't beat me, they
were harassed mercilessly about losing to a trainee.

Even though I eventually gained the respect of my coworkers, the
teasing never stopped. The men I worked with every day were more than
happy to point out—and laugh at—how my interests in science fiction
and video games made me different from them.

It was at roughly this same time that my brother and youngest sister
started calling me the milkman's son. I bore no resemblance to my siblings. They were blond, and my hair was almost black. They shared the
same eye color; I did not. They had many Lindsay features, and I had
none.

Growing up, the differences between us hadn't escaped my attention.
I often felt like I was the odd one out, even within the safe confines of my
home.

What was wrong with me?

Once, I'd even asked Mom and Dad if I'd been adopted. They told
me not to be ridiculous. Of course I wasn't adopted. I'd accepted their
answer, but still felt a need to convince myself with a few arguments of
my own. Like, it doesn't make sense for the oldest child to be adopted.
Or, the math doesn't work out. Mom and Dad met in March, married
in April, and I was born in the fall. No one adopts a child so soon after
marriage.

Besides, no matter how solid the arguments sounded in my head, my heart failed to believe it.

My brother and sister found the milkman's son bit to be hilarious. I had a hard time understanding why they gained such delight from our differences. Didn't they know how much I needed to feel like I was an important part of the family? Doesn't everyone?

Mom and Dad never talked about how different I looked and acted from the others. I didn't feel like an oddball when I was with Dad. He loved me the same as all the kids who looked like him . . .

—— ——

Memories of Dad slow the whirlwind of mental chaos blowing through my head. Dad's DNA may not have contributed to my physical form, I remind myself, but his influence has shaped my life. His natural storytelling skills transferred to me even though I am neither flesh nor blood to him. Long hours of sitting at his side as he spun tales about his youth gave me the skills I needed to tell an entertaining story. But it was his acceptance of my love for writing that set me on the path of an author and the lessons he taught me that gave me the determination to keep writing.

Dad attended an author signing for my first book. He strode up to me, beaming a smile that could light up the night, and said, "I'm proud of you, son." I cherish that memory. All I had to do to earn my dad's respect was to march to the rhythm of my own special drummer and work hard to make my dreams come true.

How much of my relationship with Dad is about to change? Will he still love me for just being me?

# CHAPTER 6

# OH, BROTHER

Does God have a sense of humor? Does He think some things are funny? This situation feels like a practical joke played on a cosmic scale. Only, I'm not laughing.

The Great Lindsay Quest was a sham. I'm not actually a Lindsay. I'm not related to William "The Immigrant" Lindsay, or John Crawford Lindsay, or any of the other family members with whom I felt such an incredible bond through my research.

For a brief moment, I consider calling Mom to find out what she has to say about the situation, but I decide I'm not ready for any more surprises. That task will have to wait for another day.

I occupy myself with housework. It isn't until everyone has gone to bed and I'm left alone with my thoughts that the hounds of sorrow begin nipping at my heels. I slip on my black trench coat and take a walk through the neighborhood to sort out what I'm thinking—what I'm feeling.

The neighborhood is quiet this late at night. Only the sounds of an occasional car in the distance disturb the silence. Vapor clouds form in front of my face each time I exhale. The cold nibbles at my cheeks in the same way the frost of stark realization gnaws at my soul. It takes a few minutes before I stop drinking in the beauty of the night and focus on the situation.

My concept of family has been ripped in two—literally. The only thing I can think about for the next several blocks is that I don't have any full-fledged siblings. There isn't another person in the entire world who has the same mother and father as I do. I feel as though I'm only half a brother, less important than the siblings who share the same set of parents.

I've always hated it when my friends refer to one of their siblings as a half brother, or a half sister. Just the mention of the term makes me feel as if those individuals are loved only half as much as the siblings who share a full genetic bond. When talking to my oldest son, I refer to my ex-wife's children as the other set of siblings. I've never felt the need to have my son think of them as anything but his brother and sister.

He isn't half a brother. He isn't half a son. He isn't halfway between here and there in some stupid metaphoric sense. And neither am I.

A gust of wind kicks up, blowing cold air inside my open coat. I take a moment to secure the two middle buttons and then continue down the street.

As I look back on my early childhood, I realize that I didn't bother then to question why my siblings looked so different from me. It was enough to simply know that my family loved me and I had my place with all of them. High school changed that. I grew increasingly aware I didn't fit in with the rest of the family. Now I know why.

A wicked thought stalks along the dark edges of my mind. "You're an intruder. You don't belong with the rest of the family."

The rational portion of my brain rejects the idea, but that doesn't stop the flow of emotional responses triggered by the thought.

I don't have a regular family anymore. I have two sets of half families.

I've missed an entire lifetime of experiences with my New Jersey family. I've been cheated!

Are the differences between me and my siblings a sign that I never fully belonged with them? And how can I ever hope to have more than half a connection with my other set of siblings? Will both sets of brothers and sisters expect me to keep a respectful distance while they share the warm, comfortable bubble of full siblinghood?

How is this going to change the family dynamics? I briefly imagine my status switching to that of extended family . . . or honored guest . . . or possibly even fifth wheel. I'd settle for them merely placing me at the kid's table during the next holiday. At least that way I'd still be considered family.

I'll find out when I drop the bombshell on them.

Dozens of opening lines flit through my mind as I try to find the right way to tell my baby sister about the situation. It reminds me of my first job interview, standing in front of the bathroom mirror, practicing how I would introduce myself. I figure I can start with Jana because I'm the closest to her and then work my way up the family ladder until I reach Dad.

Unfortunately, sharing the news with my wife failed to give me any insight on how to tell the rest of my family. She barely raised an eyebrow when I first mentioned it. Her response is a great example of why she's such an ideal match for me, but it doesn't help in this situation. What is my family going to think when I tell them I have a different dad?

Except, they're only my Arizona family. I have two families. The Arizona family I grew up with, understand, and love. The members of the other family are complete strangers, living far away. For all I know, the New Jersey family might be members of a bizarre cult who believe Elvis is still alive and operating a soda shop along the Atlantic City Boardwalk.

I sit down at the desk in my office. My hands tremble as I pick up the phone and enter my sister's number. I run through a couple more lines, hoping one will stand out before Jana answers.

Maybe a funny approach would work best. Like, "You've heard of babies being switched at the hospital . . . it turns out the nurses switched dads on me."

"Hey, big brother," says Jana over the phone. "What's up?"

"I need to talk to you." My voice cracks. So much for the humorous approach.

"Are you okay?" Her voice is instantly filled with concern.

"Uh . . . yeah. I'm not in the hospital or anything. No one over here has died."

"Then why do you sound upset?"

I take a deep breath and let it out in a long, ragged sigh. "Ah . . . well . . . it's about the DNA test I sent in a few months ago. I found out that Dad doesn't have a long-lost brother."

"Oh, really?"

My heart pounds so hard against my chest I wonder if Jana can hear it through the phone. I lick my lips. "Um, I . . . I have another family."

Jana laughs. "That's so funny."

The awkwardness of the moment flees in an instant and is replaced by a combination of rage and shock. How can my dear, sweet, little sister laugh at my pain?

"Why are you laughing?" I ask.

"You really are the milkman's son."

"It's not funny," I shoot back at her. But I should have expected this reaction. Jana laughs when people slip and fall on their butt. If they happen to struggle to stand back up and limp away afterward, it makes the situation all the funnier to her. The only thing she enjoys more than watching a stumbling display of graceless mishap is performing one. Jana laughs louder at her own accidents than she does at others'. I've never been sure if it's a nervous reaction to misfortune or if she finds pain a laughable matter.

"No. You're right." She continues to chuckle, although I can tell she's trying to silence her mirth. "I'm sure you're devastated by the news. How . . . how . . ."

"Funny? Is that the word you're looking for?"

"Noooo." She snickers. "How . . . did you find out?"

If the situation was reversed, I wouldn't be laughing. A growling voice inside my head tells me to disconnect the call. Families are supposed to support one another. Each snicker, giggle, and laugh Jana makes drives another jagged spike into my already sensitive psyche. I'm teetering on the edge of a dark place, and my sister seems all too willing to give me a push.

"You have to admit that it's funny," Jana says when I fail to respond. "And do you know why it's funny? Because it doesn't really matter."

"It matters to me," I mumble.

"All right, I'm sorry." The giggles are gone. "It's sad you didn't know you had another family, but now you have an opportunity for more people to love you. All this has done is increase the size of your family— not the quality."

"I guess."

"There's no guessing about it," says Jana. "My emotions toward you haven't changed in any way. You're still the person who looked after me when I was little. You're still the person who sat with me when we watched scary movies. You are what you are. You are my brother. That hasn't changed."

"Thanks." The heavy darkness in my chest lifts . . . some. She might be telling me all of this just to make me feel better, but I accept it because it's what I need to hear.

"Now, tell me how you found out."

"My sister in New Jersey told me I wasn't understanding the data cor-rectly." A tiny thrill charges me. It's the same feeling I have whenever I tell a story, only muted by the negative consequences of my discovery. "The DNA match is for a close relative, not a first cousin. Then she showed me a picture of her dad when he was in high school. He looked a lot like me at that age. Or maybe I look a lot like him. Either way, we look alike."

"Wow," Jana chimes in. "That's incredible. What about your new sister? Do you look anything like her?"

"Yes. We look very similar." Rather than brood over the reminder that the two of us look nothing alike, an unfamiliar sense of belonging bubbles up inside me. See, I do belong somewhere. I'm not a freak. It feels so good to have a sibling look like me. My eyes water with the threat of tears.

"Send me pictures. I want to see."

I tell Jana to hold on while I email her a copy of the picture of Mr. Petrauschke.

"Have you told Dad yet?" Jana asks.

Her question stops me cold. That's really the purpose of all this, to start with the family member I have the easiest time talking to and then work my way up to Dad. I'm not ready to share this with him yet.

"Of course not," I say. "Based on the way you reacted to the news, I'm not sure I want to tell anyone else. Everyone will laugh at me."

"Oh, come on," Jana says, all traces of mirth gone. "This doesn't change our family dynamic. I love you. Mark still loves you. Dad loves you."

"They love me now," I say, "but what's Dad going to think when he finds out?"

"He's going to think the same thing he's always thought—that he loves you. And so does everyone else. Don't let this bother you. It's nothing."

"Okay. Thanks. I love you too." A mental numbness sets in. The conversation has simultaneously gone better and worse than I expected. I end the call.

Jana laughing at the situation is better than most of the scenarios I had played out in my head, but it isn't what I need right now. Then again, the Lindsays are not a touchy-feely bunch, quick to lend their limited talents at empathy to those in emotional need. The family tends to use more of a kindly phrased "get over it" when dealing with tragedy.

I sit at my desk for a few minutes, deciding whether I should tell anyone else, when my fourteen-year-old daughter walks past the office door on the way to her bedroom.

"Lucy," I call out. "I need to talk with you."

She steps into the room and motions with her head for me to speak— one of those what-do-you-want gestures.

"I'm pretty sure grandpa isn't my biological father."

Her eyes widen. Then I show her Mr. Petrauschke's high school picture.

Lucy puts her hand over her mouth and laughs. A short laugh. Like a laugh that escaped before she could close the inappropriate-emotion gate.

"Tell me what you think," I ask her.

I can tell from her face she's struggling with her response.

"Go ahead," I say. "Tell me what came to mind. You won't hurt my feelings."

"That's funny."

I close my eyes and sigh. After a few moments I open my eyes and ask, "What do you find funny about it?"

"It's ironic that you really are the milkman's son. That picture is evidence. You can't deny the two of you look alike."

"I don't think it's funny," I say.

"Yeah, and that makes it even funnier."

"Go do your homework."

I cover my eyes with the heels of my hands and then rest my elbows on the desk. How can my baby girl think the situation is funny? Doesn't anyone care how I feel? Can't they see the pain this revelation is causing me? A single thought echoes in my mind.

It's not funny!

My wife and I drive over to my friend Alan's house for dinner and game night. We are having Hawaiian haystacks. I load mine up with coconut, pineapple, almonds, and plenty of crunchy chow mein noodles.

The women gather around the kitchen table and talk as they munch on their own special mix of the available ingredients. Black olives, chives, and cheese seem to be the popular choices. Alan's wife, Daelyn, looks up at me and says, "What's going on with your DNA test?"

I groan inwardly. The guys and I want to play our guy games. What I don't need right now is to have a room full of my friends laugh at me like my sister and daughter did. But if I don't answer Daelyn, the women are going to keep asking me to share the DNA results. I brace myself for a round of uproarious laughter with the thought that the sooner I tell everyone my secret, the sooner I can get on with the purpose for which I came here tonight . . . to mete out death and destruction to imaginary beings on a game board.

With my haystack still in hand as a sort of food-shield against the inevitable guffaws, I address the table full of women. "The DNA test matched me to my biological father in New Jersey."

The women release a collective gasp.

"No way," my friend says.

"Does your family know?" asks Stacy.

"I keep telling him," says my wife, "that you can't make this stuff up."

Daelyn leans back in her chair and sits taller. Her eyes are wide and her eyebrows knitted together in an expression that's half shock and half curiosity. "How sad for you."

Finally. Someone understands the tragedy of my situation. My heart goes out to my friend, the only person besides my wife who hasn't laughed at my misfortune. Bless you, kind lady.

"Are you okay?" Daelyn asks. "Are you okay with this?"

That's what I wonder every day. Am I all right with having another family? But so much of my answer depends on how Dad is going to react to the news.

"No," I tell her. "Not really. For fifty-seven years, I lived with a stable concept of what is family. Then overnight, I find out my family image is wrong. Rather than being a part of two families, I feel I don't belong to either."

"I still think it's funny," says Alan.

"Eat your haystack," I tell him. "The adults are talking here."

Alan chuckles and wanders off to the front room, where the rest of the guys are setting up tonight's guy game. He joins the casual debate already underway . . . what color playing pieces do you want?

"I thought you were going to tell me what country you're from," says Daelyn. "Then you tell me this. That isn't at all what I expected. I feel for you."

"Thanks," I say. "It means a lot to have someone care about my feelings."

Daelyn's words are a soothing balm to my chafed emotions. Her comments won't change the situation, but knowing someone recognizes my pain gives me strength to face the unknown road ahead. Why couldn't everyone react to the situation this way?

"How could this happen?" Daelyn asks me.

"I don't know," I tell her. "It doesn't really matter how it happened— it happened."

"You're right, but this is big." Daelyn shakes her head. "I mean, what do you do with that? Where do you go from here? All I can think of is what would I do?"

I just shrug.

"I had a cousin who went through the same thing," Daelyn continues. "The relationship started off well but then fell apart. Some people don't want to know the truth if it's inconvenient. I hope this all goes well for you."

"Me too."

I was right. It isn't funny.

I wake up in a foul mood, which seems appropriate for confronting Mother about my little surprise. I work through the morning ritual, thinking of exactly what to say when she answers the phone. Then I call.

"Hi, Mom."

"Oh, what a wonderful surprise," she says. The warm greeting and the cheerful tone of her voice rob me of a portion of my anger. Anger that I need to fuel this discussion. I draw a deep breath and continue.

"I know that Dad isn't my biological father," I tell her.

Silence.

"Mom, did you hear what I said?"

"Yes, dear."

"I want you to tell me about William Petrauschke."

Silence.

"Mom!"

"I don't want to talk about it," Mom says in the same sweet, calm voice she uses to tell me she loves me.

"This is pretty important," I tell her. "I think I deserve to know as much about my biological father as possible."

"I told you, honey. I don't want to talk about it. Maybe we can go to lunch together next week. My treat."

She isn't going to tell me anything. If I keep bothering her for an answer, she'll just turn off her hearing aid. I decide to drop the matter. "Yeah. Lunch sounds good."

"Okay," she says. "Love you. See you next week."

The conversation ends, and I'm no closer to finding an answer about my parents' relationship than before I called. I know it can't be an easy situation for Mom, but it's harder on me. I'm the one left with a tangled family situation and having to deal with a group of strangers who happen to be my relatives.

What can I do about it, though? If Mom decides to keep the information to herself, I may never know what really happened.

Six weeks pass. Lunch with Mom failed to produce any information about the situation. I know she's not going to tell me anything, so I decide to drop the matter rather than stress our relationship.

A cool breeze blows in through the screen door of my office. In another month, the wonderful spring weather will give way to the scorching desert heat. Until then, the lower temperatures invigorate me, encouraging my fingers to tap dance across the keyboard as I work on book number five.

Two sparrows chirp to one another from on top of the backyard fence. They combine with the coos of an unseen dove to form an impromptu chorus, providing background music to accompany my writing.

The house phone rings. I answer it.

"It's Mark," my brother says. "I happened to be in the neighborhood for business and thought I would stop by and visit."

"Great. I have to stop for lunch soon anyways."

"See you in a few." Mark disconnects the call.

I have difficulty pulling my attention away from the computer. My mind is still in writing mode, and I'm in the middle of a chapter. I hate being interrupted when I'm "in the zone," but this is my brother. And I always have time for my brother.

Mark is rarely in my neighborhood, and he never just stops in for a visit. Six years ago, Dad had a dizzy spell and fell off his horse. Probably the first time he's been unhorsed since he was a teen. The doctors weren't sure if Dad was going to recover, but he did. Ever since then, Mark has reached out to the rest of the family more and more. My guess is he senses all of us are getting older and any of us could pass away without notice. It seems like he doesn't want to miss any chances to visit the family whenever possible.

I have a few minutes before he arrives and make notes on where I plan to go in the story so I can pick up the writing trail later in the day. A knock sounds at the front door. I quickly type a last sentence and hop up to greet my brother.

While the two of us are exchanging updates on our families, it occurs to me that I might as well discuss the results of the DNA test with him. I don't expect him to be any more supportive than Jana, but the conversation I had with Daelyn weeks ago gave me emotional strength that I hope I can draw from now. Besides, I have to eventually tell Mark and Dad about this.

"Come on into my office," I tell Mark. "I have something to show you."

Mark follows me, and I pull up the DNA test results. I point to the screen and explain how the DNA results indicate there is a close relation within the Petrauschke family. My heart beats faster, but so far, Mark has only nodded.

"It appears that Dad isn't my dad." I show him the picture of Mr. Petrauschke. "This man is my biological father."

I brace myself for my brother's reaction. Of all the family, he can be the most blunt and least considerate of people's feelings. To be fair, he turns the same critical eye on himself. But that doesn't make it any easier for me to shrug off his occasional astringent comments.

Mark lets loose with a loud blast of laughter. "You really are the milkman's son."

"I'm so happy I could brighten your day with my misfortune. Maybe I can step in front of a moving bus and totally make your month." To make it worse, I can't even get mad at Mark. He and Jana are so much alike. I realized I should have expected him to think the situation is funny. Is it too much to expect them to have an understanding word for me? All I really need is for them to give one simple acknowledgment of the complications this has caused in my life.

"Oh, come on," says Mark. "Get over it. You're making too big of a deal about this."

"Yeah, that's what everyone in the family keeps saying."

Mark raises his eyebrows and gives me a shrug, his way of letting me know he's right. And the truth is, I'm not as upset about his reaction as I had been with Jana's. I feel more numb to the situation than pained by it. Maybe even a little annoyed. All this laughter is getting old.

"All right," says Mark, "I think this is funny. If I hear something crazy I'm going to laugh, but we live in a day where crazy is normal. And if you don't laugh it off, the crazy can drive you insane."

"That's crazy talk," I tell him, but at the same time it makes sense.

"Whatever." Mark grins and shakes his head. "You'll have to do better than this if you want to blow my socks off. I mean, it's not even a negative thing. Nothing changes the situation here, and you have more family in New Jersey. Boo-hoo-hoo. Randy has a whole new batch of people to love him. They might even be rich."

"I don't care if they have money." I roll my eyes. Why does everything have to be about money? It can't buy happiness, and it doesn't determine a person's worth. "I'm worried about how Dad is going to react to this."

"Ask him and find out," says Mark. He looks at the picture of Mr. Petrauschke and snickers. "It's funny how much he looks like you. Now we know where you got those lips."

Everyone who looks at the picture notices the lips. And it isn't funny that I look like Mr. Petrauschke—it's tragic. Why isn't anyone dealing with the elephant in the room? I'm not the person everyone thought I was. Or at least I'm not the person I thought I was.

The only thing left to do . . . is to tell Dad.

It takes a month to work up the courage to make the trip to see Dad. I wait for the next school holiday and load up the kids in the van. I'm hoping Dad will take the news better if I'm surrounded by his grandchildren. He might have his reservations about me, but surely he can't say no to the lovely, lovely grandchildren.

Dad offers the kids Popsicles as soon as we arrive. I give him and my stepmother a hug and walk inside the living room. Dad and Judy each have an easy chair with a prime view of the television. Everyone else sits on the visitors' couch. If more than three people come to visit, the rest have to sit on the floor.

A western is on the television. I raise my voice to be heard over the sound of a cattle stampede. "Can you turn off the idiot box for a few minutes? I have something I want to talk to you about."

"Sure," says Dad. "Is everything okay?"

"I guess that depends on your definition of okay."

He turns off the television and sets the controller down on the cluttered table next to his easy chair. His expression is all business. I can tell he thinks something bad has happened, which makes it harder for me to start talking. How do I tell the man who has been my dad for all these years and is sitting across the room from me worried about whether I'm all right that he isn't really my dad?

I think back to my calf-riding days. As much as I dreaded giving the okay to open the chute, I found it easier to get it done with than to wait in fear. I stare straight into Dad's eyes and, in a single rapid-fire blast, tell him, "The DNA test results I told you about don't show you have another brother; they indicate I have a different biological father."

The worried expression on Dad's face fades immediately. He claps his hands together and laughs. "Yeah, isn't that a hoot?"

A hoot? No, it isn't a hoot!

I sit on the sofa, staring across the room at him. My mind is frozen in place. This not the way any of the scenarios that have run through my head over the last few months played out. He hasn't rejected me. He hasn't asked for any details. He isn't even upset.

Dad thinks this is funny.

This is unreal. Laughter is not a viable option for my dad, or any dad, in this situation. He's supposed to be shocked—not me.

"You guys hungry?" asks Dad. "I'm thinking of ordering pizza."

"Pizza's good," I say, but my mind still stumbles along, looking to make sense of Dad's response. How can he be thinking about food at a time like this? I've just dropped the biggest family-relation bomb of all time, and he wants to order pizza. For the amount of emotion he's showing over this, I might as well have told him the weather in Phoenix was going to be warm and sunny over the next few days.

If I were him I . . . I don't know what I'd do. Fifty-seven years is a long time to think someone is your son—or father. Is it even reasonable to expect those feelings to go away, immediately and completely, as soon as you find out the truth? Do fifty-seven years of hugs, kisses, and family events blow away on the breeze of a few words?

Isn't there an element of feeling cheated, like I felt cheated when I heard the news? Then again, that isn't the way Dad operates. He taught us to focus on what's important. I remember him telling me, "It does no good to worry about things you can't change."

It isn't as if I want him to be upset. I love this man. Dad raised me. He protected me. He supported my decisions to be different from the rest of the family. I'm glad I didn't hurt his feelings with the news, but even with his philosophy on life, it doesn't make sense. He isn't even surprised.

Ah! That's it.

He isn't surprised because someone already told him. I feel better . . . I think.

"How'd you find out?" I ask.

"Jana and her family came over a couple of weeks ago to help me clean out the barn. She mentioned you told her about the DNA results, and I about died laughing."

"You thought it was funny?" I ask. No . . . not Dad. Why would he think it was funny?

"It was hilarious," says Dad. "Then I asked Jana what she said to you when she found out, and she told me what a good time she had harassing you about being the milkman's son. The same thing happened with Mark. We just sat around laughing about it. You want pepperoni on your pizza?"

Does anyone in my family not think this is funny?

"I don't get it, Dad. I thought you would be upset."

Dad leans forward in his chair and turns his head so he can look at me with his good eye. "What do you want me to do? The situation has reached a point in time where something like that isn't important in my life. You were my son. I loved you. And that was all that mattered. And as far as getting a DNA test done . . . Who the hell cares? Nothing changed in my life. I raised you, and that's all that really counted. You are still my son. It's never been a big deal. It's just a fact."

Tears fill my eyes. How could I have thought Dad would react any differently? He has always been there for me. It was stupid to worry he might possibly stop loving me. And in that light, with the knowledge my family doesn't care because nothing has changed, I finally see how the situation is funny.

I am the milkman's son. Apparently God does have a sense of humor.

CHAPTER 7

# THE MILKMAN'S FAMILY

Tammy's latest message sits in my email inbox. I still haven't dealt with what it will mean to have a new family. As long as I focus on my current novel, I can block out the emotional bugbears that keep flitting around inside my head.

Unfortunately, it's late in the afternoon and my brain is mush from writing all day. I save my file, lean back in my chair, and close my eyes. Hollywood thrives on weird situations and abnormal families. The stranger the better. That's why Jerry Springer has been on the air all these years. But I don't enjoy having my life turned into a drama-filled reality show. If I don't like what's going on, I can't change the channel or fast-forward to the happy parts. There isn't even background music to advise me of the appropriate mood for whatever situation in which I might be involved.

The part of my personality that flinches at the thought of being rude tells me to respond to Tammy. I want to believe it won't bother her if we stop exchanging emails, because that means I can stop right here. If she doesn't care whether we're family, then I don't have to either. But I'm not feeling it. Her previous messages have been considerate of my emotions. The least I can do is return the courtesy.

Then again, I'm not sure what to say to Tammy. I don't know anything about the woman other than we share the same father. Is that, by itself, enough reason to move forward from here and work toward a meaningful relationship? I already have a family I love. I don't need another one. I don't need the Petrauschkes complicating my life. I'm not sure I even want to learn how to spell their name. Or pronounce it properly.

I recoil from the prospect of emotionally embracing a clan of strangers who live on the other side of the country. I try to picture myself casually walking up to Mr. Petrauschke to give him a big father-son hug, like I do my dad, and find the idea a bit creepy. It feels wrong.

Not that I think there's anything wrong with Tammy's dad. But even if he is the greatest father in the world, how would I go about blending in with a new family this late in my life? Do I want to be related to these people? What if I don't like them? What if they don't like me? What if they're weird? I mean, weirder than I am.

Too many questions bounce around inside my head to make a decision. And I know this is too important of a matter to hide from. My best bet is to continue the casual conversations with Tammy. Uncomfortable with the seriousness of the situation, I decide to start my reply to Tammy with a joke, to break the tension I'm feeling.

I switch to my email and write, "Thanks for the pictures of your dad and brothers. That certainly helped confirm the DNA tests were correct. My family has always kidded that I'm the milkman's son . . . I don't suppose your dad is a milkman, is he?"

I hit the send button.

Doh! I slap my forehead.

I instantly regret not taking a moment to consider if what I wrote was appropriate. Tammy may not think the joke about the milkman's son is funny. This is her dad, the one she's known all these years. She might think my comment is making fun of her father being overly friendly with the ladies. Tammy might take the comment as an insult to his character. And what if it brings up uncomfortable memories?

Having her think I'm insensitive to the delicate nature of this situation is probably not the best way to start a relationship with my new sister. But the message is already on its way, and all I can do is wait for her response.

A new sister. When I refer to her that way it sounds as if my mother just gave birth. Tammy's not new. Just the connection. I'm not even sure what I think about having another sister. The relationship doesn't feel real at this point. If I were asked to talk about my sisters, Tammy's name wouldn't come to mind. I suspect that over time my feelings about the situation will change.

My knees crack as I rise from my desk. A series of pops from the left one, a single pop from the right. Then I stroll into my bedroom and change shirts for my Wednesday critique group. The comfortable, worn, bright-green Grinch T-shirt goes into the clothes hamper, and I don one of the Hawaiian-style shirts my wife made for me.

The group holds our weekly meetings at a local bookstore. I hurry inside and admire the massive number of books that fill the shelves. The path to the group weaves through the romance section, past the overstocks table, and on to the back of the store. I love meeting in a place where I am surrounded by books. It seems almost karmic to discuss my writing in a setting where people come to buy the finished works of accomplished authors. I hope some of the skill and success of those famous writers rubs off on me.

Most of the group is already there, sitting around a white, plastic fold-up table.

"You ready to be roasted?" asks Jeannie.

"Sure," I say. "The criticism will be a welcome diversion from real life."

The grin on Jeannie's face fades. "Are you all right?"

I hesitate, not sure if I should tell everyone. The notion of revealing my secret to a small group of my writing buddies doesn't bother me nearly as much as telling my family did. Maybe because their reaction to the news isn't going to change my life. At worst, they will find it ironically funny, and I've already come to terms with that.

"Earlier this year, I found out that my dad isn't my dad." I watch the faces of my fellow authors. They all raise their eyebrows. A couple of them give me openmouthed stares. It's quiet around the table as they look at one another.

"I imagine that came as quite a surprise," says Carlene.

"You could say that," I tell her. "My family is my life. For fifty-seven years, I had a clear and stable understanding of what my family was and what it meant to me. Then those dynamics changed overnight. And since I'm the only one who had a parent switched, it feels like I'm facing the situation by myself."

How can a man with two families feel alone? It doesn't make sense. More people means more options. A bigger family means a larger support network and a greater chance that someone within the two groups will understand whatever crisis I might currently be going through. Except that none of them are in this situation—my situation. I'm the only one who knows what this feels like.

"Are you?" asks Jeannie.

"Am I what?" I ask.

"Are you facing this situation alone?"

I think about this. Despite their laughter, I know Mark, Jana, and Dad are concerned. All three of them love me for who I am and not what I am. The fact that my DNA isn't an exact match for my siblings, or any kind of match for my dad, doesn't change the way they feel about me. We have shared too much of our lives to think of one another as anything other than family.

"Not really," I answer. "My baby sister has always been there for me when I need someone to talk with. It doesn't matter if I need advice or just want to vent. All I have to do is call, and she makes time to listen. I guess it's only a matter of me realizing that it will take some time to work this out."

"Is your biological father alive?" asks Anthony.

"Yes."

"What's he like?" asks Ruth.

"I don't know," I tell her. Curiosity wells up inside me. I should know, but I don't.

———

Every day I check for Tammy's reply. This is different from the time I spent waiting for my DNA test results. A thrill of discovery filled me as I waited for the DNA to return and unlock the secrets of Lindsay family history. Each day brought me closer to those revelations. But every day I fail to hear from Tammy gives weight to the fear that I've upset her.

It takes a week before Tammy replies. "My dad was not a milkman."

I knew it. She didn't think it was funny. I spend a few moments giving myself mental uppercuts to the head, making sure I feel appropriately stupid.

Tammy's message continues. "I think he was doing insulation work when he was in Phoenix. He was working in a hot attic and then had an ice-cold drink, which caused a blood clot, which caused the stroke."

What stroke? The way Tammy mentions the stroke makes it seem like everyone knows about it. As if that one event sculpted the rest of my biological father's life and the family he raised uses it as a common navigation point for who he is and what they are together.

"My family has been in south Jersey for many years," Tammy writes. "Dad lived in Phoenix from about the age of nine until a little after his stroke in 1958. My grandmother was living on East Madison around that time. I'm not sure if that is where she took care of him while he recovered.

"Some time after recovering from the stroke, Dad moved back to NJ, and then my parents got married. He worked at the local mill. When I was a baby, he had an accident. He fell off the scaffolding, went through the safety net, and hit his head on the concrete floor. The doctors put a plate in his head. While this is bad, I was too little to remember, and we have always known dad the way he is. If you have any more questions, please feel free to ask. I will answer to the best of my ability."

First the milkman joke and now reminding her of the stroke. I have plenty of questions to ask Tammy, but I'm not sure how much this might be upsetting her. On the other hand, the only way I'm going to find out more about my biological father is to ask questions, and Tammy said I should feel free to do exactly that.

I imagine this isn't any easier on Tammy than it is on me. That's something else the two of us have in common. As I get to know her, I might discover we have even more similarities. That would certainly make it easier to bond with her and the rest of the New Jersey folks . . . if I decide that's what I want to do.

"I'm sorry about your dad's stroke." I wonder why Mr. Petrauschke moved here as a child, and why he and his mother returned to his native New Jersey. He triggered my arrival into the world—to impact my entire life—and then abruptly left. Was it fate that he sired me . . . or just a mistake?

My head is full of questions, but two stand out. "Why did your dad move here? And why did he go back to New Jersey?"

I send the message to Tammy.

The part of the city Tammy's dad lived in is close to the area where I spent most of my childhood—not living there but visiting my mom's side of the family in the trailer park where my grandmother and great-aunt lived.

Images of catching toads in Aunt Max's garden bubble up from my memory. More scenes play out in my mind; exploring the overly large ditch just to the west of the trailer park, walking up to the corner grocery store with my aunt and grandmother, and the laundry room with the old-fashioned washers that had a pair of rollers to wring the clothes dry.

I loved playing with those wringers.

These are good memories. When I think of Tammy's dad living nearby, he seems less of a stranger. Not only have both of us lived in Phoenix, we shared a common stomping ground. For the first time, I feel a connection with my father.

— • —

I check my email before I head off to my Tuesday meeting. No response from Tammy. Her messages are friendly, but she seems to be in no hurry to get back to me. I wonder if she's sharing my emails with the rest of her family and that's causing the delay in her responses.

Maybe tomorrow.

As part of a community outreach program, I meet with a group to discuss employment opportunities for people in the neighborhood. I arrive at the meeting a few minutes early. The normal crowd of volunteers is sitting around the large sectional table in the conference room of a local church. Old black-and-white pictures of Mesa around the turn of last century adorn the wood panel walls.

"Hey, Randy," says Tom. "What's new with you?"

"I found out that my dad isn't my dad."

The room is silent. Tom raises his eyebrows. The others all look at one another. Eventually, Tom sputters the question I'm sure everyone wants to ask. "Um . . . How did you find out?"

I tell him about the family history research and my DNA test. It turns out to be way easier than discussing it with my family. No one in the room laughs at me. No one jokes about me being the milkman's son. And unlike my family, the group has plenty of questions.

"How did you feel when you found out?" asks Tom.

I do my best to imitate the *Twilight Zone* theme . . . and fail miserably. "I felt as if my whole world dropped out from underneath me. Someone could have told me the Earth was flat and I would have been more likely to believe it."

"That had to be rough," says Jeff.

"Yeah, it's a lot to process," I say.

"Does the rest of your family know?" asks Scott.

"Unless my sister has spread the word, it's just my parents and my siblings who know."

"What about the new family," Scott continues, "do they know?"

"It was my sister in New Jersey who told me," I say. "At least, she's the one who figured out the connection. I don't know if she's shared the information with the rest of her . . . I mean, our family."

Does my biological father know about me? The group's questions reveal how little I actually know about the situation. My situation. Hopefully, Tammy has the answers.

"What did your siblings think when you told them?"

At last, an easy question. "They think it's funny." I explain the joke.

"What about the man who raised you?" asks Jeff. "How did he react?"

"He thought it was hilarious too," I say. "My whole family busts out laughing over the idea that I really am the milkman's son. I'm not quite as amused as they are, but feel free to chuckle if you find it funny."

A couple members of the group smile, but at least they don't laugh.

Tom interrupts the discussion to start the meeting. I only half listen to the employment reports the others give, then I breeze through a quick version of my own. No one shows up for help with job searches, and so we dismiss early. I drive home and let my wife know I'm going for a walk.

It's warm outside. In another month, it will be too hot to enjoy my nighttime treks through the neighborhood. I let my feet pick the route for tonight's walk.

My thoughts drift back to how long it takes Tammy to respond to my messages. Maybe it's an indication that she isn't interested in connecting with me in any significant manner. Since no one else from New Jersey has bothered to contact me, maybe none of them want anything to do with me.

Even though I have thoughts about keeping the Petrauschkes at an emotionally safe distance, the prospect of them rejecting me leaves an aching hole in my chest. It's not my fault things are the way they are. I had no part in creating this situation . . . other than being born. I'm their brother, their son. Shouldn't that be enough for them to want to know me better?

Shouldn't that be enough for me to want to know them better?

I turn around and head back to the house. My wife looks up from her crocheting as I stroll through the living room. "That was a quick walk."

Rather than wait for Tammy to reply, I decide I need to let her know I'm interested in getting to know all of them better. A thin fog of darkness in my mind lifts as I accept my connection to them. For some reason I can't explain, I feel better already.

"Tammy," I write. "I got to thinking, after I responded to your message, that this turn of events may have upset you and the rest of your family. I'm sorry if that is so. I definitely don't want to contribute to your sorrows. The news of the test results has impacted my family. They worry I will feel left out, but it hasn't changed anything for them.

"That being said, I am willing to go along with whatever path you choose to take on the matter. If you would like me to remain a faceless family history contributor, then I'm all right with that. And if you, or the rest of your family, want to take a step toward getting to know each other a little, then I'm all right with that as well. Just let me know."

I lean back and look the message over to make sure it's what I want to say and to ensure I haven't mentioned anything that might upset Tammy. I read it, then reread it, then reread it again. Then I hit the send button. A sense of relief floods through me. The Petrauschkes might not be ready for a relationship, but at least I have acted in the way that's right for me.

——— ———

A message is waiting for me the following Monday.

"Dad didn't meet my mother until 1961," writes Tammy. "They

married in 1962. The discovery isn't as big a deal for us since it happened before the two of them met. One of the reasons I started on Ancestry was to find my father's family. I certainly wouldn't stop anyone else from learning as much as they want to about their family.

"I was a little shocked when I found out. It took a little while to sink in. I was not sure how you were going to react to all of this. I would like to get to know you, but only if you are comfortable with that."

My lips tremble as I read the message. I release a breath I didn't realize I was holding. My new sister wants to get to know me. She hasn't rejected me. I'm engulfed by the warm, comforting blanket of acceptance. Hopefully, the rest of the family will want to find out more about me as well.

"Tammy," I type. "I have to admit this has really been a weird experience. You see this sort of thing in the movies and scoff at the situation as being unrealistic. Or, at least, I do. Then all of a sudden—boom. I have three new siblings. I don't suppose anyone in the family is a successful Hollywood director looking for a talented author to write the next big mega-hit?

"How many in your family know about this situation?" I share a couple of paragraphs of information about myself as part of the getting-to-know-you process and end with, "If all of that doesn't scare you off, then I'd be happy to tell you more."

Send.

Tuesday passes.

Wednesday passes.

Most of Thursday passes. No response . . . so far.

I fix a quick dinner of tuna-salad sandwiches and sliced apples for the kids. We eat together and discuss which of the candidates is our favorite for winning this season of *The Great British Baking Show*. As usual, the two youngest boys wait for me to state my pick and then agree with me. A quarter to seven rolls around. I kiss my wife goodbye and make the five-minute drive over to the monthly book club meeting.

My friends Dave and Deb host the meeting at their house. Other than the three of us, the attendance varies from month-to-month. Charlie, their big white poodle, greets me at the door. I can expect him to spend most of the evening with his chin resting on my lap. Dave will try to keep Charlie from bothering me during the meeting, but I'm all right with the attention. The arrangement gives me all the benefits of having a dog for two hours a month without any of the responsibilities.

A win for me. A win for Charlie.

The group engages in a discussion about an upcoming writer's conference while we wait for everyone to arrive. Deb looks over at me and asks, "Everything all right? You seem kind of quiet."

"Nothing major," I say. "Just a few things on my mind."

"Oh, really? Like what?" she asks.

I can already picture the expressions on their faces when I tell the group about my secret DNA discovery. My previous tellings of the story have given me a few clues about how to add some dramatic touches to make it even more interesting than it already is.

First, the power punch to get their attention. "I found out this year, at the not so young age of fifty-seven, that my dad is not my dad."

I wait for the ripples of shock to circulate through the room.

"No way," says Deb. Her eyes look like they're going to pop out of her head.

"What?" Dave sits up straight in his chair.

"That's right," I tell them. "For years, my brother and sisters have teased me about being the milkman's son, and it turns out they were right."

I shake my head as if it's all a grand joke, letting the group know I don't mind if they find the situation funny. None of them laugh. The women in the group give me their unique versions of the you-poor-thing look. I find that with a little sympathy from my audience, I don't mind revealing the intimate sentiments of my soul.

"Are your parents still alive?" asks Deb.

"Yes, they are," I reply. "All three of them."

"Have they said why they never told you the truth?" asks Dave.

"I'm not sure who, if any of them, knows the real situation," I tell him.

"Then why did your siblings call you the milkman's son?" asks Rebecca.

"Because they have a sick sense of humor," I say. "And because they're little brats. I mean, what do you expect from younger brothers and sisters? You'd think they would eventually grow up, but they don't."

"Have you met your biological father?" asks Deb.

"No," I say. "Not yet. I'm not even sure if he wants to meet me."

"Of course he will." Deb waves her hand as if batting away the suggestion like an annoying fly in the room. "You're his son."

But will he? Tammy hasn't given me any sort of indication that the members of my New Jersey family want to meet me. None of them, besides Tammy, has reached out with an email or a text message. How hard is it to add me to their list of contacts and send a text that says, "I hear you're my brother"?

"Enough about my surprise family," I tell the group. "Let's talk about books."

We switch topics. I try to focus on the book discussion, but my thoughts drift back to the Petrauschkes. If they aren't interested in getting to know me better, then why did Tammy contact me about the DNA results? Is there something wrong with me? Did I say something that made the majority of the family flinch at the idea of establishing a relationship?

Eventually, the meeting ends and I go home. I check my email and my inbox on Ancestry, but there are no messages waiting for me in either place.

The weekend passes.

I wake up and start my Monday morning ritual. Shower. Breakfast. Check my email. A message is waiting for me. It finally clicks for me. I see a pattern. It doesn't matter what day of the week I respond to Tammy, she usually writes to me on Mondays.

Maybe, like me, that's when she schedules a block of time to answer emails. But another idea sticks in my head. What if she meets with the rest of her family on Sunday and shares my messages with them? I can almost picture the family gathered around the kitchen table, anxiously waiting to hear from the long-lost son/brother.

Nah! That's just wishful thinking on my part.

Her message reads, "It's been weird, and I'm not sure it has all sunk in yet. We do not have any directors in our family."

I scan the rest of the message. Then I stop. What did I just read? I go back to Tammy's last paragraph.

"I think it's time for you to know that my dad is in the same situation as you. Twenty years ago, he found out that his dad is not really his dad."

# CHAPTER 8

# DNA TEST ROUND TWO: LIKE FATHER, LIKE SON

Give me a break.

I'm the guy who writes stories about people who have incredible, unusual lives and are forced to suffer through ironic situations that seem realistic but should only exist on the pages of a gripping, page-turning novel. That's known as . . . fiction. Real lives, especially mine, are not meant to resemble the events from one of my books. I resent actually living in one of those absurd scenarios.

Not only am I a milkman's son, but so is my father. And for an even more surreal plot twist, my father made his discovery at roughly the same age I am now. Even I have limits to what I'll do to one of my characters, and this crosses the line. I would never put one of the precious products of my imagination into such a cosmically ironic predicament like this.

Okay, I would . . . but I'd feel conflicted about it.

At least the family name I grew up with is easier to spell than my father's. The surname Petrauschke seems like the universe decided to kick the poor man while he was down. Definitely over the line on that one.

I'm having a hard-enough time grasping the complexities and dealing with the emotions of my own situation. I can't conceive the level of torment I would have if I learned I have a son in the same predicament. In twenty years, am I going to receive an email, or whatever replaces email in the future, and find out I have a child I didn't know anything about? Ironic boundaries must have a limit, and I hope a third-generation milkman's son, or daughter, falls beyond that border.

But knowing Mr. Petrauschke probably went through many of the same difficulties I'm going through now creates an instant bond. I find it easier to accept him as my father because we share a few life experiences. And that's what family is all about—sharing difficult moments together.

I have to meet this man.

Another look at Tammy's email and I'm ready to respond. I decide to pass on telling any more jokes that might drag additional skeletons out of the family closet.

"Thanks for sharing pictures of your family," I write. "It allows me to think of all these individuals as people rather than just a list of names. When I see the pictures of your dad, I can't help thinking he looks like a nice guy. Isn't that weird to be in a position where something like that goes through my mind? Where I can only make guesses about him based on old pictures?

"I believe I see a family resemblance between the two of us. Which is unusual for me, because I don't look anything like my siblings here in Arizona. You might as well know I tend to tell a lot of jokes . . . some of them even funny."

Hopefully, my warning will be enough to prevent Tammy from being horribly insulted by one of my comments-gone-astray. The family I grew up with find me fairly harmless and know to err on the side of comedy when they're not sure what I mean. But Tammy isn't familiar with my sense of humor.

"If you, or any of the rest of the family, have questions about me, or the situation, please don't hesitate to ask." I check my comments for potentially insulting overtones. Then I check it again. I consider a third pass, but decide to just send it.

Before I exit out of my email, a notice from Ancestry catches my eye. It's one of the DNA alerts that inform me about another records match. I receive at least one a week. Most of the time I just file them away for future reference, waiting for the time when I feel like working on my family history again.

My family.

The phrase comes so easily to mind but no longer represents my life. I find it annoying that I have to identify which family I mean . . . even to myself. Do I mean the family I'm emotionally connected to or the family I barely know and who share half of my genetic code?

And does it really matter?

I haven't done any family history research for months. The Great Lindsay Quest has seemed pointless if I'm not a Lindsay. Almost as if the Lindsay pedigree is none of my business. As I stare at the email alert, William "The Immigrant" calls to me. In my mind, I hear him say, "Find my home. Find my family."

A part of me argues that I should dive into the Petrauschke line and learn as much about my new family as I can. Whether I like it or not, their blood flows through my veins. The interest just isn't there, though. I may be part of the Petrauschke bloodline, but the Lindsays have my heart. Besides, the Petrauschkes have Tammy. The Lindsays need me.

The struggle to learn and memorize the previous generations of my New Jersey family can wait until after I know the living ones better. I might even finish the Great Lindsay Quest by then. If technology can reveal the secret of my biological father, it should be able to help me find where William "The Immigrant" was born.

Ancestry is always adding new records to their database. I move the new email over to my family history folder and then start a search for Lindsays in Tyrone County, Ireland. A check on Google Maps gives me towns in the immediate vicinity of Fintona. That still leaves hundreds of results to study for clues to William's birthplace.

Omagh is the largest town within twenty miles of Fintona. Strabane is only thirty miles away. I know from my previous searches that both towns have numerous records available. If I don't limit myself to just mentions of Fintona, I might find my William.

Six hours of research fails to give me any new leads. I close the program and amble into the kitchen to start dinner. A quick search of the refrigerator reveals there are plenty of leftovers from the weekend. The kids are more likely to eat whatever my wife makes than my humble culinary offerings. Fried meatloaf, mashed potatoes with cream cheese, and broccoli. I place the meatloaf in the microwave and nuke it. Then I holler down the stairs to the basement. "Get ready to eat."

"What's for dinner?" asks my youngest son.

"Last night's leftovers."

"Yay," sounds the chorus of Nick and Rick together.

Food snobs.

At least I don't have to figure out a menu I think they might enjoy. We have dinner, and I return to my research. I pull up Google and try combining names of Lindsay ancestors with the names of towns around Fintona. Trillick, Dromore, Kilskeery, and Clogher are all close enough to have been William's home and still be linked to Fintona. Two hours of sifting through the results gives me the name of a book that should provide me with useful information.

The book was published in 1884 and is no longer in print. Amazon lists the title but doesn't show any actual copies for sale. That figures. The book's title includes Lisnacrieve, the name of the farm built by the original James Lindsay when he emigrated from Ayrshire in 1678. The extensive farm is only a mile from Fintona, where I suspect William "The Immigrant" was born. If any book has information on my . . . on the Lindsay ancestors, it has to be this one.

It takes another hour to find that none of the online book sellers has a copy of the ancient tome. This is just another dead end. I stretch my muscles, close out my programs, and then drive over to Alan's house to see if he wants to take a brisk stroll around the block. If I can't make any progress on the quest, then I might as well walk the neighborhood for some much-needed exercise.

"How many pages did you write today?" Alan asks.

"None. I got sidetracked with family history research."

"Which family?"

"My dad's ancestors," I tell him.

"Which dad?"

I want to load my voice with sarcasm and snap, "My dad." But it isn't Alan's fault I have two men who qualify for the title. I can already tell this is just the first in a long line of conversations that will include that same question.

"The dad who raised me," I say. "The dad who's name I can pronounce."

Alan chuckles. "You could just call your biological father P-Daddy."

"I don't think so." Although it doesn't sound half bad when I mentally repeat it to myself. At some point, I will have to decide what to call the two of them. Unless Mr. Petrauschke rejects me as his son. Then the problem is solved. I can just refer to him as the Paternal DNA Donor—PDD for short—and Dad will continue to be Dad.

"Correct me if I'm wrong," says Alan.

I don't know what's coming, but I'm sure I won't like it.

"But isn't the family history stuff responsible for you finding out you have two families? You start snooping around again and you might find out your uncle isn't your uncle. Or that your mother isn't your mother."

"I suppose you find that funny."

Alan laughs. "Yeah, I do. Maybe you'll find out that your—"

"Enough. I get it. There's a possibility that further research could uncover even more family secrets. Like in your case, you might find out you were given to your adopted parents by little green men from Mars."

"More like big purple men from Jupiter."

"It doesn't matter," I say. "I've already opened Pandora's box. My DNA is out there to match me to whatever secret relatives might still exist. It's not like I'm submitting another DNA sample to be tested."

Alan snaps his fingers, then points at me. "Maybe you should. Not your DNA. Have your dad take the test and send that in."

"Which dad?" I ask.

"The one who raised you. Isn't it his ancestral line you're researching? Use his DNA to find the right Lindsay family in Ireland."

"Not bad . . . for an adopted space alien." All I have to do is convince Dad to spit into a tube and I'll be right back where I left off when I decided to test my DNA. What's the worst thing that could happen?

———

A new email is waiting for me the next morning. It's from my sister Jana. "Just opened the email with your dad's picture. Yeah, I think you look like him. That's so funny. But it is nice to see that other people look like you. I think it's awesome to see these people."

I'm not sure how my looking like the siblings in New Jersey is funny, but at least it doesn't bother me that she thinks so. It is nice to feel that I belong somewhere. I'm glad Jana is happy to see me fit in with my new family. At least I don't have to worry about her feeling jealous over the situation. My Arizona family tends to avoid bouts of trivial drama.

Jana's comments brighten my mood. I send off a quick thank-you. Then I switch over to Facebook to find out what's happening with my author buddies.

I have a new friend request. It's from my brother Joe . . . in New Jersey. The level of my internal bliss meter soars. I realize it's only a friend request. People send them to me all the time—people I don't even know. But this is different. A friend request from a member of my new family is a sign of acceptance. Or at least a first step in establishing a relationship with another of my New Jersey relatives.

Even though it's a tiny step, it creates an emotional connection. As the fear of rejection fades, my desire to love these people grows. The reaction confuses me. How can I start to love people I don't even know?

I accept the friend request. My fingers hover over the keyboard as I try to figure out something appropriate to say to Joe. Since these will be my first words to a new family member, they have to be just right. They have to be clever. And maybe even wise. Like Neil Armstrong as he prepared to walk on the moon. I consider using a horribly cheesy spoof of Mr. Armstrong's quote that immediately comes to mind, then reject the idea. There will be no "One small step for Randy—one giant leap for Petrauschke-kind."

Ten minutes pass. Nothing clever, wise, or remotely close to being just right comes to mind. I settle on something safe and dull. "Hey, bro."

Then I look through the pictures on his account. The first is the old-time photo of him, his brother Bill, and our father. They are dressed in Civil War–era costumes, and the photo is black and white. This is the same picture Tammy sent me when she was trying to convince me Mr. Petrauschke was my father. Sort of a guilt-by-family-resemblance tactic.

The second image is of a younger man I don't know. Maybe his son. And finally, there is a picture of Joe, wearing a T-shirt with a crudely humorous cartoon and tagline. He's a rough-looking character with dark, uncombed hair and a salt-and-pepper ten o'clock shadow. But he has a smile that says, "You've got to love me."

I shake my head and laugh at the T-shirt. From just that one picture, I feel I know him already. Not intimately, but at least a little bit. I write another message, "Love the shirt."

A single click of the mouse, and my message is on its way. I lean back and study Joe's picture for a few minutes. This is my brother. His image gives me the impression of a gruff, uncultured sort of fellow. Am I going to like him?

As an author, I like to drive over to the shopping mall, find a seat by the high-end soda vendor, and then watch people as they walk past.

I develop descriptions of the shoppers to sharpen my writing skills. I imagine interesting character relationships between couples, or groups of friends, as they stroll along the shops.

But that doesn't work with the picture of my brother. It only works for passersby at the mall, who I have no connection to. I can't invent personality traits for Joe based on the impressions I receive from looking at his photo. I don't know how he is going to act, how he's going to sound, or whether I will feel at ease around him. I will have to spend time with him to know any of that. All I know at this point is I like his smile.

I shake myself out of reflection mode and call Dad. With all of the positive energy being generated from my social media exchanges with Jana and Joe, I'm ready to ask him about taking the test. He answers on the third ring.

"Que pasa, amigo?" he says.

"I hope you're staying out of trouble."

Dad laughs. "I'm too old to have any fun, so you don't have to worry about that. Besides, Judy keeps me on a short leash. If I cause any problems, she beats me."

"Somehow I doubt that." I wait for him to finish his chuckle. "Dad, would you be willing to take a DNA test for me?"

"No," he says in an extra-firm voice.

That wasn't the answer I expected. I struggle to think of a reason why he would refuse such a simple request. It's not as if I'm going to discover he isn't really my father. The chance has already passed for keeping that skeleton hidden in the closet.

"When are you and the kids going to come out and visit?" Dad asks.

"Probably next week," I tell him, then switch back to my original topic. "The DNA test is super easy to take. All you have to do is spit in a tube. I'm even going to pay for it."

"Not interested," Dad replies, his voice gaining an uncommon firmness to it once again. "Those grandkids of mine are growing like weeds. It'll be good to see them. What day are you planning on coming out?"

His response catches me by surprise, leaving me too shocked to ask why. I mumble, "Monday. They'll be out of school for the holiday."

"Good. I'll make sure to stock up on Popsicles. Love you," Dad says. Then he terminates the call.

This is just a guess, but I think he doesn't want to take the DNA test.

— —

Halfway through Thursday, I check and find an email from Tammy. Her messages have gone from simple dialogues with a stranger to much-anticipated discussions with someone I like. It takes a moment to remember she usually writes to me on Mondays. I hope the change in her regular routine isn't an indication of a problem.

"After I sent the last message," writes Tammy, "I realized I should have explained more about the situation. Dad grew up, for the most part, without a father. He thought Frank Petrauschke was his dad. Then in 1996, my grandmom finally told him the truth. His real father was a Lodge. The other family name would have been a lot easier to spell."

Even though the two of us were both milkman's sons, my father had gone through a much different experience than I had. I'd grown up with a dad who loved me and took care of me. Mr. Petrauschke had not. Instead, he had two men, his father and his stepfather, who had failed to provide for him. If that had been my childhood, I would have wondered what I'd done to drive away my fathers. It would have crushed me.

Is that the way my father felt about the situation? And if so, does it still bother him?

"My grandmother remarried and moved to Arizona," Tammy continues. "I don't think my dad and his new stepfather got along very well. Then, like I mentioned before, Dad moved back to New Jersey sometime after his stroke.

"As for your comment, Dad is a nice guy. Although, when we have parties, he is usually in the living room away from the noise. I too find the situation weird. I'm thankful that you have a loving dad who raised you . . . and yet it is a little sad that we didn't get to know you before now. I don't think my dad knew he had another child. He seemed a little confused when we talked last night. I'm sure it will take awhile to figure things out.

"We can be pretty goofy too. Laughter is the best. And we did get a laugh at the milkman comment. It would have been funnier if he actually was one."

I feast on the information Tammy has given me. It helps dull my hunger to know as much about my New Jersey family as I can. There are a lot of lost years to cover. I reread the section about my father hiding away from the noise at parties. That's me. Even when I'm with the family I grew up with I tend to find a corner and let people come to me to visit. Every message from Tammy seems to reveal another way in which my father and I are alike.

A warm fuzzy settles in my chest. It isn't as though I've ever felt unloved by the dad who raised me, but being able to see the similarities with my biological father makes me feel like I belong in a way I never have before. I have to meet this man. I have to find out what he thinks about me.

"Tammy," I write. "Please tell me more about you and your family. What hobbies do you have? What does your family do for fun? What's your favorite flavor of ice cream?"

I send off the email and try to return to my writing. It doesn't work. My mind continues to drift away from the story. I keep wondering what it would be like to get together with my New Jersey family. My anxiety over meeting people I don't know is still there, but it fades with each email, text, and picture I receive from them. They are starting to feel, a little bit, like family to me.

My children trickle home. First the youngest, as he walks in the house from grade school. Then, later, my two high schoolers. And finally, the lone junior high student. All of them stop in my office so I can find out about their days.

Their replies range from a simple grunt by my oldest to an overly detailed account of my youngest son's every move during the day. I'm not sure which is better. I send each of them off to do their homework while I prepare for my book club meeting.

A sign on the front porch asks members of the group to let themselves in. Charlie the poodle greets me as I step inside Deb and Dave's house. I scratch his head and stroll over to my usual seat. My path takes me dangerously close to a pan of brownies.

Hmmmm . . . brownies. One of my three publicly known forms of kryptonite. And sitting next to the pan is a bowl of M&M's. I rationalize with myself that I have this opportunity only during book club and transfer the smallest brownie in the pan to a snack plate. Then I take a scoop of the candies and drizzle them around the brownie.

"What's the latest news on your family in New Jersey?" Deb asks.

Why is everyone so fascinated with the story of me having two dads?

"Yeah, what did your Dad say?" Rebecca asks.

"Which one?" Now they have me doing it. In my mind, Dad means the man who raised me. The man in New Jersey is my biological father— or just father. But that is a distinction no one else seems to understand.

"Have you contacted your biological father?" Deb asks.

Pam straightens up in her chair. "Right. Have you stalked him on Facebook?"

Stalking? Since when did looking at a few pictures on the internet count as stalking? The word has such a negative connotation. My activities so far fall more into the category of social browsing or possibly a long-distance, impersonal introduction. But definitely not stalking.

"I don't stalk people," I tell Pam. Then I turn toward Deb. "As much as I would like to have a discussion with my father, I've only been able to exchange emails with my sister out there."

"Has he accepted you?" asks Dave.

"No," I answer and then look down at my plate of goodies. My friends seem to have an endless river of questions. Then again, so do I.

The problem is that I don't have all the answers. This situation is still too new, too unsettling.

How long are people going to ask me about my two dads? Will this become the favorite topic of discussion between my friends and me? Is this unusual family dynamic going to dominate my social interactions for the rest of my life?

And is it going to bother me if I'm perpetually known as the milkman's son?

Dave starts the meeting, saving me from any further questions. It isn't as if I mind the attention that comes from being the milkman's son. I don't even mind most of the questions. But sometimes the probing into my life, my feelings, strikes a sensitive spot. They serve as reminders of things I'd rather not face. Like the possibility of my own flesh-and-blood father rejecting me. During those moments, I'd rather not be the milkman's son.

The meeting passes quickly. Two hours of book discussion is barely enough time to engage in one of my favorite passions. That must be why they invented writing conventions and book fairs. Everyone in the group tells one another goodbye, and the meeting is over.

I drive home and check my social media before bed. There's a message on Facebook from Joe. It's about my comment on his picture, "Yeah, got to have fun."

Then in a second message he gives me his cell phone number. I've already responded with my own before it hits me that we have taken the next step in our relationship. We have gone from Facebook messaging to brothers with the potential to call one another. It seems incredibly nerdish to get excited over a little thing like exchanging contact information, but when I spend every day wondering if my family in New Jersey is going to accept me . . . it feels like a big deal.

I send the message and then open a pending friend request. It's from Mrs. Petrauschke. I check the picture on her account and verify this is my new stepmother—not a sister-in-law or other New Jersey relative.

Why is she friending me?

She has posted a picture of her, Tammy, and several other women/girls who must be the daughters-in-law and the granddaughters. Mrs. Petrauschke is short. Only the youngest of the granddaughters is shorter. I have the same reaction as when I looked at pictures of my father. She seems nice.

If she's willing to connect with me on social media, maybe she really is nice. Based on my status as a child of another woman, I expect her to resist any effort to include me as part of her family. Or part of her husband's family. I wonder what sort of thoughts are running through her head.

Of all the efforts by my New Jersey family to connect with me, this one impresses me the most. This single request, from someone not related to me by blood, does more than all the rest to make me feel accepted. The only thing missing is an acknowledgment from my father. A simple message or email from Mr. Petrauschke would validate my membership in his family.

I go to bed, happy with the way things are progressing with my other family.

On Monday, I rush to the computer as soon as I awaken. As usual, there's an email waiting for me from Tammy. Maybe this will be the one that contains the confirmation from my father that I am his son and he wants to meet me.

"I think we are pretty boring. We gather together as much as possible. We have Sunday dinners after church and picnics in the summer. That is what I like to do for fun. We all live close to one another. My parents and daughter live just down the street from us. My son lives just a few blocks away."

What Tammy describes as boring is an image from a Norman Rockwell painting brought to life. A scene that could easily be placed in a handbook for the American lifestyle during the '40s and '50s. Families living close together and participating in one another's daily routine is something I thought existed only in fiction . . . or my dreams. That sort of existence isn't boring. In my eyes it's heaven.

She continues to write. "I'd like to know more about your family also. And my favorite flavor of ice cream is vanilla and chocolate mixed and stirred until it's like soft serve."

Amazing. That's what I like to do with my ice cream. No one else in my Arizona family does that. But my sister in New Jersey does.

"I haven't had a chance to sit down and talk with Bill. The last time he was over, there were a lot of people around. I'm sure he'll want to contact you.

"My kids haven't said a lot. I did show them the pictures you sent me, and my son thinks your younger son looks a little bit like him when he was younger. We used to call him Scrawny Shauny because he was so skinny.

"Dad seems to be having a hard time with the situation. I think it's because he didn't have any idea that he had another child. It's hard for him to wrap his head around it. I think we might have to resign ourselves to the fact that we will probably never know exactly what happened with our parents. We will just have to keep moving forward.

"We keep mentioning the DNA test to Dad, but he doesn't believe it. He thinks it has to be a mistake. It looks like the only way we're going to convince him you're his son is to have him take a DNA test and match it to you."

# CHAPTER 9

# ANOTHER SKELETON
# IN THE CLOSET

The man can't be serious. Who needs a DNA test? All anyone has to do is look at the high school pictures of me and Mr. Petrauschke to see that we're father and son. Look at the lips. A DNA test should be necessary only if a person is determined to avoid the embarrassment and inconvenience of having to recognize me as his son.

I push myself away from the computer and march out to the kitchen. Last night's leftovers are in the fridge. None of them hits the right gastronomical note for the eating binge I have in mind. I decide I need tacos. Or possibly a quesadilla. Maybe both.

It takes a couple of minutes to dress and grab my car keys. As I drive, my mind returns to the subject of Mr. Petrauschke's DNA test. The initial flare of anger over being rejected fades. I mentally put myself in his place.

I try to imagine what it would be like to wake up one day and find out I have a son who is fifty-seven. Especially with no memory of how that might have happened. A son who grew up without my guidance. A son who grew up without ever having heard me tell him, "I love you."

A host of similar regrets floods my mind. If I were him, I wouldn't want the news to be true because it would mean I wasn't there for my child. It would mean I had failed him as a father. I feel for the man, just like Daelyn felt for me when the gravity of the situation weighed uncomfortably on my shoulders.

Let him take the DNA test. The results aren't going to change the past. All it will do is destroy his current fortress of denial and force him to accept the truth . . . that I am his son.

I return home and call Jana. "What's up with Dad?"

"Other than being his usual cantankerous self," she says with a question in her voice. "It might help if you clue me in on what you're talking about."

"Dad refused to take a DNA test."

"I can't imagine why he would want to," Jana says.

A creeping suspicion tells me that Jana and I aren't having the same conversation. Or, at least, we aren't addressing it from the same direction. I ask, "Is Dad not interested in me doing anymore family history research?"

"Family history?" I can clearly hear the confusion in her voice. "What are you talking about?

"The whole reason I took a DNA test was to help me find which branch of the Lindsays in Ireland belongs to us. And since I'm not a Lindsay by blood, I need either Dad or Mark to take the test. What did you think I was talking about?"

"I . . . thought . . . you wanted Dad to take the test to prove he isn't your biological father. Or something goofy like that."

Now it's my turn to be confused. After all the time I've spent worrying about how the family will react to my news, how does it make any sense for me to want to prove Dad isn't my blood relative? "That's the silliest thing I've heard all day."

"It's only 9:00 a.m."

"And your point?" I ask.

"As late as you sleep," she says, "how many silly things have you heard already?"

"You're changing the subject," I tell her. "I need Dad to take a DNA test."

"Then ask him again. Make sure you tell Dad it's for family history work. He's just worried about your feelings being hurt. He doesn't care that you're not his biological son, and he wants you to know that."

"Absolutely," I say. "I got it already. None of us cares. All of us love one another. Dad is my dad, and I am his son. And at the next family gathering we can all sing 'Kumbaya.'"

"You're such a dork."

"Yep. Love you too."

I decide to call Dad later in the week, or even next week, to arrange another visit. Confident in my ability to talk him into taking the test, I order another DNA kit from Ancestry. Then, with that concern out of the way, I open my email and respond to Tammy's last message.

"I don't think your life sounds boring. I think it sounds great. I love to spend time with my family, whether it's my children, or my siblings, or my parents. It's great that all of you live so close together. If I lived that close to my siblings, I'd probably never get any work done. When we are together, we talk for hours.

"My dad is the real-life version of John Wayne. Take all those westerns and war movies John Wayne was in and roll them together. That's my dad. He did competitive roping until about two years ago. Now, the doctors won't let him ride horses anymore. Boy, is that killing him."

I send the message off without checking it. Much like the siblings I grew up with, I'm feeling comfortable with Tammy. There is no longer a concern that one of my failed attempts at a joke is going to drive her away.

The conversation with Jana is still clunking around inside my head, making it difficult to concentrate on writing. I stare at the nearly blank page of a new chapter for fifteen minutes. The only thing on the page so far is "Chapter 6."

Eventually, I write a few lines of humorous dialogue. It's funny but doesn't actually have anything to do with what I have planned for the chapter. I delete the witty banter between my two main characters and start over.

Some description would be nice. I stare at the blank page. It stares back at me. After a few minutes of this, I turn my head and gaze out my office window. Brown brick wall, some of my neighbor's hanging vines, a few mismatched trees, and the roofs of the houses on the next street over. Nothing I can use for my current story.

What I need is inspiration. I load up my liked videos on YouTube and watch "Feel It Still" by Portugal. The strange and seemingly unrelated scenes mesmerize me as I try to figure out what über-cosmic message the video might contain for those chic enough to figure it out. And what's with the pig dude? The beat reminds me of "I Feel Love" by Venus Hum and the Blue Man Group, so I listen to that video next. Twice.

An hour passes as I work through my list of favorite tunes. It isn't as much a waste of my morning as it is a sign that I need to work on something else. Something that allows me to play videos in the background without distracting me.

Family history.

I ignore the Lindsays. They've caused me enough frustration and have eaten away more than their fair share of my valuable research time. The lack of forward progress with them convinces me to work on a different family line. It even prompts me to try something different in my search. I log in to Ancestry and find a family tree with a common ancestor and see how far back my extremely distant cousin has gone with their family quest.

Most of the pedigree charts match the information I already have. Then I follow one on the Matheny line and find they have tapped into royalty. I check the citation of their sources to make sure they haven't simply invented an impressive line of dead relatives for the purpose of connecting to history's rich and famous.

The information comes from parish records in Virginia. Those records extend back to 1584 and are a reliable source. The Matheny line eventually merges with the Wentworths around 1660 in Canterbury, England. I work back as far as I've ever seen any of my family lines go, the citations now listing King William the Conqueror's commissioned Doomsday Book, which was completed in 1086.

I follow the Wentworth family tree back through the 1700s and the 1600s before bumping into an ancestor with an attached portrait. Thomas Wentworth, first Earl of Strafford. The commanding figure in the portrait impresses me. He's a good-looking guy . . . or was. A bolt of excitement shoots through me as I wonder which of England's royals lent their rarified blood to the Lindsay line.

"Dad," one of my sons says from my office door. "I have to be at school in ten minutes."

I look up. It's Nick. His band concert is tonight. I drag myself away from the computer and rush to put on my shoes and a clean shirt. We arrive early. Nick runs off to the band room, and I look for a seat in the auditorium.

The seats are small and uncomfortable. Lovely. At least it should keep me from nodding off during the beginning band's hour-long performance. I want to show Nick my support and intently listen to every note he makes . . . sour or otherwise.

After the concert, the two of us drive over to the local soda shop and order a congratulatory drink for my budding musician. We talk about songs the band performed and which part of the concert I liked best.

And then we're back home. Nick heads to the living room, where the rest of the family is watching reruns of *Highlander,* and I grab a salad from the fridge and then return to the office. The royal hunt awaits me. I sit down and fork a generous portion of salad into my mouth. My fingers tap ancestral names on the keyboard as I dive back into the search.

Somewhere during the evening, my wife enters the office. I give her a quick kiss and mumble, or think I mumble, "Food . . . kitchen . . . microwave. Love you."

She leaves me in the thrall of my family history fever.

The line of royalty meanders through Markingfields, Sothills, and Cromwells before reaching John Marmion, the fourth Baron Marmion of Winteringham, in 1292. A coat of arms with three red diamonds on a blue-and-white checkered field reminds me of the Lindsay crest, even though there's no connection between the families.

Eager to skip the third, second, and first barons of Marmion, I switch to the pedigree view of the family tree. I do a double take as I notice the title of "King" attached to a member of the family four generations previous.

I let out a whoop loud enough to disturb the rest of my family in the kitchen. Then I call for them to share this discovery with me. As I wait for them to trudge into my office, I click on the record of the king.

King John Plantagenet, born December of 1166 as the youngest of eight children to King Henry II and Eleanor of Aquitaine. He is the younger brother of King Richard the Lionhearted.

Wait a minute! That's the jerk in Robin Hood.

King John's life sketch continues: his father gave him the nickname "John Lackland" because it was suspected that he'd never inherit any land. He was later known as "Joh Softsword" because of his military bungling. It turns out King John is widely considered one of the worst rulers in England's long and glorious history, having lost Normandy to France and then being instrumental in plunging England into a bloody civil war.

I finally connect the Lindsays to a royal line and it happens to be one that includes an infamous villain in popular fiction. Does that mean the next time I watch a Robin Hood movie I need to root for the bad guy? That isn't any fun. I already know he's going to lose. And it will make me look like an idiot if I sit there during the movie and chant, "King John. King John. Go-o-o-o-o Lackland."

Wait until the rest of the family hears about this. They may not be excited about being related to King John specifically, but they should still enjoy the royal connection. I close out of all of the genealogy programs, websites, and documents.

What about the Petrauschkes? Do they have a royal branch in their family tree? I consider checking Tammy's research on Ancestry to see if she has been able to track any of her lines that far back but decide against it. I can only imagine what sort of tarnished historic figure might be connected to me through that line.

— —

On Monday, like clockwork, I receive another email from Tammy.

"The description of your dad made me chuckle. My dad has been collecting John Wayne movies and memorabilia for years now. He has quite a collection. You probably didn't know this, but the Cowtown Rodeo is fairly close to us. It's been around since 1929."

Not much of an email. I hope it's only a matter of Tammy being extra busy and unable to spend too much time exchanging messages with me. The alternative is that, along with her dad's reluctance to accept me as his son, the Petrauschkes have taken our relationship as far as they intend to take it.

It takes several tries to compose my response. "For the most part my kids are like yours; they haven't said much about the situation. Although Merlin asked me today, 'Does this mean our name really isn't Lindsay?' I told him this situation wasn't going to change any of that.

"I look forward to establishing contact with Bill. I hope you won't mind me speaking my mind. The shock of this revelation has worn off, the event itself has settled in my brain, and I want to embrace all of you as family . . . at least to the extent any of you may want to do that. Obviously, it's not my fault I was born. Nor is it my fault I didn't know about you. Or your fault that you didn't know about me. You, Bill, and Joe are just as much family as the siblings I grew up with here in Arizona.

The only difference is that we have not been given the chance to celebrate, or curse, our relationship with one another. I hope the three of you feel the same way. Or will feel that way eventually.

"I hope taking the paternity test will help your dad. I don't want to push myself on him, but I can't help thinking that if I were in his position, I would want to know that I had another child and at least have one chance to meet that child during my life. I am concerned for his position in this situation. I know it has to be tough on him. Even though I'm okay with having a new batch of siblings, I'm still kind of jittery about having a second father."

Am I making a mistake opening myself up to Tammy? Once I hit the send button, it will be too late to change my mind. I go back and forth between thinking it's time to move forward with our relationship and worrying that the Petrauschkes will reject me. Friendly email chats are one thing, but deciding to embrace them with the email equivalent of a family hug is something else altogether.

The decision boils down to the fact that I want to know these people better. They are my family, and families are supposed to love one another. I can't let the fear of them possibly rejecting me prevent me from reaching out to them. The potential emotional rewards are too great to let my insecurities stand in the way.

I send the message.

Then, since I'm feeling brave, I call Dad and arrange for my visit next week.

━ ━

Midway through the week, Joe sends me a text. "Hey, bro, how are you? Haven't been on the PC, so I figured I'd just say hi."

It's just an ordinary message, I tell myself. The kind siblings send to one another all the time. But what makes this so special is that it comes from a brother I've never met. A brother I've never shaken hands with. A brother I've never hugged. A brother who barely knows me. And Joe makes it sound as if we've known one another all our lives and he simply wanted to drop me a quick reminder that he's thinking about me.

Not only that, but I've been "bro" from the beginning. How can he accept me so quickly? Maybe he's just as conflicted about this situation as I am, but he doesn't show it. All I know is the message chokes me up more than I think it should. I feel even closer to this family I've never met.

I respond, "Doing well. I've been planning to call you. How are you?"

"I'm alive," texts Joe.

"I should hope so, or else I'd be texting a ghost."

"True," says Joe.

I watch for five minutes, but no more texts come through.

—◆—

The DNA test kit arrives on Saturday.

On Monday, I send all the children off to school and call Dad to let him know I'm driving out to see him. He's disappointed I'm not bringing the grandkids but happy I'm coming over. The long drive gives me plenty of time to think of a good argument to convince him to take the test.

When I arrive, I knock on the glass back door and let myself in. They have a new dog, an Australian shepherd, who barks at me as he hides behind Dad's easy chair.

"Quiet, Billy," Dad growls. He struggles out of his chair and gives me a hug.

"You named the dog after your brother?" I ask.

"Yep. I thought they kind of looked alike."

Dad sits back down and turns off the television. "Where are the kids?"

"School," I tell him. "The state gets upset if I don't send them on a regular basis. Besides, I can only put up with so much of their fighting before it drives me insane"

Dad grunts and nods like he's been there a time or two in his lifetime.

"I've been working on family history again," I say. "It turns out that one of the Lindsay branches leads to King John of England."

Dad arches an eyebrow. "Really?"

A grin spreads across my face in anticipation of Dad being on the other end of a genetic bombshell. "They call him King John of Lackland. He's the worst king England ever had. When you watch the Robin Hood movies, he's the bad guy."

"That doesn't surprise me," says Dad. "Your grandfather always claimed we were descended from horse thieves. This fits right in with what he told me."

"Whoa there, cowboy," I tell Dad. "The way I see it, the advantage of having two dads is I can pick and choose which family dynamics apply to me. You are my dad, but King John isn't related to me—just you. And, of course, Mark and Jana, when I tell them the good news."

Dad laughs. It's the same laugh he used when he heard the news about me being the milkman's son. The same laugh that lets me know Dad never takes himself too seriously.

"Can't argue with that," he says.

"Since we're on the topic of family history," I say. "I need you to take a DNA test."

"What the hell for?" Dad growls. "It doesn't matter if I'm your biological father; you're still my son. I love you, and that's all there is to the matter."

"I love you too, Dad. But this isn't about proving whether we are related by blood. I need your DNA so I can continue with my genealogy research. I'm at a dead end with finding out where the original Lindsay immigrant is from. All you have to do is spit into a little tube, and I can match your DNA to other Lindsay families and gain a better idea of where to look for more records."

"Oh." Dad nods. "Why didn't you say so?"

The instructions on the kit state to avoid eating or drinking anything for thirty minutes before the test. Dad turns the television back on and watches an old western. He takes a swig from his insulated cup, and we have to start the timer over.

"Dad, no eating or drinking for thirty minutes."

"That's a stupid rule." He sets the cup as far away as he can reach. Then he gives me a disapproving look. "Why do you even do family history?"

"Because you asked me to," I remind him.

He grunts and returns to watching television. I stop him—twice—from putting anything in his mouth that will spoil the test results. Thirty minutes pass, and I hand him the tube. He fills it to the halfway mark and then says, "It'd be easier to spit if I had something to drink."

"But then the lab would be testing your drink and not your spit," I tell him. "Unless you want me to find the ancestors for your drink, I suggest you keep at it. Just imagine how good that beer is going to taste when you finish."

It takes another five minutes, but he manages to reach the this-is-enough-spit line on the tube. I seal the tube, pack it away, and hand Dad his drink. "See, that wasn't so bad."

I give him a hug and then drive home. The kids are in the house, playing video games when I arrive. I don't see any blood or severed limbs, so I figure they were all right while I was gone. We exchange a shortened version of our usual ritual greeting as I pass through the living room. Then I fill out the return envelope, drop the tube inside, and take it out to the mailbox.

The kit says to expect results in six to eight weeks.

Previous experience tells me otherwise. I really hope there aren't any more surprises.

—— ——

Tammy responds on the following Monday. "I was surprised at all the emotions I felt when I first found out I had another brother. Now that it has sunk in, it's exciting to get to know you and your family. Although a sister would have been nice. (LOL) I have been blessed with wonderful sisters-in-law. And I'm not the oldest anymore.

"I think it might be sinking in for my dad. He really had no idea he had another child. He didn't recognize the picture of your mom. That would have been only about five or six months after his stroke. I don't know if that would have anything to do with him not remembering. I haven't really talked much about it with him.

"When we found out who my dad's dad was, Bill was going to change his last name. But after that long, it didn't make sense to do it, and he forgot about the idea. Good luck with your dad's DNA test. Hope nothing too shocking shows up."

If I had Petrauschke for my family name, I'd want to change it too. I'm still not sure how to pronounce it. The situation is different for me, though. From what Tammy has written, her dad basically grew up without a father. He didn't have an emotional connection with the man whose name he was given. But in my situation, I love my dad, and I like our family name. Before this moment, I hadn't even considered changing my name. It'd be a slap in the face for my Arizona family.

Even if I decide to change my name to match my actual bloodline, it won't be Petrauschke. It'd be Lodge. My New Jersey family and I would still not have the same last name. I mouth a silent "Thank you" to Bill. His decision to abandon the name change makes the matter a nonissue for me.

"One last thing—Mom found this song and thought it was funny. At least we are not this bad." Tammy included a link to YouTube.

The link takes me to a video of "I'm My Own Grandpa" by Ray Stevens, complete with an illustration of the family tree described in the song. I laugh as I listen to the lyrics about the ridiculous family in the song. And while the situation in the song is vastly different from my own, it feels somewhat relatable.

It amazes me that my new stepmother knows about this song and suggested Tammy send me a link to it. Of all the people in my New

Jersey family, she's the one who has the most reason to resent the situation. Instead, she has the uncommon presence of mind to approach our relationship with humor. What an astounding woman. Her action reminds me of the teasing my brother and sisters give me on a regular basis. The fact that she can laugh at all of this makes her feel like family. It makes me feel closer to all of the New Jersey crew.

"I'm glad to hear you're excited about having an older brother," I write. "When you get around to talking to your dad about the situation, I'd be interested in hearing about it.

"Thanks for the song. It makes me feel better knowing the situation could have been even stranger than it is. Besides, I was talking to my brother, Mark, and he mentioned how awesome all of this is. He looks at it as a bigger family and lots of fun getting to know one another. Now that I've communicated with you, I'm glad to have another sister. I expect the same will hold true for Bill and Joe being my brothers. Have a great week. Chat with you more soon."

Months pass as I wait for the results of Dad's DNA test. Tammy and I continue to exchange emails, sharing more and more details about our families. The folks in New Jersey are no longer just a list of names pinned to a location on a map. They have lives and personalities.

I find out that Tammy's mom is called Babe by most of the people who know her. Tammy doesn't tell me why, but I imagine it has to do with her mom's petite size. I can't picture myself walking up to her someday and saying, "Hey, Babe." It just sounds creepy when it applies to anyone besides my wife. I already have two women I call Mom—my mother and my mother-in-law—why not three?

The decision about what to call Mrs. Petrauschke is much easier to arrive at than the one I'm still struggling with. The one about what to call my father. In time, that one should work itself out as well.

Babe . . . I mean Mom, posts cooking tips on Facebook. They don't inspire me to cook them for my family, but they look delicious. She posts a recipe for Crock-Pot beef vegetable stew that catches my attention. I'm making a mental list of how many ways I could unintentionally massacre the simple instructions in the recipe when a notice pops up. There's a message from Ancestry in my email. Dad's test results! The way my alert system works—or doesn't work—it's likely that the message has probably been there for at least a day.

I switch to my Ancestry account and spend a few minutes figuring out how to pull up Dad's test results instead of mine. As expected, his DNA summary looks entirely different from my own. He has fewer ancestors in Great Britain than I do and none in Eastern Europe. Of course, this isn't about comparing our heritage for differences, it's about finding where the Lindsays lived in Ireland.

The section on DNA matches should be the key to unlocking that mystery. But as I move the cursor to access the matches, I notice a message waiting for me. The message is from a person named Susan. A person I don't know. With the hope that it contains a piece of evidence that will take me closer to solving the Great Lindsay Quest, I open the message.

It says, "Greetings, cousin!"

Oh no. Here we go again.

# CHAPTER 10

# THE JOKE'S ON ME

How many DNA surprises can one person have? Logic dictates an individual should be limited to just one. A family member takes the test, a few weeks later the results arrive, and BOOM. It turns out someone in the family isn't related to the others. Or that they're related, but not in the way everyone thought.

I'm the milkman's son. Surprise! I get it. Let's move on. There's no need to drag any more of my family members into the cruel joke. When is this going to stop? I mean, how many stinking skeletons can be in my family closet?

The argument of whether I should read the rest of the message or just delete it rages inside my head. I've had enough surprises for one year, thank you very much. The cosmic agency in charge of unexpected events and situations is certainly welcome to spread its drama-inducing works to other families and leave me alone.

Curiosity wins out and, even though I should know better, I read the rest of the message.

"I am writing in regards to our DNA match," writes Susan. "For several years, I have been searching for members of my mother's family, most importantly her father. DNA will be my best chance, and I think finding you is a real breakthrough.

"My mother was born in Lawrence County, Arkansas. As far as I can tell from DNA testing, she and her brother did not have the same father. I was wondering if you might help us find out who my grandfather may have been?

"The closest match to my mother is your account. Will you help us with our search?"

It's not as bad as I thought it would be. In fact, this seems to be my chance to help someone connect with their family. I guess DNA testing has a few positive uses after all.

In this case, the DNA match is for dad. Several of his ancestral lines pass through Arkansas. Since I submitted my dad's DNA for testing, the results are tied to my account, so any queries people have about the Lindsay DNA are sent to me.

I open the file Susan included and look at the family names. None of them are familiar, but I do recognize several of the locations where they lived. The most important information is about her mother. Looking at where she was born will tell me the general area where Susan's grandmother was likely to have connected with the mysterious grandfather.

A search on Ancestry shows that Susan's mother was living in Craighead County, Arkansas, during the 1940 census, along with her mother, Anna. I remember that being the same neck of the woods where my paternal grandmother's side of the family lived. I open Google Maps and find that Craighead is the county just south of where my dad was born. Susan's family and several branches of my dad's family lived within thirty miles of one another. Definitely close enough for a guy to meet a girl and produce a baby.

At least the skeleton is in someone else's family closet this time. Tracking down Susan's grandfather sounds like fun. This won't be like the search for William "The Immigrant." I have records for these people. I know who they are and where they lived. All I have to do is sort through the data and find a match.

I respond to Susan, "I'd be happy to help as much as I can. My dad is from Arkansas. His mother's side of the family spent several generations in Randolph County. When I searched for information on your mother, I found her in Craighead, Arkansas. That's where my family is from. (Which makes sense since we are looking for a common ancestor.) Let me do some looking through my files, and I'll get back to you."

The appeal of a family mystery taunts me, but I have other things to do. Laundry. Shopping. Dishes. Not interesting things, like a lost grandfather hunt, but they still need to be done. And as soon as I finish all the household chores, I have to work on my latest novel. The big science-fiction convention is next month, and I still have to prepare two presentations, research agents, and order all my normal author supplies before then.

I shower, dress, make the bed, and put the first batch of clothes in the washer. Then I start on the grocery list. As busy as I'm going to be this week, I consider stocking the freezer full of the usual fast-and-easy menu items. The top of that list would, of course, be corn dogs and cheap frozen burritos. But I did that last week, and growing children need good, nutritious meals that include plenty of lovely, fresh vegetables . . . or so I've heard.

The house phone rings, saving me from making any difficult food decisions for another few minutes. It's my brother Mark.

"Hey, Randy. I'm going back to school to earn my nursing license," he says. "By the time I graduate, the kids will all be out of the house. Then I can work anywhere in the country as a traveling nurse. Jana and Cheryl are thinking about doing it as well."

Cheryl is Mark's wife. She was best friends with Jana in high school. All three of them are close. Closer than I am to anyone in the family, but that's probably due to Mark and Jana being so near in age and having gone through the family experience together. The age gap between us always put me one life stage ahead of them. I was grown and out of the house before they entered high school.

"Great," I say, putting as much sarcasm into my answer as I can muster. "I can see the three of you at Christmas, sitting around Jana's kitchen table, talking about who saw the most gruesome injury in the last month. That should put a pleasant, warm holiday touch to our family get-togethers."

Mark laughs. "I thought you might appreciate it. Anything to help a brother."

"Thanks," I say. "If I can ever find out what gives you the creeps, I can return the favor."

The phone is silent.

I wait a few seconds before asking, "Mark, are you there?"

"Yeah. I was just wondering if you've heard anything from your family back East?"

"I exchange emails with my sister Tammy. And my little brother Joe has sent me a few texts over the phone. I haven't had any contact with my biological father. Or my other brother Bill."

"Your brothers are Joe and Bill?" Mark laughs again. "That's hilarious."

"I thought so too," I tell him. "But where Dad has a Joe and a Bill for brothers, I have a Bill and a Joe. Bill is the oldest of the two in my set of siblings."

"Is he older than you?"

"No," I say. "I remain the old man. I'm older than all my siblings. At least, all the siblings I know about."

"The reason I called," says Mark, "is I wanted to make sure you're all right. Jana and I were talking about the situation, and we don't want you to feel as if anything has changed with our family. Dad and all of us have always loved you, even though you were the milkman's son."

Mark's comment hits me like a twenty-pound bowling ball. It doesn't make any sense for him to tell me they have always loved me when we only found out that I was the milkman's son a couple of months ago. But maybe I'm reading more into what he said than is really there.

"What do you mean?" I ask, confusion swirling inside my head. "I only sent in the DNA test a couple of months ago. Why wouldn't you have loved me before then? Nobody knew I was really the milkman's son."

"Well, we kind of did."

What! A mixture of emotions competes for my attention, but anger flares to the top.

"And no one told me?"

"We didn't want to upset you," says Mark. "We thought it would hurt your feelings."

"But teasing me about it for years was all right?" My voice rises. "Where was your concern about my feelings then?"

"See? This is what we were worried would happen," says Mark. "You're upset."

"Of course I'm upset," I respond sharply. "I just found out that the rest of the family withheld a secret from me. My secret. Something I deserved to know. I have a right to be upset about this."

"Jana and I didn't actually know," says Mark. "We only suspected Dad wasn't your biological father. We didn't know for sure until you took the test. That's why Dad didn't want you to do it."

"Dad knew too?"

Mark snorts one of those duh-snorts. "Yeah. We're not stupid. You don't look like anyone else in the family. We did the math. And so did Dad."

My mouth hangs open. I didn't think it was possible to have the floor fall out from underneath me a second time—on the same topic. But it has. Mark, Jana, and Dad apparently discuss this when I'm not around. It looks like the joke was on me all along.

"You knew all along, and nobody told me," I say.

"We didn't want this to bother you," says Mark. "It doesn't matter to us. You're still our brother. We love you the same way. And what if we had told you our suspicions and it turned out we were wrong?"

"I don't want to talk about this anymore." My hand lowers the phone toward its cradle, jerking the receiver back up at the last second. I croak out, "I love you, too."

This hits me harder than finding out Dad isn't my dad, even though it shouldn't. The first discovery changed the perspective of my entire life. Another set of family was plopped right into my lap. New relationships sprang up, and the question of whether to accept these strangers into my life, into my heart, had to be made. That's big.

But news of my family keeping me in the dark about this strikes at the very center of my insecurities. The fear of the milkman's child is being different from the others. To not fit in with the rest. Mark and Jana have always been close, making me feel like an outsider in my own family. Their secret . . . my secret, pushes me even further outside the intimate family circle to which I don't belong. To keep my own secret from me, as their private little joke, makes me feel more than ever before like the milkman's son.

Who do I turn to in this emotional crisis? Where do I go to seek solace? In the past, Jana was always willing to listen to my problems, but she's in on the joke. She's one of the insiders. I can't go to her, and if I did, she would only laugh. Now I see why everyone found the situation so funny. And for the first time, the barbs of the milkman taunt have the power to harm me. They isolate me. They show me how very alone I am.

Maybe helping Susan isn't such a good idea after all. I certainly don't want to open the doors of rejection and heartache to her. Especially knowing how it feels.

Anger struggles to take emotional center stage but is unable to break through the shell of sorrow that has encrusted me. "This is my life," Anger reasons. "I deserve to know the truth. Good or bad, happy or sad, it is my right to know something this important. It was wrong to keep it from me. It was a greater wrong to turn it into a joke."

I cannot deny the arguments Anger gives me. The choking tendrils of isolation are too strong to ignore. What do I do next? How can I make the hurting stop? I want to call one of my family and seek their help, but that will do no good in this situation. Either they are one of the insiders or they lack the level of empathy I need at the moment.

I should go to a movie.

That isn't going to solve my problem, but it will temporarily drown out the voices in my head. I can bury my emotions for a short time by immersing myself into the sensory overload that is theater entertainment. The vibrations of a supercharged sound system. The soft relaxation of sitting in reclining easy chairs. The pervasive smell of popcorn. And either the bliss of masterful storytelling or the horrible dagger to my brain that is a poorly executed script.

With summer just a few weeks away, there is a decent selection of movies. I decide on the only science-fiction offering they have and drive to the theater. The aroma of freshly popped popcorn hits me as soon as I enter. My eyes are so busy checking out the movie posters that I barely notice the doorman as he tears my ticket.

"Theater seven is on your left," he says.

"Thanks," I say and then shuffle over to the concession stand. I order a large soda, a small popcorn, and a box of Hot Tamales. It takes me five minutes to reach theater seven. Posters for upcoming movies keep grabbing my attention.

*Baywatch*. A remake of *The Mummy*. And *Wonder Woman*. I allow the mixed bag of reactions to occupy my mind. How many pirate movies are they going to make? I picture a white-haired, wrinkled Johnny Depp using a cane to shuffle across the deck of his ship and decide I would probably watch that. I know I could write a hilarious script about Captain Jack Sparrow as a senior citizen on one last adventure. Hopefully, someone else can do the same.

I take my seat just in time for my favorite part of the movie-going experience—the sneak previews. *Thor: Ragnarok* gets a thumbs up from me as I toss a handful of popcorn in my mouth and enjoy the buttery goodness of fluffy carbs. Trailers for remakes of *Blade Runner* and *It* fail to ignite my fires of interest. Then again, I rarely enjoy remakes. A classic is a classic for a reason. The successful combination of script, actors, and a director with a solid vision cannot be duplicated just because Hollywood has run out of original ideas.

A couple of Hot Tamales go into my mouth during the trailer for *Justice League*. The sweet cinnamon taste of the candy is extra good after the salty flavor of the popcorn. I don't know the science behind alternating between salty and sweet for an extra amazing level of flavor, but popcorn and Hot Tamales is my favorite combination for that particular gastronomical experiment.

Popcorn. Hot Tamale. Groan at the horribly cheesy dialogue. Take a drink of my not-nearly-large-enough soda. Wonder what the writer was thinking when he/she wrote the script. I repeat the routine a couple of dozen times before the credits roll. I leave the theater, thinking of ways to fix the numerous plot holes in the story. Halfway home, I decide the movie is beyond reasonable efforts to salvage and give up.

As soon as I stop complaining to myself over the choice of viewing entertainment, thoughts of my siblings return. The feelings are not as strong as they were before the movie. My anger has been downgraded to a low simmer. They shouldn't have kept me in the dark about having a different biological father. No matter what their motives, it was a part of my life they kept from me.

I phone home and tell the kids I'm stopping for pizza. They cheer. That's another meal I don't have to cook and they don't have to eat. In other words, a win-win situation. My wife is home by the time I arrive. I set the pizzas down, give her a kiss, and then holler for the children to come eat.

"Let's go to Florida for our anniversary," says LuAnn.

"You mean, let's go see the new grandbaby," I tell her.

"Maybe."

She doesn't fool me. Twenty years of marriage has taught me a thing or two about how my wife thinks. Our anniversary is more of an excuse to travel than it is a desire to celebrate many successful years of marriage. She sees me every day, but this will be the first chance she has to see our newest grandchild.

"Okay," I tell her. In my sour mood, I don't really care. "We can do that."

I load my plate with pepperoni pizza, apologize for not having dinner with the rest of the family, and then head to my office. Taking the time to visit with the family during meals is important to me, but when I'm in a mood like I am today, it's better if I don't.

Between bites of extra-cheesy goodness, I navigate to my Ancestry account. My fingers act on their own while my mind still broods about the earlier conversation with Mark. I open the DNA tab and stare at my Ethnicity Estimates just to have something to look at while I eat. A new color has been added to the map.

An orange blob covers Delaware, Maryland, and New Jersey. It's listed as the Delmarva Peninsula Settlers—an area settled by immigrants from Germany, Wales, and Ireland. Pretty much the same nationalities I would have expected before I received my DNA test results. But these results have to represent my biological father's side of the family.

I decide to work on Susan's family mystery and check my inbox for her latest message. It has a list of family trees that share DNA with both her and the Lindsays. I look through the trees for familiar surnames.

The first account has no family chart connected to it but looks to be a close relative of both my dad and Susan. I notice the account hasn't been active for a couple of years. Too bad. A quick message to the owner of the account might be all it takes to solve the mystery of Susan's unknown grandfather.

Three of the remaining matches have no family names I recognize as being related to the Lindsays. There are two more with no family trees attached, but one of them lists a Byrd as the administrator of the account. Byrd is a family name in Arkansas.

The Byrds are part of the Williams line. They belong to Dad's mother. I make a list of all the males that extend from Alonzo Williams who are approximately the same age as Susan's grandmother and lived nearby. That leaves me with six names; three Williams, a couple of Spikes, and a Brown. Two of the men are six years younger than Susan's grandmother, making them unlikely matches, but I include them anyway.

I compose a message with the names I found and where they lived around the time Susan's mother was born. "Do you have any idea where I should be looking on my family chart, based on how distant the relationship is to my dad?"

That's all I can do without more information. I send the message. The mystery of Susan's grandfather is interesting, but not as exciting as the Great Lindsay Quest. I check the clock. It's past my normal bedtime, so I shut down the computer and head to bed.

Jana calls in the morning. "How are you doing?"

"I'm all right," I tell her. Suspicion prickles the back of my mind. First Mark, and now Jana. As close as the two of them are, they have to be up to something. At the very least, they've been discussing Mark's conversation with me the day before.

"Have you spoken with your biological father yet?" she asks.

"No. He doesn't have any memory of Mom and doesn't think it's possible for him to have a child he didn't know about."

"Don't worry, he'll come around," she says.

My curiosity gets the better of me. "Did you know that Dad wasn't my dad?"

There's a pause. "Yeeesssss." She draws out the word as if my question confuses her.

"How did you know?" I ask.

"You mean aside from the fact that you don't look anything like the rest of us?" There's a hint of laughter in her voice, reminding me of the milkman's son comments I've lived with most of my life. "Really, it wasn't that hard to figure out. You were supposedly born four months early. Except that you were a fat baby and premature babies are not fat."

Her comment stops me cold. Why hadn't that ever occurred to me? All my life I had been focused on the possibility of being adopted. My mind had never entertained the possibility that my mother had hooked up with someone before my Dad. "I never thought of that."

"Duh." Jana laughs. "You're a guy. Guys don't think that way. It never occurred to Dad either, until we told him. That's okay. We still love you, even if you aren't the sharpest knife in the shed when it comes to babies."

Oddly enough, I find her sarcasm comforting. It's the same sort of humor she uses with Mark. It's the same sort of humor she uses with Mom and Dad. And having her treat me the same way she does all the other members of the family feels good.

"That still doesn't explain why you didn't tell me."

Jana sighs. "Because we didn't want this to happen. You're upset about a stupid situation. It doesn't change who you are or who you are to us. We just didn't see the need to tell you about something that wasn't important."

"It's important to my other family," I say.

"Well . . . we didn't know about them until after you sent in the DNA."

"I'm still upset that you didn't tell me."

"You'll get over it," says Jana with a laugh. "You love us too much to stay mad. Mark and I just want you to know that we support you and hope that your new family loves you as much as we do. If not . . . they're crazy."

"Thanks." I end the call.

I'm not as mad as I was yesterday, after talking to Mark, but the idea of my family keeping such an important suspicion from me is still upsetting. The urge to reach out to someone I trust returns. Then an idea flashes through my head. Why not reach out to Tammy? She's my sister.

"I received calls from my brother and sister in Arizona," I write. "They wanted to support me in this situation, but the reason I mention it is I found out my dad has known for a long time that I'm not his biological child. He loved my mom and decided to accept me as his own son. And he always has. What's funny about the situation is I've been worried about how my dad would react when he already knew. I was worried about nothing. Life can be comical that way."

———

My wife walks into the office. "Have you made a decision about the trip?"

"What trip?" I ask. My mind barely registers her presence as I focus on the computer screen and finishing the last page of the chapter I've been working on all day.

"Our anniversary trip."

"Right." It takes a moment to realize LuAnn is going to need more of an answer than I've given her. "It sounds good."

"What part of it sounds good?"

I pause. This must be how our youngest son feels when we catch him not paying attention to one of our discussions about his behavior. "All of it."

"You don't have any suggestions on what else we can do besides visit Alex?"

"We could see if they still have that paddleboat tour in Miami. The one we went on during our honeymoon."

She nods and leaves.

I return to my writing and finish the chapter. It's too late in the day to start another one, so I make the social media rounds. Mother Petrauschke has posted some crafting videos. I don't like them as much as the ones she posts for creative food ideas. I switch to my email and write to Tammy.

"You mentioned that your dad likes John Wayne. I happen to have a John Wayne story that he and the rest of you might like. Whenever I'm at a party and they play the tell-us-something-most-people-don't-know-about-you game, I answer that John Wayne fed me lunch. The story behind that answer is that one of my dad's friends worked on the Red River Ranch that was owned by John Wayne. When I was about ten, the ranch had their annual barbeque and stock auction. Employees and friends of employees were all fed barbeque as part of the event. Of course, the Duke didn't do any of the cooking or serving. During the auction, John Wayne was out in the feed pen with the cattle. Dad had my mom sitting on his shoulders so she could snap a picture of the Duke. After a few minutes, Dad shouts, 'Hey, Mr. Wayne. Can you look over this way? My wife is getting heavy.' John Wayne turned and posed for the picture.

"I love rodeo. Who would-da thunk there were any rodeos in New Jersey?

"My dad's DNA test resulted in another family member who no one knew anything about. I'm still working out which member of dad's family is the grandfather. I'm going to have one of the men on my mother's side of the family take a DNA test so I can do more genealogy work for the Andersons. I'm kind of worried about what we might find. LOL."

I pause. I need to know more about what my father is thinking, and my mother still refuses to tell me anything. If I'm ever going to find out about my parents and their relationship, it will have to be from my father.

"About your dad. A friend of mine brought up an interesting point. He suggested the possibility that this isn't a case of your dad not remembering, but rather a situation he prefers to leave in the past. I don't know, so this isn't a matter of me accusing him of anything. Is it possible that my mom told your dad she was pregnant and he walked away and is now too embarrassed to admit it? Like I said, I'm not suggesting that is what happened. I'm just curious. I hope that doesn't offend you."

One way or another, that should get me a better idea of the real situation.

Tammy's response is waiting for me the following Monday. "My dad liked the John Wayne story. It made him laugh.

"I think my dad just doesn't remember. Maybe with it being so close to his stroke, he feels it might not be a possibility. I'm not sure. I think if he knew, he would have admitted it by now.

"It's a process for all of us. You and I have been processing the situation longer than the others have. My mom is fine with everything. She said you are more than welcome in our family—as long as you don't mind a second mom. I wonder if all this just brings up memories for my dad. He was always told that Petrauschke was his dad. He tried having a relationship with him, but Mr. Petrauschke didn't want anything to do with him. I'm not really sure how he feels.

"I also wanted you to know that Dad took the DNA test. I will let you know when I hear anything. Although, I'm pretty sure what it will say. Talk to you soon. Your sister, Tammy."

Your sister. It surprises me that something as small as ending a message with "your sister" can emotionally impact me. But it does. That simple acknowledgment of our blood bond means more than I would have ever expected. She is my sister, and I love her. Now, if I can only gain the same acceptance with my father.

"I'm glad your mom is all right with the situation," I write to Tammy. "I was a bit worried about that. And I'm glad your dad agreed to the DNA test. I'm already convinced, but it should settle the matter for him. I can see how he might be unsure about the situation.

"Maybe when he finally accepts me as his son, I can come out and visit all of you. I mean, if that's all right with everyone out there. Please tell the rest of the family hello."

—● ●—

"Randy," my wife says, from the office door. She waits a few seconds and repeats my name—louder. "Randy, have you made up your mind about our anniversary trip?"

I turn my chair around to give LuAnn my full attention. It takes a few seconds for my mind to switch from writing-mode to world-aware-mode. "What's left for me to decide?"

"All of it. Will the dates I picked cause any problems with your schedule? Do you care which airline we take? Are there any places you want to see while we're out there? It is our anniversary; I want to make sure you enjoy the trip."

"I thought we were going out to see the grandbaby."

"Don't forget Alex. We're going to see our daughter too," says LuAnn. "And to celebrate being married for twenty years."

"Whatever you decide should be fine," I tell her. The truth is she cares more about traveling than I do and always has better suggestions on how to make the trip fun. But I know I should have some sort of input on the plans so I don't hurt her feelings. "Let me think about it overnight. Maybe I can come up with something appropriate to do for our honeymoon."

LuAnn walks off to start dinner. A dinner the children will actually eat as opposed to my experiments in culinary disaster.

I check my email and find a message from Tammy. "I don't want you to feel that my dad doesn't accept the situation, because we have talked about some of the similarities between the two of you. I think he just needed to know for sure.

"Oh, by the way. The results from the DNA test came in last night. They confirmed what we already knew. Welcome to the family, brother."

I read the last part of Tammy's message again to make sure it says what I think it says. I'm officially part of the Petrauschke family. Which probably means I'll have to learn how to pronounce the name correctly. I hop out of my chair and run into the kitchen.

"I'm in," I tell LuAnn. "I'm in."

My wife smiles at me and says, "That's nice, dear."

"No, it's not nice. It's awesome. Tammy sent in a DNA test for her dad and it came back positive. Mr. Petrauschke is my father."

"You already knew that," she says.

"Yeah, but now he does too. Which means . . . we need to go to New Jersey during our anniversary trip."

# CHAPTER 11

# STALKING THE FAMILY

LuAnn and I penned the opening chapter of our lives together with a trip to Florida—a place neither of us had been to separately and which we encountered for the first time as a couple. As such, it seems fitting for the two of us to make a similar trip, twenty years later, to meet my New Jersey family for the first time.

A vision of what it will be like to meet the Petrauschkes plays in my head. First the children—my nieces and nephews—will come running out of a perfectly crafted house, youngest to oldest. They'll surround me, jumping and shouting with joy. Then Tammy, Joe, and Bill will make their way outside with happy, bouncy steps. Ear-to-ear smiles will adorn their faces. Finally, my father will stroll out the door, a fashionable pipe clenched in his jaws, and laugh at the sight before him as he offers a pithy remark . . .

The story in my head comes to a screeching halt when I have to come up with a glib, yet still wise, comment to respond.

When writing a novel, I have the luxury of spending hours thinking up those spontaneous quips. It's not quite as easy when I'm operating in real time.

I realize my first meeting with the new family probably won't be anything like my dream scenario. Tammy and Joe seem nice enough in their emails and their text messages, but the experience might be very different in person. Long-distance communication could be concealing a veritable encyclopedia of socially unacceptable behaviors.

Meeting anyone for the first time is an awkward event. Meeting my immediate family for the first time only multiplies those uneasy feelings. Will they like me? Will they get my sense of humor? Or will they decide I'm a thorn in the family's back end? What if we just stare at each other in endless, awkward silence?

Maybe I shouldn't be in such a hurry to go to New Jersey. The state will still be there next year . . . and the year after.

The only question is whether all of the Petrauschkes will be around in a couple of years.

I decide that putting off the visit will haunt me for the rest of my life if something happens to a member of the New Jersey family before I have a chance to meet them. Besides, all families have unique behaviors that others find odd. My Arizona family certainly has its share of quirks, eccentricities, and outright bad habits. Those peculiar bits of strangeness are often what I love most about them. I'm sure it will be the same with this new batch of characters.

I open my email and respond to Tammy. "I have to admit I was worried about whether it'd be all right for me to come out and visit. I'm really looking forward to meeting everyone. I will let you know when my wife schedules our flight so you know what dates we will be there."

The daydream still lingers in my mind. I have a mountain of author work that needs to be done over the summer but decide to open Google Maps and take a look at the section of New Jersey where my family lives. Just a quick look—not a full-out distraction. I'll be back to work in a minute or two.

I find the place where my family lives. The town is tiny. Only six streets going east to west, fewer going north to south. I don't see any hotels or motels listed and make a note to book a place to stay in one of the larger towns nearby.

Typing in my father's address fails to take me to the street on which he lives. A marker on the mini-map shows his house is on the next street over. Apparently Street View doesn't consider the road important enough to photograph. I have to settle for a view from across a lawn. The image is blurred, and all I can really tell is that my father lives in a white, two-story house.

I cruise down a few streets to look at more of the town. It's definitely rural. The rustic homes and wide spaces between them lend a Mayberry feel to the place. I half expect Sheriff Taylor or Barney Fife to appear in one of the images. There's even a lake, named after the town, on the outskirts.

A few clicks along the street and I'm back on Main. The images have gone from dim, blurry, and overcast to bright, clear, and sunny in the space of a block. Apparently, it took more than one day to map out this tiny town. I spin the image around and click on the previous street.

Dim and cloudy.

I do another about-face and click.

Sunny and bright.

Cloudy. Sunny. Cloudy. Sunny. It takes a couple of minutes before the novelty of instant weather change wears off. I resume my internet drive through town and notice there's hardly any traffic. After searching several streets, I determine that three cars on the same section of road constitute a traffic jam.

I type in Joe's address in the adjacent town. Street View shows me a two-story home with a guesthouse in back. Less than thirty feet away, a railroad track runs along the side of the property. The railway line is bracketed by trees, forming a green tunnel for the trains to pass through. Why would anyone live in a house positioned this close to the train tracks? I hope Street View is wrong and Joe doesn't actually live here. Otherwise, my visit to his place will be . . . interesting. And not in a good way.

My writer brain runs away from me again and I imagine us sitting at Joe's place as a train rattles past the house. Everyone rushes around the room, grabbing items on the shelves before they have the chance to fall, just like in the movie *Mary Poppins.*

I check the clock. An hour, rather than a few minutes, has passed while I've been playing with Street View. Time I can't afford to waste with all the writing that needs to be done. I close out the program and open an unfinished chapter in my latest middle-grade book.

My cell phone rings. It's my brother Joe. A member of my New Jersey family is calling me! I hesitate for the briefest of moments, wondering if I should answer it. Then the excitement over one of the Petrauschkes calling me wins out. I hit the green button on my phone to accept the call. "Hey."

The chance for me to give Joe an outstanding first impression through the clever use of dialogue goes out the window. I regret not having thought about what I was going to say before I accepted the call. It's too late now. All I can do is work on not sounding like an idiot.

"It's your brother . . . Joe." His voice is deep and gruff. "Tammy says you're coming out to visit us."

"That's the plan," I tell him. "I mean . . . if that's all right with everyone out there."

"Of course it's okay. You're part of the family."

His words stun me. To have any of the Petrauschkes accept me, a stranger, into their family without us ever having met is beyond my comprehension. His reaction feels like a bear hug of approval while simultaneously forcing me to scratch my head in disbelief. How can Joe, or any of the Petrauschkes, bring me into the family that quickly, that easily?

I shrug off my doubts and enjoy the moment. A first phone call moment with my brother. The bliss lasts mere seconds before I realize that neither of us is talking. What do I say to him? I can't tell him I hate talking on the phone because he might take that as a rejection. I don't dare ask him anything too personal until we know each other better.

"What went through your mind when Tammy told you about me?" I ask.

Joe humphs. I'm not sure if it's the I'm-still-thinking-about-it sort of humph or the why-did-he-have-to-ask-me-that-question variety. "I thought it was great."

The phone is silent. I wait a moment to see if Joe is going to say more and then ask, "Could you expand upon that a little?"

"Another brother means more family, and it's good to have more family."

"That's it?" I ask for some reason. I realize I'm expecting more.

"Yeah," he grunts. "What about you?"

"More family is good . . . I guess." I sort through my thoughts, wondering which of them to share with Joe and which of them to keep locked away. For me the situation isn't as simply defined as it seems to be for him. My approach to relationships is more cautious.

Joe chuckles. It's a low, raspy affair that should belong to a dastardly villain in an Edgar Allan Poe story. "Our family is close. It surprised us that Dad had another kid running around in Arizona, but you are our brother, and that means we love you. That's what families do."

Can it be that simple?

In a perfect world, that's the way it should work. Families would support one another without question and without hesitation. The Hallmark Channel is loaded with stories that focus on the very same sentiment. Even though I find those movies cheesy, the messages they convey ring true in my heart. Joe's right. That's what families do.

Time to move on. I switch to my go-to topic. Food. "Are there any foods LuAnn and I should try while we're in New Jersey?"

"Depends on what you like," says Joe.

"What we would like is to try some foods that are popular in New

Jersey and we can't find at home." I open up my browser and search for regional foods in New Jersey. Several lists come up, and I select one that includes plenty of pictures.

"Pork rolls," says Joe.

"Pork rolls?" An image pops into my mind of dinner rolls made out of bacon, or ham, instead of wheat. I know that can't be what they are, but my imagination often takes me in odd and nonsensical directions. "Is that round gobs of baked meat?"

"No." Joe chuckles again. It's definitely a villainous sort of laugh. "It's like ham. It's sliced, cooked up, and served on bread with egg and cheese. I have it for breakfast."

I Google "pork roll," and a picture of what looks like an Egg McMuffin pops up. Another site shows the "meat" in its packaged form, with a description of the product. In this form it reminds me of salami or bologna. The information page gives a history of the food. Pork roll dates back to 1856 and is a cultural staple in New Jersey, I read.

There's another silent pause as I wait for Joe to ask me something. He doesn't. I gulp and search the internet for a list of popular foods in the state. One site shows a picture sloppy joes that don't look anything like the sandwiches my mother made when I was a child. I move past the obvious moral crime against gastronomy they represent and on to the next item.

"Tomatoes?" Oops. That was meant to be an internal thought. I quickly scramble to recover from the faux pas and ask an actual question. "Are you guys known for your tomatoes?"

"Yeah. We have the best tomatoes in the country."

I look for something on the list that Joe might talk about for longer than thirty seconds. Jersey-style hot dogs are deep-fried and prepared in seven varieties. Pass. Disco Fries. The name alone causes me to scroll by without reading any further about them. I find it interesting that the Trenton Tomato Pie places the cheese and toppings directly on the crust and saves the tomato sauce for last, but I somehow doubt it will excite Joe enough to shift him into conversational high gear.

Saltwater taffy? No.

Fat sandwich? No.

Texas wieners? Why are Texas wieners considered a New Jersey food? Still a—no.

"Where you going to stay when you come out here?" Joe asks.

His sudden, unexpected question startles me. "We haven't decided."

To my surprise, the call lasts an hour. During that time, Joe tells me a few things about himself. I listen to the details, and it sounds as if he's had a rougher life than I have. Apparently, Joe can contribute something to the conversation. I decide it isn't so much a matter of him not having anything to say as it is me being too impatient to wait. In my opinion, casual conversation should be saved for sitting around the kitchen table.

Despite the awkward pauses in our conversation, I find myself liking Joe. An hour is much longer than I normally speak with anyone on the phone, and I'm at my limit. I am unable to keep a conversation going on the phone, which seems crazy because I can talk for hours in a face-to-face situation. "I have stuff to do. Good talking with you, Joe."

"Yeah, I can't wait to see you."

I disconnect the call. After spending this time talking on the phone with Joe, I find myself looking forward to sitting around a kitchen table with him to have a proper conversation. Or, at least, a proper round of sitting in silence, waiting for conversation.

It takes the better part of an hour to fully submerge myself in my writing. The story flows from my head, through my fingers, and onto the computer screen. I make good progress and stop when my brain starts to feel like mush. Pounce, the hero of my latest novel, has been tricked into accepting a dangerous quest to a faraway land.

That's going to be fun. Poor Pounce. He has no idea what I plan to do to him.

It's almost dinnertime. Before I head to the kitchen, I check my emails and find a new message from Susan. "Thank you SO much for helping me. I think I'm very close to finding my grandfather, and you are my final link. Attached is a Word document I put together. I have lots of questions after you have time to review the information."

I open the file and scan through Susan's research. It includes mini-family trees for all of the close matches on Ancestry. I'm surprised she's done this much work on researching the families in my ancestral tree. That level of effort echoes the excitement I felt in the early stages of the Great Lindsay Quest. Susan and I share the genealogy bug; but in her case, she has the personal motivation to find her grandfather. It's a bond that connects us, if not by blood, then at least through our common love for the ancestry of the same family.

I hit the reply button and write, "Susan, I read through your document. Go ahead and ask me whatever questions you like."

I figure it will take a week or so for her to read the message and get back to me. Until then, I can mine through the mountain of author work that needs to be done.

Lucy leans against my office door. "What do you want for dinner?"

"Lasagna . . . no—stir-fry," I tell her.

"I don't know how to make either of those," she says.

"Hamburgers?"

"We don't have any hamburger. Unless you want to run to the store and get some."

"Peanut butter and jelly sandwiches," I suggest.

"Dad!" She rolls her eyes with the expertise and precision only a fourteen-year-old can manage. "I'm going to make tuna salad."

"How about tuna salad?" I call after her quickly retreating form.

It appears to be Lucy's night to make dinner. I won't have to stop working after all.

The top spot on my to-do list is a writing workshop I'm scheduled to teach at one of the local libraries. Back when I struggled with the publishing process for my first novel, several established writers were kind enough to aid me. The workshops are a way to pay their kindness forward.

Who am I kidding? I may tell everyone I do the workshops to help writers at the beginning of their creative journey (and I do), but I'd be more honest if I'd just admit to thriving on the time I spend with other writers.

If I come across an exciting article on developing read-on prompts or a brilliant method of adding depth to one of my characters, I can't rush out to the living room and tell my wife. She'll only say, "That's nice, dear." I hate that phrase because what it really means is, "I don't care, but I love you too much to tell you."

Writers care about storytelling stuff. They smile when I mention the try/fail cycle. The room is filled with oohs and aahs as I talk about methods of plotting a novel. An electric thrill passes through the crowd as we share stories of our favorite examples of successful foreshadowing.

I put all thoughts of family history aside and sit back down at my desk. There's another email. Boy, she's fast. She must be really eager to find her grandfather. Despite all the work I have to do, I open the email. Family always wins out.

Susan writes, "Wow. After five years, someone to talk to. Here is my first set of questions:

"Did you note any inaccuracies in the genealogy I sent you?

"Does a connection with Lloyd Williams seem plausible as my grandfather?

"Any thoughts about who the mystery account might be? This first cousin can't be a half-sibling since everyone who fits in that category is dead, right? It would be nieces, nephews?

"Did Buster Williams have any children?

"Are Lloyd Williams's grandchildren still alive?

"Who do you think would be most open to doing a DNA test?"

It takes a half hour to look through the files on the Williams branch of the family tree and then answer her questions. "The genealogy you cited was mostly correct, except that Albert Lindsay Jr. is my deceased grandfather—not my great-grandfather."

Susan seems focused on Lloyd as the most likely candidate to be her grandfather. However, from the little I know of his brother Buster, that matchup makes more sense. Buster is closer to her grandmother's age and had a reputation in the family that supports the idea of having a child out of wedlock. Maybe Susan knows something I don't about the situation.

I continue. "The DNA match is with my dad. Lloyd is the right age and in the right area, but since we're looking for a second cousin, I don't think it can be Lloyd or Buster."

Item by item, I go through the rest of the questions on her list. It takes me more time than I can afford right now to spend on anything that isn't writing related. As soon as I hit the send button, my phone notifies me that I have a text message.

Joe writes, "Have you ever had a cheesesteak or a sub?"

I tell him yes.

Then I wait. Experience has taught me to not even try to write while my mind is expecting an interruption. A minute passes. Five minutes pass. Everyone has quirks. I accept the random, drive-by texting as part of Joe's offbeat personality. After ten minutes, I give up on waiting for a response from Joe and I give up on writing for the night.

With any luck, the rest of the week will be free of interruptions and I will make some serious progress on my novel.

— —

The summer drags on. It's hard to concentrate on what the characters in my story should do next when my children are reenacting the Battle of Gettysburg in the next room. Plus, it's 115 degrees outside—who can concentrate in this heat? I keep the office door shut, but that doesn't stop the phone from pinging whenever Joe texts me. Nor does it stop the computer from posting a message bubble as each of Susan's emails arrives. I usually ignore the vast majority of the notifications I receive . . . but these two are from family. A pesky voice inside my head offers snide comments about how I can't ignore family.

Despite the distractions, I manage to force my protagonist through a series of grueling challenges and even leave him near death on the forest floor. Poor Pounce. I almost feel sorry for the heroes in my stories. My goal is to make them suffer. And I do that well. Of course, the good news is that they make it through the story alive . . . most of the time.

The weeks pass, and life reminds me there is more to the world than just my writing. LuAnn marches into the office with the schedule for our trip. Her suggested itinerary has us in Florida for most of the anniversary celebration and then arriving in New Jersey on Saturday and leaving for home the following day.

"That's not going to work," I tell her. "You need to schedule more time in New Jersey. I have a family I've never seen, and spending one afternoon with them is not enough. This may be the only chance I have to spend time with my father."

"Okay." She smiles. "You seemed a little nervous about meeting them. I wasn't sure how long you wanted to stay there. Should I book the flights for convenience or to save money?"

Later in the month, Joe texts me. "Hey, big brother. What two days are you going to be here? I want to make sure I don't have anything planned on those days."

I text, "We arrive on the 29th and go home the morning of the 1st."

"What time do you arrive in Jersey?" he asks.

"Friday, about 1:00 a.m."

"Awesome. I can't wait to see you, bro."

Joe's excitement warms me emotionally. I find myself looking forward to seeing him. Tammy too. Anxiety still nibbles at my chest when I think about meeting the rest of the family. Even though Joe and Tammy have both said my father has accepted me, I need to experience that for myself before I can believe it.

I'm close enough to finishing the book to spare some time to respond to Susan. I email her, "Lloyd is my dad's uncle. If Lloyd were your mom's father, then her and my dad would be first cousins. That would be three degrees of separation from each other. One degree to go from my dad to his mother, one degree to go from my grandmother to Lloyd, and then a final degree of separation to go from Lloyd to your mother.

"The chart on Ancestry shows second cousins as moving up the family tree three times, giving my dad and your mother five degrees of separation. As I mentioned before, that rules out Lloyd as your grandfather."

An hour later, Susan responds, "If I'm not mistaken, there will be an extra stage of DNA separation when half-siblings are involved. Siblings will appear as first cousins, first cousins will appear to be second cousins, and so forth."

I slap my forehead. Why hadn't I thought of that before? It's the same reason my brother Bill had shown up as a close relative rather than a sibling. Only half of the regular amount of DNA was being connected to the Lindsay family. The other half belonged to Susan's family. I go to Ancestry and check the family relations chart, keeping in mind that any relation I see should be one stage closer than is listed.

Only two individuals could possibly be Susan's grandfather. Lloyd and Buster Williams. Adjusting for the extra step puts both of them in line with the chart. She has more work to do before she'll know which of the men is her grandfather, but at least Susan can positively identify her great-grandparents.

I write, "Congrats. That means Lewis and Cora are your great-grandparents. All you have to do now is convince one of Lloyd's grandchildren to take a DNA test, and you should be able to determine which one of the brothers is your grandfather. Here's the email address for Lloyd's grandson Terry."

Susan's quest is nearly at an end. A grin spreads across my face as I think about how Dad's DNA has helped her find the lost portion of her family. Maybe his DNA will be the key for others to connect with the Lindsays and the Williams in the future. The fact that I played a part in putting some of the missing pieces together gives me a sense that I have filled a hole in Susan's soul.

A spirit of peace settles in my chest. My portion of this quest is done. DNA testing has helped a woman find a grandfather she didn't know. Even though a victory dance is in order, I decide to walk through my neighborhood and reflect on this journey. In other words, I take a moment to enjoy this victory.

My next adventure awaits me in Florida and New Jersey.

# CHAPTER 12

# FLORIDA

The nights before a big event are long, miserable affairs. My mind is so focused on ensuring all of the details of the Florida trip have been properly planned that I can't sleep. No matter how firmly I tell my mind to shut down and sail off to dreamland—it doesn't listen. I roll around the bed for a couple of hours, trying to find a comfortable position to rest. Eventually I give up, trudge into my office, and jiggle the mouse to wake up the computer.

Twenty minutes of solitaire fails to silence the demons of doubt. I give up on the game and launch Google Street View. I check the addresses of Joe and my father so I can recognize their homes when we reach New Jersey.

I spend ten minutes studying each house and the surrounding neighborhood. Then I do a search for restaurants in the towns we plan to visit. The browser search gives me results that feel more like paid advertisements than honest testimonials for landmark restaurants. I switch over to the website for *Diners, Drive-Ins, and Dives.* The kids and I watch the show often and have vowed to visit a recommended restaurant if we are ever in the area. Now I have that chance.

Most of the Florida restaurants are in Miami and Orlando. None of them are close to where our daughter lives. I search for New Jersey eateries and only find a diner in Clifton that offers burgers and world-famous disco fries. There are plenty of words that don't belong on a menu, and *disco* is pretty high on that list for me. I move my search to Philadelphia. None of the results grabs my attention.

A memory bubbles up from the edible-goodness section of my brain. One of the other food shows I regularly watch featured a pair of restaurants, across the street from one another, that served cheesesteaks. I'm not going to find a more authentic slice of the Philadelphia food scene than cheesesteaks. This is exactly the sort of culinary pit stop I want to make. I enter the address for one of the restaurants in my cell phone and then shut down the computer.

The flight doesn't leave until late-morning and has a layover in Dallas. My oldest son drops us off at the airport, and we go through the usual security procedures. Then we wait. LuAnn plays solitaire on her phone. I sit next to her as a parade of thoughts keeps me occupied.

Our oldest daughter, Alex, and I haven't always maintained a calm and stress-free relationship. She has her opinions, and I have mine. Her teenaged years marked a period of drama-induced turmoil in our household.

Technically, Alex is my stepdaughter, but I don't think of her that way. I've been a part of her life since she was two, and most of the troubles in our relationship have arisen because she takes after me. The moments, good and bad, I've shared with her have made us family—not our bloodline, not any shared DNA. Knowing one another, as only family can know one of its members, is what has forged our bond.

This trip will be a test of our fragile, distance-induced truce. I feel I've matured enough to turn this verbal ceasefire into a permanent peace and hope she will give me the chance to mend our precious daddy-daughter relationship.

While the emotional forecast on Florida is still foggy, the situation in New Jersey has taken a decidedly sunny turn. I still have the first-meeting jitters, but I feel a real connection to my new family. The ease with which they've accepted me has settled a couple of concerns in my mind. I plan to hug them and not just shake hands. I plan to call Mr. Petrauschke Dad instead of Father. In other words, I will treat them the same way I do my Arizona family.

We board the plane. LuAnn takes the middle seat, allowing me to sit on the aisle. She pulls out her cell phone and says, "Smile for the camera. I'm going to post the start of our trip on Facebook."

LuAnn takes the picture and then works on sending it out to family and friends. The journey has officially begun.

The plane arrives late in Dallas, giving us five minutes to reach the other side of the airport. We don't make it. The plane is still docked, but the door is closed.

"It's not our fault the other flight was late," I tell the attendant. "What's it going to hurt to open the door and let us in?"

"Once the door is shut," she says, without looking up from her computer terminal, "no one is allowed onboard."

"No one?" I ask. "So if the head of the FBI walks up and tells you it's a matter of national security for him to enter that plane . . . you would stop him?"

LuAnn leans over and says, "You're not helping matters any."

The attendant prints out a new boarding pass and hands it to my wife. "The next flight to your destination is in three hours. That should give you plenty of time to reach the correct boarding gate."

It looks as if our luggage will reach Florida before we do.

LuAnn and I find a restaurant and order some food. I'm tired, hungry, and upset about the delay. As usual, my wife is unfazed by our travel hiccup. She slides over next to me, matches my sour expression, and snaps a picture of us with her phone. Then she posts the image on social media with the caption "Missed our connection; now spending three hours eating dinner."

Her unsinkable spirit disperses my dark mood. We share a meal and some conversation. The time passes quickly. Then again, any time I spend with this woman feels like a fleeting moment. I suspect she has a secret superpower that gives her control over the passage of time. Before I know it, I find myself boarding another plane.

The flight into Florida lands us at a small airport just before midnight. We barely exit the plane when a tired voice announces over the intercom that the airport will close in ten minutes.

Close?

LuAnn and I glance at one another. The airport back home never closes. Whenever the television news reports the cancellation of flights due to weather, they show crowds of people sleeping overnight in chairs and on the floor. The same thing happens in movies and television shows. Airports are not supposed to close.

I panic. What if there aren't any taxis waiting outside? How will we get to our hotel? An image lodges itself in my brain of LuAnn and I spending the night on the sidewalk outside the airport doors.

*Don't be silly,* the cool, rational part of my brain says. *Airport security won't let you stay the night on their sidewalk. They'll call the police and have you escorted off the premises.*

I wonder if the police will give us a ride.

"Honey," I say to my wife, "if this town is small enough to have the airport close at midnight, then they might not have a line of taxis waiting for us when we exit the building. How about using the app on your phone to find us a driver in the area?"

I take her luggage and drag it along, freeing up both of her hands to search for a ride. The signal is weak, and we are nearly out the front door by the time she connects. She frowns. "The app says there are no drivers in the area. No one is available within twenty miles."

Oh no. Our only hope for reaching our hotel tonight rests in finding a taxi outside.

We walk through the sliding glass doors and see a taxi. Just one. I rush forward, ready to throw elbows to block anyone else who might be thinking of taking it. Another couple follows on my heels. They apparently have the same idea.

"Are you still accepting fares?" I ask the driver from ten feet away.

"Yes," he responds. "The last one of the night."

"Excellent," I tell him. Then I turn to the other couple. They walk past me to the parking garage across the street. I guess they didn't want a taxi after all.

"Well, I would have been willing to share," I mumble to their retreating forms.

The driver opens the trunk, and I load our luggage. I open the door for LuAnn and then slide into the back seat beside her. Tension ebbs from my body as I slump in the seat. It takes less than a minute for the taxi to exit the airport.

Darkness reigns in the immediate area. I watch the slouched silhouettes of trees during our drive through the hot, muggy night. Our last visit to Florida was during February and through portions of the state that could apparently afford to pay their electricity bills. The Sunshine State isn't impressing me this second time around.

After a few minutes, I spot signs of civilization through the windshield. Lights. Buildings. Buildings with lights. Even a few tall buildings. The driver stops in front of a bright, beautiful beacon of architectural refuge and identifies it as our hotel.

I pay the driver, grab our bags, and stumble inside. A cheerful smile greets us from the front counter. There's a face attached to the smile, but the information that rolls out of the woman's mouth has me too enthralled to care.

Yes, this is our hotel.

Yes, they have our reservation and will take us immediately to our room.

And yes, they know where the car rental place is located and can give us directions in the morning. Hallelujah! We have escaped the murky wilds of Florida and are safe.

Our room is clean, brightly lit, and decorated by someone who knew what they were doing. Even though it's only ten o'clock back home, I struggle to keep my eyes open. The soft bed and cool sheets lull me to sleep within minutes.

＊ ＊ ＊

Alex lives a little more than forty miles from our hotel in Gainesville. The countryside between towns is green and still bears the scars of Hurricane Irma. Spanish moss hangs from the branches of trees, like seaweed on the undead crew of the *Flying Dutchman*.

When we reach the outskirts of town, LuAnn calls Alex for directions. One scenario after another plays out in my mind. Alex and I haven't had an argument in years, but one careless comment from me could shatter our unspoken alliance and ruin the vacation.

*Keep your mouth shut and smile.* I continue to mentally repeat the plan until we reach Alex's apartment. Trees surround the complex. Trees thick with Spanish moss. If it's this creepy during the day, I can only imagine what it must be like after dark. I can picture zombies walking through the fog-enshrouded woods.

Why would anyone want to live here?

Alex opens the door to her apartment and greets her mother. I smile, say nothing, and follow them inside. Alex has the most beautiful baby girl cradled in her arms. She looks over at me and says, "Hey, Dad. I hope you didn't have any trouble finding the place."

Sweeter words have never been spoken than "Hey, Dad." They represent acceptance. They represent a maturity that is willing to leave the past behind us. But mostly, I just love it when any of my children call me Dad. It doesn't feel as much like a name as a term of endearment.

"No trouble at all," I tell Alex. "You gave us great directions." Tension that's been building since we left Gainesville flows out of me in seconds. It looks as if we're going to have good visit after all.

A young man with dark hair and a bold mustache walks out from one of the other rooms. Alex puts her arm around him and says, "This is Derick, the baby's father."

I shake Derick's hand and look him over. He's well-groomed and neatly dressed, but his mustache makes him look like a train conductor from the 1880s.

Alex gives us a tour of their home. Walking from one end of the apartment to the other takes less than a minute. Her showing us Derick's collection of World War II military relics and a closet full of war games takes closer to half an hour. My opinion of her baby daddy jumps several notches. I love military board games. While the others are talking about the neighborhood, I'm thinking of a way to fit one of the lengthy games into our visit.

LuAnn takes the baby, and the four of us sit around the kitchen table. Derick lingers near Alex as we visit. It's as if nothing has ever come between Alex and me. We talk. We laugh. We swap nerd stories about superhero movies, collectible action figures, and board games unknown to the general public.

Alex may not have any of my genetic code, but she is definitely my daughter.

While Alex and LuAnn talk about the baby's sleep schedule, I watch my daughter and remember how adorable she was as a child. Images of vacations, movies, and even pulling weeds together on Saturday mornings slowly scroll through my mind. We've shared so many good times together. We've also shared more than a few unhappy moments.

When we struggled as a unified family, we grew stronger. When we struggled against one another, we grew apart. I'm happy to take the bad memories with the good as long as it means I can continue to include this amazing young woman as a part of my family. As a part of my life. Every moment I spend talking with my daughter is a treasure I will take back home.

The ladies glance over at me, noticing that I'm watching them.

LuAnn winks. After twenty years of marriage, she's caught me quietly observing her enough times to know the sappy portion of my brain is in overdrive. I wink back at her.

"What?" Alex asks.

"Nothing," I tell her. "I'm just admiring my beautiful granddaughter."

"Well, then," says Alex. "You can hold her while Mom and I make lunch."

I watch to see if LuAnn is going to object. Once a grandbaby is placed in her arms, it just about requires the Jaws of Life to pry the child loose. LuAnn nods toward the wooden rocking chair in the front room and then gently transfers the baby to me.

Beautiful.

It's been years since I've held a baby in my arms. Only a few seconds pass before I decide Adelaide is my favorite grandchild. All right . . . not my favorite, because grandparents are not allowed to enjoy one of the grandchildren more than the others. But if that sort of grandchild bias were allowed, she'd be my favorite.

I gently rock her in my arms as she sleeps. I whisper conversations to her I know she won't understand. Mostly I tell her stories of fantastic creatures in faraway lands. But I sneak in a few questions about her future plans. Is she interested in becoming the first woman president of the United States? I try to talk her out of that choice. Politics is bad business and not really what our family is all about. Go into the arts . . . if you don't mind being poor all your life. Or you can be a strong, capable woman like Granny LuAnnie. Become a big shot in the company where you work and boss people around. Just don't tell Granny I said that, though.

We eat a late lunch while the baby sleeps. The protective part of me wants to grill Derick and make sure he's good enough for my daughter, but I'm not willing to risk putting my relationship with Alex in jeopardy. Instead, I settle for asking a few casual questions.

"Why do you live in Florida?"

"Why do you work in a bank?"

"When you play a World War II board game, do you play the Axis or the Allies?"

The more I talk to Derick, the better I like him. Except for the mustache. He has manners, shows no sign of being a threat to my daughter, and works a respectable job. By the time we finish eating, I find myself hoping their relationship works out.

Best of all, I've managed to interrogate him without starting a new feud with Alex.

LuAnn and I stay until dinnertime and then prepare to leave so we can find our motel. Alex and Derick escort us to the rental car. In the growing twilight, the moss-covered trees look even more sinister than when we arrived.

"That Spanish moss is kind of creepy," I say.

Derick shrugs. "You probably want to stay away from it. Chiggers live in the stuff."

"Chiggers?" I don't know much about the pests except they bite.

"They attach themselves to warm-blooded hosts that pass by the vegetation they inhabit. You should be all right as long as you don't touch the Spanish moss."

I make a mental reminder to park our rental car at least ten feet away from any moss-laden trees or shrubs. An umbrella might even be a good idea. Not that I'm afraid of bugs. We have plenty of the poisonous variety back home. I'm just uncomfortable dealing with hostile life-forms when I don't know the rules of engagement.

Scorpions. Centipedes. Tarantulas. Bring 'em on. But chiggers—no, thanks.

We drive past our motel before we notice it's there. A quick U-turn and we pull into the tiny parking lot. Just outside the office, a wicker lawn set sits under a canopy, surrounded by potted trees and plants. It's quaint . . . in an upscale, redneck sort of way.

The office is filled with curios and knickknacks, making it look more like a museum dedicated to the *Antiques Roadshow* than a motel front desk. An older woman wearing an airy flower print from the '70s offers us a cellophane-wrapped mint and then takes us on a tour to pick our room.

"Each of the rooms is decorated in its own unique style," she tells us. Then she opens the first door and I see . . . pillows. A mountain of them is piled on the bed, and more sit atop the two chairs in the room. There's even a pillow on one of the tables. The room's predominant color is sea-foam green. If I were the decorator, I would have forgone the purple trim and highlights, but that's just me.

"This will be fine," I tell her.

"You haven't seen the other available rooms yet." The next room is pink and frilly. A four-poster bed draped with sheer white curtains immediately snags my attention. Life-sized Barbie probably stays here whenever she and Ken pass through on their way to the Florida Keys.

I make sure our host is looking straight at me when I tell her, "I really liked the first room. If it's all right with you, we'll take that one."

We return to the office, and LuAnn chats with our host while I unpack the car. I find a spot in one corner of the room and stack the pillows to make room for us to sleep. The room reminds me of the *Star Trek* episode where Tribbles invade the ship. At least these pillows shouldn't make any trilling noises at night. If they do, I might have to consider moving to Barbie and Ken's room.

I turn on the AC and kick off my shoes. LuAnn joins me in the room. We spend a few minutes chatting about Alex, the baby, Derick, the humidity, chiggers, and the motel manager's fascination with pillows.

Then she goes to sleep. Lucky her. She has a talent for being able to sleep anywhere. Less than a minute after she closes her eyes, she's out.

I sit on the bed in front of the AC unit and sweat. A weak flow of marginally cool air flows out of the vent, but the room remains hot and sticky. There's no use trying to sleep, I know it won't work. With a heavy sigh, I move over to the antique desk, push aside the army of figurines, and pull out my laptop. I might as well work.

Half the night passes as I write my main character into one horrible situation after another. This time I'm working on one of my adult novels. The words of my biggest fan echo in my mind. "What horrible thing are you going to do to Robert in this book? Why do you pick on him? He's a nice guy."

The miserable heat has me in the right frame of mind to put Robert into all sorts of terrible trouble. I march him through the middle of Georgia in August. It takes no imagination at all for me to describe how he feels.

Around three in the morning, the room cools enough for me to sleep. It's not actually cool, but it's close enough. I look forward to a nice, long visit in Alex's air-conditioned apartment the next day. Maybe I can even curl up in a corner and catch a short nap in comfort.

We spend two more days in Florida. Most of the time, we sit in Alex's apartment and visit while she feeds the baby, changes the baby, and comforts Adelaide when she cries. LuAnn and I do our part by playing with the baby.

It brings back memories of when my own children were little. I'm glad I don't have to go through all of that again. The grandparent gig is where it's at. I can hold the baby when she's happy and then hand her back to my daughter when her diaper is full. And best of all, I'm not staying up all night while the baby adjusts to a daytime schedule.

No wonder young people have babies. It's exhausting.

The hours and then the minutes slip away. Before I know it, our time in Florida is over. I don't want to leave. I want to stay with my daughter and granddaughter. I've missed too many precious moments with Alex because of our disagreements. The longer I stay in Florida, the closer I come to making up for some of those lost opportunities.

But I'm also pulled to New Jersey. A whole new family awaits me there, including my biological father. Even if we could make last minute changes to our itinerary, this is something I have to go through with. It's something my inner voice pesters me to do. If only I could be in two places at once. Eventually, I comfort myself with the thought that there will be plenty of visits with these two amazing girls, but the time for meeting my new family is now.

# CHAPTER 13

# HELLO, JOE

It's close to midnight when we arrive in Philadelphia. People crowd around us as we walk through the airport corridors to the luggage claim. Every few minutes, the overhead speakers announce a new departure or arrival. Outside, a fleet of taxis lines the street, waiting to take us to our hotel. In fact, there are enough taxis to transport the entire 8th Army if that becomes necessary.

The hotel has air conditioning that actually works, but the room smells like an old closet filled with dirty sweatshirts and grimy gym socks. I test the bed. It's harder than my couch back home. That gives me an idea. I sit on the couch and find it much more comfortable.

As usual, LuAnn has no problem falling asleep.

I'm too tired to work on my current novel and I have difficulty sleeping away from home, so I spend half the night watching an *Iron Chef* marathon. This is why I don't like to travel. At least the room is cool and the sofa is somewhat comfy. I eventually manage to snooze for a few hours. LuAnn lets me sleep in, but a rumbling in my stomach forces me out of bed much earlier than I'm used to waking. Besides, we're in New Jersey and my family is waiting.

"They serve a continental breakfast from seven to nine," says LuAnn.

I glance over at her. We both shake our heads. I can tell she's thinking the same thing that's going through my mind. If a place smells this bad, it's probably safer to eat elsewhere. My stomach growls again. I decide to pass through the dining area on the way out. They have prepackaged yogurt cups. That seems safe enough. I take one for LuAnn and another for myself. Those will have to tide us over until after we pick up our rental car and reach our first stop. Cheesesteaks. We're going to decide for ourselves whether Pat's or Geno's has the best cheesesteaks in Philadelphia.

The drive through Philly plunges us into a world vastly different from our own. In Phoenix, most homes are single-story affairs on individual lots and spread out over a good portion of the available ground. They represent the wide-open spaces of the American West.

Philadelphia is the complete opposite. LuAnn and I pass through a neighborhood that is one long, continuous building. The individual units are tall, narrow, and packed in like sardines. Five giant steps could take me from one side of the home to the other.

Even the roads are cramped. Many of the streets barely have enough room for two cars to drive. In each direction, there is a narrow lane for parking and another for driving. Mere inches separate our car from the traffic moving in the other direction. I flinch with each tiny gap I have to thread.

We find our destination after a couple of wrong turns. Geno's and Pat's sit diagonally across the street from one another. Geno's is an A-shaped building, painted orange and white. It's only midmorning and already there's an impressive line to order food.

While LuAnn and I gawk at the menu, customers line up behind us. I wave them forward in line. Since LuAnn and I plan to compare the cheesesteaks here with the ones across the street, we want to make sure we order the real, original one. In other words, the cheesesteak.

Ordering the classic cheesesteak turns out easier than I thought. "Cheesesteak" is listed at the top of the menu. It has Whiz, American, and provolone. I hope Whiz refers to cheese. We buy a single cheesesteak and some cheese fries to split. Then we look the place over as we wait for our food.

The restaurant has celebrity pictures on the walls. Elton John, Danny DeVito, Joan Rivers, and the Philadelphia Eagles' mascot have all apparently dined at Geno's. I'm still working through the picture monument to Geno's cheesesteak mastery when our order comes up. They hand us a bag and point to the condiments table. A scowl from the server tells me just what the true fans of the original and best cheesesteak think about tainting the sandwich with ketchup or other vile flavor-altering substances.

We cross the street to Pat's. The restaurant is an island unto itself, bordered on three sides by streets. Painted red and white, Pat's King of Steaks claims to be both the inventor and originator of the cheesesteak. I order an original and some cheese fries. Pat's has an equally massive wall of fame.

As soon as the order comes up, LuAnn and I walk around to the back side of the restaurant and sit at one of the tables. I unwrap the Geno's cheesesteak, pass half to LuAnn, and then notice someone standing next to me.

A man wearing a Pat's T-shirt and a frown points to the cheesesteak in front of me. In a stern voice, he says, "Hey, pal. What's that doing here?"

I mentally scramble for a response and blurt out, "We're from Arizona."

What kind of response is that? That makes it sound like people from Arizona are simple country bumpkins who can't be expected to make intelligent choices in dining. To make matters worse, the frown on the man's face fades away, and he nods as if he's come to the same conclusion.

"We heard about this place on television," I continue, "and wanted to see which restaurant has the best cheesesteaks."

"I could've told you that," says the man. "We do. Pat's is the king of steaks."

"That's what I heard." I grab my half of Pat's cheesesteak and take a bite . . . and mmmmmm.

The man relaxes. It appears the wife and I are out of danger of a cheesesteak beating. He points to the building, "I started working here when I was twelve. That was fifty years ago."

Clearly, this is a man dedicated to cheesesteaks. For fifteen minutes he tells us how Pat's is home to the best cheesesteak in the world. Dozens of celebrities can vouch for the supremacy of the food here, he says. And it's an honor to work at a culinary landmark like Pat's, he goes on. Then, with one last sneer at the impostor sandwich sitting in front of me, he goes inside to continue his shift.

I grab my half of the Geno's cheesesteak and bite into it. The sandwich has a savory beef flavor that is missing in the cheesesteaks I've tried back home. Caramelized onions accentuate the steak, and the Whiz gives it a tang that adds a welcome level of complexity to the flavor.

Both cheesesteaks do Philly proud. I enjoy the one from Geno's slightly more but prefer Pat's cheese fries. LuAnn has exactly the opposite opinion.

We finish our meal and waddle back to our rental car. I check my cell phone and see that I've missed a text from Joe. "Did you look up the Jersey Devil?"

I text back, "Not yet. Is it a popular nightclub?"

"LOL," Joe texts. "No. Look it up. I'll make sure he doesn't get you."

"We are up and moving about in Philly," I text.

"Hmmmmm . . . cheesesteak. Enjoy. Give me a shout when you are headed this way."

LuAnn and I decide to take a detour south. According to the map, we can take the I-95 down to Delaware before crossing the river to New Jersey, which will allow us to put another check mark on our fifty-states bingo card. It's much greener than Arizona, but otherwise, Wilmington reminds me of just about any other city I've passed through at sixty-five miles an hour.

We cross the Delaware River, and the landscape turns rural. Large fields occupy the side of the road. Some of the fields are green with growing hay. Others are filled with apple orchards. Still more have square plots with corn or collard greens. Each home seems to have its own combination of produce and flower beds. I can see why they call this the Garden State.

"Where are we going?" LuAnn asks.

"To see my family."

"Who are we going to see first?"

I hand LuAnn my phone and have her text Joe.

"Should we head to your place or Tammy's house?"

"It's up to you. Do you want to go straight to Dad's?"

The suggestion to head straight to my father's house brings immediate clarity to the decision. I don't want to go there first. Over the last eight months, I've shared a lot of texts and phone calls with Joe and a large number of emails with Tammy. I already have a bond with them. I'm comfortable with the idea of meeting them.

My father, though, hasn't made any effort to communicate with me. I have only Tammy's opinion on the matter to indicate that he wants me here. Other than knowing what he looks like, he's still a stranger to me. And a first meeting with a stranger always makes me nervous. Plus, if I head to Joe's first, it will be a one-on-one meeting rather than a crowd fest.

I have LuAnn text Joe back: "We'll come to your place first."

We pass a farm with a red barn. It's an image I've seen only in paintings. Rural Arizona looks much different from the landscape around us. On the other side of the road is a farm with a pair of greenhouses shaped like Quonset huts. The fields we pass are bordered by trees. Skinny trees. Fat trees. Baby trees. Tall trees. All of them green. Real green. Not the brownish, faded green of the trees back home.

It's not that I don't find Arizona beautiful. I do. Nothing I've seen in New Jersey compares to the palo verde trees back home. And Arizona has a greater diversity in terrain than any place I know. But to be thrown in the middle of all this green thrills me. The roadside stands stocked with apples and signs advertising apple cider donuts add to the thrill.

Joe finally returns our text. "How long until you get here?"

LuAnn texts back, "We just passed the Cowtown Rodeo place."

Joe responds, "Cool. Not too far."

When LuAnn reads the texts back to me, my stress level decreases. I'm jittery over the idea of facing the rest of the family in one big mob. But I can handle a one-on-one first meeting with Joe.

The homes where Joe lives are spread out on large, spacious lots. Groves of trees separate the houses. It's an amazing sight for a boy who grew up in Arizona and is used to the soulless designs and bland stucco that make all the tract homes look alike. The houses here vary in shape, giving each one in the neighborhood its own distinct look and personality.

I watch for the railroad tracks that run along the side of Joe's house and find them easily enough. I call Joe. "We're here."

He responds after a few seconds. "I don't see you."

"I don't see you either," I tell him. "We're parked to the side of the railroad tracks."

Joe chuckles, "We don't live by the tracks. They changed the addresses a few years back. You need to turn around and head toward the edge of town. There's a red car in the yard."

No railroad. No loud, rattling noises to interrupt our visit.

Two minutes later, we pull up to a house with deep-red brick and a steeply sloping black roof. The house is trimmed in white and has a chimney on one side. A wooded area runs along the side of the property, isolating it from the neighbor's house. Several cars are parked on the lawn out front. Joe's place has a quaint and cozy quality to it.

I park on the dirt drive with the rest of the cars on the lawn. A last-second doubt flashes in my mind. Did I make a mistake coming to New Jersey? It still feels like the right thing to do, and even if it's not, it's too late to back out now.

Joe steps out of the house wearing a T-shirt, jeans, and a ball cap. He looks just like his pictures. Scruffy, dark beard. A bit haggard from what I expect has been a hard life. His movements are slow and stiff because of a work accident years before.

Despite the ease I've felt talking with Joe over the phone, my palms sweat. I climb out of my car and open the door for LuAnn, giving me a few extra seconds to think of what I'm going to say. Hopefully, something better than "Hello, Joe."

"Hey," says Joe in his gruff voice.

"The cheesesteaks were good." It sounds lame when I say it.

"Hmmm," grunts Joe. "Cheesesteaks."

Or maybe the sound is a mmm. I can't tell for certain.

Joe walks up to me and gives me a hug. All of my first-meeting tension drains away.

Up close, I notice he's shorter than I am. Back home, I'm the shortest male by about an inch. All of the Lindsay men range from five eleven to six one. Being taller than another male family member is a different experience for me.

"I'm glad you're here." Joe motions toward the house and stiffly walks that direction. "Tammy and the rest of the family are waiting over at Dad's. Whenever you're ready, you can head over there."

No fanfare. No big scene. My first contact with Joe feels like a routine visit with one of my siblings back home. I like it. His calm, accepting reception has already put me at ease. I follow him up to the house.

"You like tomatoes?" Joe asks. He stops at the door and bends over one of the plants growing under the front window. Then he hands me a bright-red cherry tomato.

I use my shirt and wipe off the tomato before popping it into my mouth. The small, firm ball bursts into juicy goodness when I bite. It has a rich tomato flavor with a hint of sweetness. "That's really good."

"Yeah," says Joe. "Jersey has the best tomatoes. Come on in and meet Tammy."

By Tammy, he means his wife—not our sister. This is my chance to ask him a question that's been on my mind since I found out there were two Tammys in the family. "What does everyone do to make sure they know which Tammy is which?"

"You can just call our sister . . . Old Tammy." Joe offers a sinister chuckle. In other words, he gives me his usual laugh.

"I think I'd rather come up with my own way of telling them apart," I tell him. Since she's married to Joe and now a Petrauschke I can call her Tammy-P.

"Suit yourself."

Inside, a red-haired woman with a cherubic smile waits for us. As soon as I enter the house, she rushes me and gives me an enthusiastic hug. Then she hugs LuAnn. "I am so happy to finally meet the two of youse."

Her accent reminds me slightly of the scene in *My Cousin Vinny* when Joe Pesci talks about the two utes—youths. The sheer joy of Tammy-P's greeting surprises me. I certainly didn't expect a sister-in-law to be this excited about my visit.

Tammy-P motions us to a couch in the front room. "Come in. Come in. Have a seat. Everyone else is at Poppi's house. They can't wait to see youse guys."

The words fly out of her mouth in rapid succession. I'm pretty sure she's exceeding the conversational speed limit, but I relish the sheer joy she exhibits over having us here. Tammy-P strikes me as the polar opposite of Joe. Where he is gruff and takes his time to respond, she is bright, sunny, and animated. Their relationship reminds me of mine and LuAnn's. Lu is cool, calm, and collected, where I'm bouncing off the walls most of the time.

LuAnn and I sit on the sectional. There are five or six cats in the room. Two on the couch, one on the table, another on the windowsill, and at least one napping on pet furniture.

"Don't mind the cats," Tammy-P says. "They're lovers. We seem to attract strays."

Joe grunts at the statement.

"Anyways," Tammy-P continues. "I'm so glad the two of youse came out to visit. Tell me about Florida. What did youse guys do there?"

LuAnn tells them about the Florida trip. She talks about the grand-baby, our daughter, the grandbaby, the boyfriend-in-law, the grandbaby, our unusual motel stay, and the grandbaby. I toss in an occasional comment about the horrible humidity and creepy Spanish moss.

Joe stands in the kitchen while we talk. The house is small enough that a person in the living room is only a few feet away from anyone in the kitchen. He sips a cup of coffee and seems content to let his wife carry on the bulk of the conversation.

When LuAnn runs out of things to say about the grandbaby, I launch into my list of questions for the family.

"Tell me again. What was your reaction when you found out about me?"

"I was shocked," Joe says. "Dad's all about doing what's right. It surprised me he had a past. Then after that, I was glad to have another brother."

"Anything else?"

"I was worried about Pop," Joe says. "It hurt him to know he had a son all these years and that he wasn't there for you. He's excited about your visit."

Joe's answer leaves a lump in my throat.

"Did he say anything about me?"

"Dad doesn't talk much," he says.

"How did your mom take the news?"

"She thinks it's cool," Joe says.

His low, graveled voice seems better suited for a gritty battle scene in a military movie than for a heartwarming family discussion, but after a few minutes, I find it oddly comforting. He answers my questions without the need to pad his responses with extra words or information.

"You want a pork roll?" Joe asks.

"It's going to be a couple of hours before Mom has dinner ready," says Tammy-P. "You might as well snack on something until then."

"Yeah, pork rolls," Joe says.

"Sounds good to me," I tell them. Then I stand up and stroll over to the kitchen. Four tall black chairs are situated around a matching table. LuAnn joins me. We sit and watch the birth of a pork roll sandwich.

Joe pulls out what looks like a roll of bologna and slices off enough meat for the sandwiches. Then he grills the pork roll. The kitchen fills with a smell that isn't exactly ham or bacon. As much as Joe talks about these sandwiches, they must be good.

The slices of pork are set on a Kaiser roll. Fried eggs go on top of the meat, and then Joe seasons it with salt and pepper. A thick slice of American cheese finishes the sandwich. It certainly looks good. I wait a moment for condiments and eventually ask, "What about mayo?"

Joe whisks the plates away from me and LuAnn. "You don't put mayo on pork rolls."

"Mustard?" I ask.

He growls at the suggestion. "No. This is the way you eat them. I'm not going to let you ruin the best sandwich in the world with any of that garbage."

"Just try it this way," says Tammy-P. "You'll like it."

Joe and Tammy-P both watch us as we take our first bite of a pork roll sandwich. The combination of pork, egg, and cheese is breakfast nirvana. Fatty pork and gooey cheese dance on my tongue and then skip cheerfully down my throat. Joe's right. This is a great sandwich.

"Did you research the Jersey Devil?" Joe asks as we eat.

"What's with you and this devil?" I ask.

"It's a thing, man."

"Hopefully, it's not like a romantic thing," I tease him. It surprises me that our relationship has so quickly reached the stage where I feel comfortable joking with him. We are interacting just like I do with my siblings back home, and it seems totally natural.

"No. A scary thing," says Joe. "It has wings and hooves and a goat head. You have to be careful when you're walking around in the woods or else the Jersey Devil will get you."

"We have something like that back home," I say. "Old Mogy. The Mogollon Monster. He lives on the Mogollon Rim and is supposed to be like bigfoot or a mutated grizzly bear . . . or something. I'm pretty sure he could take your New Jersey Devil without working up a sweat."

Joe snorts.

I lean back in my chair and enjoy the moment. This is definitely the way to have a conversation—sitting around the kitchen table, snacking on the house specialty, and swapping stories with people you like. The only thing missing is a lifelong set of shared experiences to form a pool of casual topics for us to discuss.

Those shared experiences have to be built, one kitchen-discussion at a time. As much as sitting here with Joe and Tammy-P reminds me of the family holidays that have been an important part of my life in Arizona, I can already tell they will be different. Different foods. Different jokes. And a different set of stories . . . ones that begin with this trip.

I turn to Tammy-P and ask, "What went through your mind when you found out Joe had another brother?"

"I am really happy you have a chance to meet your family." Tammy-P looks over at Joe. "They are a wonderful family. I just love them so much. They've been such a blessing to me. And they are going to be wonderful to you as well. It hasn't always been this way for me."

"What do you mean?" I ask.

"I have a DNA story too."

# CHAPTER 14

# TAMMY'S STORY

It seems like everyone has a DNA story. If not the individual I'm talking with, then certainly a parent, cousin, or friend has taken a test and found some sort of surprise waiting for them. Apparently, I'm far from alone in discovering I have a wonky family dynamic.

"I took a DNA test to find my biological family, and it didn't turn out the way I hoped," Tammy-P tells me.

"Are you adopted?" I ask.

"No," she says. "My mother raised me, but it turned out that my father . . . wasn't really my father. I was thirteen before I found out the truth. That's enough about me, though. Tell me more about everyone back home. After all, they're family now."

She has to be kidding me. Another person who discovered the man she thought was her dad wasn't actually her dad. Does that make her the milkman's daughter? This whole misplaced-father routine appears to be more common than I thought. For months, I've been telling people the shocking news of my discovery. This is my chance to find out how someone else feels about the situation.

"Your story really connects us," I tell her. "Both of us are late arrivals to this family, and we both have DNA surprises that changed our lives. I want to hear more about what happened to you. That is . . . if you're comfortable discussing it."

She waves her hands as if shooing away flies at the suggestion that talking about this will bother her. "My family now is the one sister who I talk to on a regular basis. The others know about me, but we don't talk. They know the DNA test came back positive. It links me to my grandmother on my father's side."

"What was your like life before that?" I ask, wanting to compare our situations.

"My mother was married to my sisters' father. I thought he was my father too, but he was abusive to me. I always felt hated. I always wondered why he didn't like me. I never knew. He treated my sisters completely different. Completely different."

"Like Cinderella?" I ask.

"Yeah," says Tammy-P. "And I never knew why. "I mean, he had some deep issues, and I think he took a lot of his anger out on me. Anyways, my mom and he split up, she took me, and we lived in an apartment."

"Just you?" I ask. "Not your sisters?"

"I think it was a matter that my mom could only afford a two-bedroom apartment," says Tammy-P. "She had to take me. I wouldn't have been safe with my stepfather."

The conversation around the table has taken a decidedly somber turn. Tammy-P's perpetually sunny disposition prevents this from becoming an angst-filled gripe session. Instead, it feels like the sharing of an intimate portion of her life. A vulnerable section of her emotional center. Something a person would share only with family or a close friend.

"Mom finds an apartment across town," Tammy-P continues. "And I'm thinking he hates me, he doesn't want me. I was thirteen going on fourteen, and I guess it bothered me. Even though he'd been abusive, that rejection hurt. I was a good girl, and for the life of me, I couldn't figure out why he didn't want me. Why didn't he love me?"

My heart goes out to her. I can't imagine what it must have been like to have lived in that sort of environment. To have felt unloved by the man she thought was her father. The pressure of self-doubt during the troublesome teenage years had to have been crushing. Even though both of us have fathers who turned out not to be blood relatives, our experiences are complete opposites.

"Finally, Mom told me that my real dad was deceased. She didn't have any pictures of him. The only information she had about the family was a few names for his other children and a couple of siblings. That's all I had to try and find them. I looked for years and found nothing.

"Tammy—"

"You mean Old Tammy," I interrupt.

"Yeah. Old Tammy," she continues. "Tammy was just getting into genealogy, and she helped me look for my biological family. She found a link on Ancestry, just based on the names. I knew my dad's family was from Camden, so Tammy searched in that area for other people with the same last name. Then she and I went to the library and searched the city directories. Eventually, we found one of my cousins."

Tammy-P pauses to take a drink, giving me a moment to connect her story to mine. She too had a quest, but unlike my search for William "The Immigrant" Lindsay, this one had real consequences. She was searching for living members of her family. Success in my quest simply put another name on the ancestral tree. A failure on her part would prevent her from ever meeting and knowing the close members of her family.

"I wrote my cousin a big, private message on Facebook," Tammy-P continues. "Just asking questions. I told him I was trying to find out who I was. He gave me information on my father's brother that included a phone number."

*Trying to find out who I was.* Her statement hits me emotionally. Is that what this trip is all about for me? Am I looking to find out who I am?

Nah. I'm a Lindsay. For me, this trip is about finding out who the Petrauschkes are.

"I called my uncle, and he gave me the number of my sister, Debbie," says Tammy-P. That was six years ago. It took from the time I was thirteen to when I was forty-two to find my family. Debbie was excited to meet me. It turns out all of them lived nearby. Debbie wasn't even ten minutes from where I lived.

"Then I met her, and she told me that nobody else wanted to be involved."

"I'm sorry," I tell Tammy-P. "That had to hurt. I've been so lucky with Joe and the others. They have really reached out and welcomed me to the family."

Tammy-P nods. "Debbie and I met three times the first year to sit, and have coffee, and talk, and whatever. Then her husband retired and they moved to Florida. I still get a card from her on my birthday, and she occasionally texts me. I guess it's better than no contact.

"Four years later, Joe gets me a DNA test for Christmas. I got the results in January. I call my sister Lisa and tell her it's official. We're sisters. Once I told her the news, she wanted to have a relationship. We started talking."

"Why did it take so long for her to accept you?" I ask.

"She said Debbie jumped the gun and they were mad at her for not including them. It went back and forth, but after the DNA test, she was open arms. Now, I visit with her all the time. But she's the only one who talks to me. My other three sisters are still bitter toward our father because he was never there for them. Even though he's dead, they all still hate him except for Lisa."

"It sounds as if the others have a guilt-by-association attitude toward you," I say.

"Yeah," says Tammy-P. "I think so. As long as they hate my father, they aren't going to want to have anything to do with me."

"What about the two sisters you grew up with?"

"I still talk to them. They're half sisters. We have the same mother, but we're not close. They have their own issues they're dealing with."

A cat hops on the table. This one has an ear that bends backward. He looks like a rough-and-tumble tomcat but starts to purr as soon as I pet him. Another cat sits on the kitchen counter, not yet sure if she wants to make the leap to join us.

"Were you excited when you found out you had other siblings?" I ask.

"Yeah," says Tammy-P. "At fourteen, Mom told me about the others, and I spent my whole life looking for them. It turned out they were right around the corner. I'm glad I didn't end up marrying my brother. They lived so close my whole life and I never knew them. That was mind-blowing. I'm sure I walked past them a million times. My sister Lisa used to shop every day at one of the convenience stores I managed. With her best friend. I remember the best friend."

"What went through your mind when Joe gave you the DNA kit?" I ask.

"I couldn't breathe. It literally took the breath out of my chest, and I started crying. I was expecting it, but I was overwhelmed and scared. I just sat on the stairs and cried. It was personal, and private, and something I was going through. All sorts of thoughts went through my head. Like, I've looked so long for these people and they don't want to have anything to do with me. Maybe they're not even my family. I'm going to take this DNA test, and who knows what will happen?"

"Right," I say, "because your mom could have been lying to you."

"Sure. She had told me something that wasn't true my whole life and then didn't keep any documents or pictures so I could identify myself later in life. Nothing. Nothing. She had a couple of names and the town where we lived."

"Then my situation comes along," I say. "What did you think about that?"

"I was a little jealous at first. I knew you were walking into a wonderful situation, and my experience wasn't like that at all. I was really happy for youse and the family but sad for myself. It was, like, that really sucks. Why couldn't it be like that for me? I had a hard life. I had to deal with a lot of abuse. Just one time, why couldn't this be me? Why couldn't they love me?"

Tammy-P has lost her perpetual smile, but she's still holding it together better than I am. Tears threaten to roll down my face. I don't want to cry in front of her and Joe. They'll think I'm a big baby. It doesn't matter that I am—I just don't want them to think that.

"For people who go through this sort of thing," Tammy-P says, "youse situation is ideal. I got to tell you that it doesn't happen like this a lot of times."

I manage to choke out a response. "I'm sure it doesn't happen most of the time. I got super lucky . . . and I know that. There are going to be times when the siblings never want to hear from you, but other people in our situation are going to get lucky too. And even in your situation, which isn't ideal, you are starting to get along with Lisa. The rest of your siblings might come around. You don't know what the future holds. No one does. You won't know until the end of the journey. And maybe then it will be worth the slow buildup to sibling unity."

Tammy-P nods. "I agree. When I first found my siblings, I faithfully tried to reach, and reach, and reach out to them. Then it was, like, you have to let them reach out as well because youse can't force yourself on somebody."

"Right," I say. "They aren't going to love you just because you want them to."

"I could reach out to my dad's brothers," says Tammy-P. "And he has a sister. I could reach out to them, but with all I've gone through . . . I just don't want to. I don't want to be rejected anymore. At this point in my life, I'm going to take what I have and try to work with that. I'm not going to worry about my siblings rejecting me because they hate our father and I am a reminder of all the things he did to them. I'm going to take what I have now, and if something falls into place in the future . . . then I'll take it."

Tammy-P smiles and claps her hands. "It's time for us to head over to Poppi's."

Just like that, she switches gears. The big, beaming smile is back in place. I sit there for a moment longer, thinking about what she said. It feels as if all of our searches are connected. Separate parts of a single grand plan.

We rise from our seats and head for the front door. It's time to meet my father.

# CHAPTER 15

# DAD, I'M HOME

It takes fifteen minutes to drive from Joe's house to the town where the rest of the family lives. The scenery on the way continues to be dominated by forest and fields dotted with picturesque farms. LuAnn and I pass a line of trees and drive alongside a small lake. A roadside sign identifies both the town and the lake as our destination.

The road forks, and we stay to our left, passing a sign that warns me to watch for turtles crossing. The armored water denizens aren't common in Arizona. I scan the road but don't see any of them navigating the asphalt. It's probably for the best. I can imagine the sort of first impression I'd make if I had to explain I was late because I stopped to look at a turtle.

I drive two more blocks and then turn onto the street where my father lives. His house looks exactly like it does on Google Street View, except it isn't blurry. My stomach churns with nervous energy. This is it. This is the big moment when DNA testing comes face-to-face with reality. I'm moments away from meeting my biological father.

The house is white in front and has wood paneling, faded to gray, in the back. Several cars, including Joe's, are already parked on the lawn alongside the house. I find an open patch of grass in the backyard and follow their example.

A wood deck extends from the back of the house and serves as the porch. White lawn chairs line almost the entire the edge of the deck. There appears to be enough seats to accommodate the entire Petrauschke clan.

A magnificently large maple tree grows a few feet from the deck, casting its protective limbs over the entire porch and part of the house. This is a perfect tree for children to climb—a wooden giant that provides shade on warm afternoons. I can picture the family gathering on Sundays for their after-church dinner, the adults sitting in the cool shade chatting about the details that fill their everyday lives while the children play in the yard. If a better formula exists for building strong family bonds, I can't think of one.

Two long picnic tables sit under the tree. A swing set and a trampoline occupy the sunny open space beyond the tree. Squirrels scamper around a white shed at the back of the property. The yard has plenty of room for children to play tag or hide-and-seek, or simply run in circles until they are so dizzy they fall down, too tired to get back up.

LuAnn rests her hand on my arm. "Are you ready for this?"

I glance at her and then turn my attention back to the scenery, thinking this could have been part of my childhood and might be part of my future. This place, this family. I stare into LuAnn's eyes and say, "I'm ready."

I climb out of the car and then open LuAnn's door. Before I can close the door, three children race to us from the other side of the house. They look to be around eight to ten years of age. The oldest one has curly hair and a dark complexion. He charges up to me and asks, "Are you my uncle?"

"Yes," I tell him. Then the three children run off. The encounter reminds me of how I daydreamed this would happen. It started with children running to meet me. I wonder if the rest of the day will play out the same way.

The nervous willies in my stomach kick into overdrive. My father is just inside the house. What if he doesn't like me? What if I don't like him? I swallow down my nerves.

LuAnn and I step onto the deck just as Tammy breezes out through the door. All of my jitters melt away. I recognize her instantly from her pictures: blonde, a face shaped like mine, and the same dark rings I have under my eyes. There's no mistaking her as my sister. I feel the same connection with Tammy now that I did while exchanging emails, but even stronger. There is a comforting element about being in her presence.

Tammy gives me a dainty hug, as if she isn't sure whether or not I'm the hugging type. It doesn't feel like a hug from a stranger. It feels like I'm hugging my sister. She says, "I'm so glad you're here."

Over her shoulder, I see Mother Petrauschke. She is shorter than I imagined, but her smile is huge. P-Mom takes her time crossing the deck and then embraces me like I am one of her children. "I can't wait to hear about your trip."

Bill moves up next to Tammy. If I didn't already know the siblings' ages, I'd think he was the baby of the family instead of Joe. He has a young face, an athletic build, short brown hair, and wears a Van Dyke–style beard.

Joe comes outside and motions back through the door for someone inside to join him. He signals a second time, and finally, my biological father emerges. Father is tall compared to the rest of the Petrauschkes. His hair is darker than mine even though he's twenty years older.

He gives me a nervous smile and holds back with Joe.

My heart catches in my throat. Could it be I've come all this way only to find he doesn't want to meet me? I toss the thought aside.

Joe gives him a gentle nudge, and Father takes a slow, unsteady step toward me.

That's all the encouragement I need. I match his pace, and we meet in the middle of the wooden deck. Father and son, together for the first time.

He wraps his long arms around me, engulfing me in the father-of-all-hugs. The strength with which he squeezes me is surprising for someone his age. I can feel his love. I mean, I can literally feel the energy of his love flowing from him through his arms and into me. And at that moment, I know without a shred of doubt that this man loves me as his son.

His arms cling to me as if he's afraid to let go. As if I might dissolve into a wisp of smoke if he releases me. It takes a full minute before he loosens his hold, and then he repeats the ritual with LuAnn.

I'm not sure what just happened. Did I physically feel the emotions of a person I just met? Or did I imagine it? Either way, the experience has imprinted itself on my mind . . . and my heart. Tears well up and blur my vision. I try to discreetly wipe the excess water from my eyes before it starts rolling down my face.

Father finishes hugging LuAnn and turns to me.

I stand there, still too emotional to talk. The family members seem to notice my watery eyes and give me the courtesy of waiting until I'm ready to continue. I clear my throat. "Here I am!"

"Yeah, here he is," says Joe in his gruff voice.

"Dinner won't be ready for another hour," says Mother Petrauschke. "The weather is nice enough for us to sit out here while we get to know one another."

"Why don't we take some pictures first?" LuAnn asks. She pulls out her phone and motions for us to form a group. I put my arm around Father's shoulder and then Bill's. P-Mom stands in front of us, the top of her head inches below Father's chin. Tammy and Joe stand on the other side of Bill. LuAnn snaps several shots of the same pose and then takes another of Father and me.

Then we take our spots in the ring of chairs. LuAnn sits next to me and Father on the other side. A spry glint fills his eyes as he watches me.

"Is there anything about me you'd like to know?" I ask.

"Do you like apple pie?" asks Mother Petrauschke.

"Who doesn't?" I respond. "It's the American dessert."

"You're going to love Mom's apple pie," says Joe. "It's the best."

Father nods in agreement. He rests his elbows on the table and then folds his hands in front of him so they form an arch.

"Sounds good," I say, "but I thought you might have a few questions about me. Or the situation. There are fifty-seven years of my life you don't know anything about."

"Do they have Tastykakes in Arizona?" Joe asks.

"We have plenty of fine bakers who make all sorts of tasty treats," I tell him.

Joe chuckles. "No. That's the name brand."

"Sorry," I say, trying to force a little disappointment into my voice. "No Tastykakes."

Everyone sits in awkward silence.

Back home, my siblings wouldn't wait for an invitation to ask questions. Nor would any question be too blunt or shocking for them to ask me. Then again, they've known me all their lives. The silence bothers me, as it always does when I'm interacting with others. We're here. We should be talking.

"All right," I say, "there's been something on my mind since I first found out about all of you. I have the spelling down, but how do you pronounce your last name?"

They all laugh.

"It's a toughie," says P-Mom. She carefully pronounces Puh-trau-ski for me. "When your father found out he wasn't really a Petrauschke, the kids considered changing their name to Lodge. It's a lot easier to spell, but by then they were used to being Petrauschkes. When the kids were young, I had a song to help them learn how to spell their name.

"P - E - T . . . "

I recognize the song right away. It's the Mickey Mouse song from the old black-and-white television show that the cast sang at the end of every episode. I listen to P-Mom sing it. She leaves out all of the extra lines.

The song plays through my mind, but I add my version of the non-spelling portions.

*Come along and sing this song 'cause now you're family*
*P - E - T*
*T is for terrific.*
*R - A - U*
*You belong here with us*
*S - C - H - K - E*
*Petrauschke*

All right, it gets sort of hung up on the last verse, but I wish I would have known about the song sooner. It would have made it so much easier to learn how to spell the name.

In true Lindsay fashion, I pop out the first real question of the visit and go straight to the heart of the matter. After all, none of my Arizona siblings are here to launch the conversation into the blunt-mode that has been a traditional part of all my family outings. I look over at my father and ask, "Do you remember anything about my mother?"

The smile fades from his face. He opens his mouth and says, "Well . . ."

Father struggles through several false starts and finally stalls. It's painful for me to watch him put this much effort into answering my questions and then abandon the attempt because the words escape him.

"Dad doesn't remember much around the time of the stroke," says P-Mom. "He used to be better about it, but over the last few years, his memory has gotten worse. His mom had to help him. He couldn't walk or write. He had to learn that all over again. I can tell you that the only thing he mentioned to me was that I reminded him of a girl he dated in Phoenix."

A jolt of excitement shoots through my body. Maybe he does remember my mother. I look at P-Mom and try to imagine how she looked as a young woman. There's a vague resemblance between her and my mother, but it's more of a general senior-citizens-look-alike similarity. They are both vertically challenged, though.

I abandon the thought and move on to my next question. An easy one. I feel guilty for having made my father struggle with his memory. "Were you surprised when Tammy told you about me?"

Father chuckles. He softly speaks. "Yeah, I was surprised."

The warm glint in his eyes tells me the question hasn't offended him.

Tammy stands up and says, "I have to go inside and finish dinner."

I want to ask P-Mom how she felt when she heard the news that Father had another child, but I don't want to upset her. She's been very warm and accepting of me, both here and on social media before the trip. The situation has to be uncomfortable for her.

Instead, I toss another question to my father, "Why did you leave Arizona?"

Father's eyes light up at the mention of home. He raises a hand to gesture. "I . . . lived on the east side of town. I went to . . . high school there. I can't think of the name of the school."

His words are slow. I can tell he's struggling to locate the bits of language that will allow him to communicate the thoughts that are so clearly in his head. Eventually, he stops and looks to P-Mom.

"He lived in Arizona with his mother," says P-Mom. "When she moved back to New Jersey, he came with her. There wasn't any family in the state once she left. And he's been here ever since."

Bill asks, "What went through your mind when you found out you had a different father than the one you knew?"

There it is. That's the sort of question I would expect from my siblings back home. It's the same question all of my friends have asked me. The fact that it took the Petrauschkes so long to get around to it speaks of a gentler nature than most of the people I associate with in Arizona.

"At first, I thought Tammy was crazy," I tell Bill. "There was no way

I could have a father in New Jersey. Then I saw pictures of you, Tammy, and Dad, and that convinced me."

I said it. I finally said it. I called my father . . . Dad.

Part of me feels as if I have betrayed the man who raised me by giving them both the same title. Another section of my brain argues that it insults Father to call him by any other name.

As long as Dad—I mean my Arizona dad—never finds out, I should be all right.

Tammy pokes her head out of the house and announces that dinner is ready.

I follow the rest of the family inside. It reminds me of a carnival fun house for short people. My head almost scrapes against the kitchen ceiling, and I have to duck to pass under the support beams that run from one side of the room to the other. The floor slants to the left. Then as I cross over from kitchen to dining room, I notice that this floor slants to the right. The walls are painted the same shade of key-lime green as the fruit used in my favorite pie.

Despite the blatant architectural flaws, the house feels cozy. It feels like home.

"You can sit wherever you want," P-Mom says. She motions to a small table at the center of the kitchen, then to a pair of longer tables in the dining room. The nieces and nephews have already taken over one of the long tables.

I make the obvious choice and pick the spot closest to the food. Pork roast, mashed potatoes and gravy, creamed corn, lettuce salad, fruit salad, and dinner rolls. The same kind of meal that has been a staple for family gatherings all my life.

A familiar aroma fills the kitchen, beguiling my mouth into a Pavlov's-dog response. I get up and saunter over to the stove. The smell is coming from a pot of homemade gravy. If the gravy tastes even remotely as good as it smells, I may not be able to walk away from the table at the end of the meal.

LuAnn sits next to me, and then Tammy, P-Mom, and P-Dad join us. The abundant quantities of food on the table prevent anyone else from squeezing in. Not that it makes a difference; everyone is within a few feet of us as we eat. All I have to do is look to my left or my right and include them in any conversation we have.

Mmmmmm. The gravy is every bit as good as it smells. I roll my eyes in ecstasy.

"Do you like it?" asks Mother Petrauschke.

Since I don't want to stop eating long enough to answer her, I just nod.

"I hope you don't mind me asking," says Mother Petrauschke, "but what's the man who raised you all these years like?"

I stop eating. That isn't a question I had expected from my New Jersey family. Sure, it points out the elephant in the room, but it also puts me in the awkward position of deciding what to tell my father about my dad. How much of the relationship with the man who raised me do I share with a group of relative strangers? And how is it going to make my father feel if I talk about how much I love my dad?

Then it occurs to me that Mother Petrauschke is more than Father's wife and loving companion. She is also his mouthpiece. She speaks for him when he cannot find the words. I can sense this is a question that's important to my father. For fifty-seven years, he was unaware of the son he had in Arizona, and he needs to know that someone was there for me. That somebody took care of me. That I didn't suffer because of his absence.

Father stops eating and watches me.

"The man who raised me is a good man," I tell Father. "He protected me. He taught me to work hard and think for myself. He loved me. All this time I thought he was my biological father because he never treated me any different from the children he had with my mother. You don't have to worry, because I've been in good hands all these years."

Father nods. He seems happy to hear my report.

"My dad . . . I mean, my dad in Arizona," I quickly correct my statement. "He's like a real, live John Wayne. Dad operated a mule train in high school to help feed his brothers and sisters. Then he joined the Marines and served his time as an MP. He was even on the boxing team. Not only that, but he kind of looks like John Wayne."

Father's eyes light up at the mention of John Wayne. "I have a hundred and . . . a hundred and . . . I have over a hundred John Wayne movies."

"I love John Wayne movies," I tell him. "Do you have *Rio Bravo* or *True Grit*?"

"Most of the movies are . . ." Father struggles for the words. "When he was young."

"Ah, the John Ford trilogy," I say. "*She Wore a Yellow Ribbon* and *Fort Apache*."

"Yeah," says Father. "Like those."

"Dad loves Mexican food," says Tammy.

"Me too," I tell them and then look over at Father and wink.

"Bill, do you remember your favorite place to eat in Arizona?" P-Mom asks.

Father motions with his hands. The words come out slowly. "It's been so long."

"And it's probably gone by now," I tell them.

I finish off a second helping of potatoes and gravy. Then I bus my dishes over to the sink and rinse them off. By the time I finish, P-Mom has an apple pie on the table and is slicing it into generous pieces. It looks amazing. Sugar and cinnamon sprinkled over a perfectly browned crust.

Apple ranks midrange in my dessert listing. I love pie, but I usually eat apple only if I can have it à la mode. Mom slides my piece over to me. It smells delicious. I wait until everyone has been served and then take a bite.

Oh . . . my . . . word! This isn't apple pie. It's sweet perfection on a plate. The tartness of the apples offsets the sugar. And the cinnamon adds an extra dimension to the taste that makes this one of the best desserts I've ever had. Definitely the best apple pie that has ever crossed my taste buds.

"What else can you tell me about yourself?" I ask Father.

"Bill used to draw pictures of space aliens when he was a child," says Mother Petrauschke. "We still have them somewhere. He was very creative before his stroke."

The world freezes in place for me. In the span of a single moment, the answer to my life's biggest mystery—Why don't I fit in?—falls into place.

It turns out I do fit in. I was just comparing myself to the wrong family. As a child, I drew pictures of monsters, dinosaurs, and other oddities. My interest in fantastic creatures was uncommon during the years of my youth. I can only imagine how much more that would have been the case in my father's time. Both of us shared a fascination with the strange and unusual when it wasn't popular to do so.

The discovery excites me. I wonder what other traits I share with this man. "Did you ever have an interest in writing?"

Tammy answers, "Dad writes Bible articles."

"He writes?" This is big. My mind reels with the revelation that the very things that make me stand out from my family in Arizona are the same traits I share with my biological father. Despite the problems Father has communicating, he is writing . . . in his limited way.

"He picks a topic from the Bible," says Mother Petrauschke, "then he researches the topic and writes about what he finds. Tammy calls them articles, but I think a study, or a devotional, is a better description. It's not the same kind of writing that you do."

"But it is," I say. "At least it's in the same ballpark. I pick an idea to write about. Then I research the facts I'll need to make the story authentic. And my books may be longer than Dad's, but it's still the same process. We are still doing the same thing. I find it amazing that we have the same interest. The same passion."

For nearly a year, I've resented the DNA discovery that changed my life. I would have rather continued my life in blissful ignorance than know the truth. But this revelation changes everything for me. I no longer need to feel like an outsider because I'm different from my siblings in Arizona. I'm not different because I'm weird or defective. I'm different because I inherited a different set of genes than the others.

Just knowing why I'm different from the rest of the Lindsays calms my inner doubts. The comfort this brings outweighs the agitation and confusion caused by the discovery of an additional family. For the first time since this rollercoaster ride began, I'm glad I took the DNA test.

We spend another hour around the kitchen table, sharing family stories. We talk until I can barely keep my eyes open. Then LuAnn and I say our good nights and leave.

"What do you think?" I ask LuAnn as we drive to our hotel.

"I think you're lucky," she says. "They're a lovely family. I like them."

"Yep, I agree."

We sit in silence for a few minutes. I play the events of the day through my head. Partially, to make sure I didn't misjudge the importance of anything they said. Partially, to enjoy the experience a second time.

I can't wait to see what mind-blowing discoveries another day with the Petrauschkes will bring.

# CHAPTER 16

# NOT ENOUGH TIME

Will my life ever be normal again?

I survived the first contact with my new family, but if this unexpected turn in my life has taught me anything, it is that things can change in an instant. The Petrauschkes have met me and had all night to decide whether they like what they saw. I wonder if the meet-and-bond experience will be different on day two.

Strike that. I know it will be different. I'm just not sure how.

LuAnn and I wake up and then quickly work our way through the morning routine. I want to spend as much of my limited time in New Jersey with the family as possible. With that goal in mind, we pass by a tempting continental breakfast in the lobby in order to head straight to Joe's. The plan is to arrive early enough for another round of pork roll sandwiches.

The drive takes less than ten minutes, and we skip the detour to the house by the railroad tracks. Joe answers the door. "About time you sleepyheads made it over here."

Tammy-P rushes out of the kitchen and hugs us. "Well? What did youse guys think about the family? Did you have fun?"

"It was great," LuAnn says.

"It was a lot to process," I tell Tammy-P. "Everyone was super nice to me. I really felt welcomed . . . and loved."

"That's the way they are," she says. "They're a very loving family."

I walk over to the kitchen and take a seat at the table. The bent-eared kitty strolls over and plops himself down in front of me. I scratch his back.

"Yeah," Joe offers in an especially low and gravelly voice. "Dad was excited to see you."

"Excited? Are you sure? He hardly said anything."

"Dad doesn't talk a lot," says Joe. "What you saw yesterday was a good day for him."

"Okay," I tell Joe and file the information away for further use. "What are the chances of LuAnn and I scoring another pork roll sandwich before we head over to Dad's?"

Joe chuckles. "I told you they're good. Now you're hooked."

"Did you get to meet everyone?" Tammy-P asks.

"I don't know," I tell her. "No one has given me a list of all the nieces, nephews, and significant others, so I'm not sure which of them might have been missing yesterday. I know that Old Tammy's husband wasn't there."

"He never attends the family dinners," says Tammy-P. "And the only reason Bill and Shelly are here is because you came out. They live in Delaware, and that's a long drive for them."

"I thought Bill was only an hour away from here," I say.

"He is," she says. "That's a long way. He's in an entirely different state."

That's one way of looking at it. In Arizona, the trip out to see my sister takes nearly an hour, and she only lives on the other side of town. A trip to any of the neighboring states takes almost three hours just to reach the border. An hour's drive time would be no barrier to me if the payoff was dinner with the fam.

The second pork roll sandwich is even better than the first. Since Joe made both of them the same way, the only explanation I can come up with is that I'm expecting deliciousness to ooze from my new favorite breakfast offering. And the sandwich doesn't fail to deliver.

LuAnn and I take our time eating and visiting. We tell Joe and Tammy-P about Arizona, and they tell us about New Jersey. Two hours are gone before I know it. The limited amount of time we have here is passing too quickly. With the day already halfway over, we drive to Father's place.

Children are playing in the yard and come over to greet us before running off again. LuAnn and I let ourselves inside the house. A tantalizing aroma embraces us as soon as we walk through the door. It smells spicy. It smells meaty. "I hope we're not too early."

Tammy and Mother Petrauschke are busy in the kitchen. P-Mom turns from the stove and smiles. "Come on in and have a seat. Food should be ready in a few minutes. Dad's in the living room if you want to go in and see him before we eat."

The primary purpose of this trip is to meet Father and establish a relationship with him, but I feel more comfortable around Tammy. It's P-Mom's talkative nature that wins the internal debate, though. If I want any questions answered, the information will have to come from her. I sit down on one of the dining room chairs. There will be plenty of time to see Father during the day.

"After everyone left yesterday," says P-Mom, "I got to thinking about the questions you asked us and had a few ideas on how I could have answered them."

"Like what?" It occurs to me that the family seems a little more relaxed today. With the first contact jitters out of their system, they might be ready to answer the questions I still have. Mother Petrauschke stops fussing with the food on the stove and turns to face me. She raises her hand to her chin, obviously thinking about her answer. "We talked about a lot of stuff. I'm having a hard time remembering a specific topic."

"What went through your mind when Tammy told you about me?" I ask.

P-Mom sits across the table from me. She looks at me over the top of her glasses. "Tammy came in and said to Dad, 'I have something I want to tell you. I don't know exactly what to say. Did you know a girl in Phoenix?'"

I lean forward in my chair, eager to hear the other side of the story. How did they react? What did they think about having a new addition to the family who was fifty-seven years old?

Mother Petrauschke continues. "He said, 'No.'

"Then Tammy said, 'Well, we found out you have a son in Arizona.'

"Then Dad said, 'I do?'

"She told him, 'Yeah.'"

Not exactly an earth-shaking response.

"Tammy kind of hesitated to tell us," Mother Petrauschke continues. "I think she knew about you two weeks before she told us. She didn't know how Dad would take it. She cried a little bit. She didn't know exactly how to break it to him."

"What was Dad's reaction?" I ask.

"He took it well," says P-Mom. "He took it better than I did. I felt kind of sad. All these years he had a son he didn't know anything about. We found out you had a family, and Dad has grandchildren he's never met. There's all this family we didn't know about. All the times the two of you could have been together. Gotten to know each other. It was sad."

"I was really concerned about how you were going to react," I tell her. "I felt like an intruder. I didn't want to disrupt the whole family. I especially didn't want to upset you."

"For me," says Mother Petrauschke, "I felt it was something that happened before I knew him. It had nothing to do with me and our relationship."

"That's sensible," I say and then sigh in relief. In my experience, people do not usually act sensibly. I had expected a much more emotional reaction. It amazes me that this woman is so open to having me join her family. Rather than brooding over a forgotten fling, she is worried about including a person who might feel left out and alone.

"Let me tell you about how Dad and I met." Her eyes sparkle with excitement. "We worked together, uptown. The men made boxes for sewing machines, and the women put on the covers, hinges, and latches. My sister-in-law worked there. I told her one day, 'Do you see that guy back there? I'm going to marry him. One of these days, I'm going to marry that guy.'

"I said hello to him one day. Then he had his cousin ask me who I was. Asked me my name. So then he calls me. We went out for three months before we got married."

"You impulsive lovebirds, you." I laugh. "Is there more to the story?"

Mother Petrauschke waves her hand. "His proposal was really cute. We were at a movie, and he said, 'If I asked you to marry me, would you?' and I said, 'Yes.' He didn't know I already planned to marry him.

"Anyways, I'm happy to have extended family. I'm glad he has the chance to meet you. He didn't have a chance to meet his dad. He didn't know about him until he was already gone. He didn't have a chance to find him while he was still alive. I'm glad you, at least, had a chance to meet and find out a little bit about one another. And meet the family."

"Yesterday," I say, "you asked about the man who raised me. Was it a mistake for me to talk about that in front of Dad? Should I not have mentioned that a good man raised me?"

"See, that made Bill happy because he didn't have that kind of relationship in his life. You know, he didn't have a daddy. I think that affected how he treated his kids. He was a good dad, but I think he would have been a better dad if he had had a father to teach him. I'm sure he's happy you had that chance."

"I get that," I tell her. "It's weird how both of us discovered late in life that the men we thought were our dads were not actually our biological fathers. Sort of like the universe was playing a trick on us."

"Yeah," she says, "but it's not that funny of a joke."

The kitchen door opens, and a young man steps in. He has a little girl in his arms.

"This is my son," Tammy says. "Shaun."

"Scrawny Shauny?" I ask.

"That's me," he says and then walks over and shakes my hand. He isn't scrawny anymore. That gives me hope that my own son will fill out some day. Shaun is tall and has an average build. I've seen pictures of his father and see a strong resemblance between the two. His manner is calm and gentle. I find myself immediately liking him.

"This is your uncle Randy," Tammy says, "and his wife, LuAnn."

"The lost uncle from Arizona?" Shaun asks.

"One and the same," I tell him.

"Dinner's almost ready," Tammy tells Shaun. "As soon as everyone arrives, we can eat. Why don't you go into the living room and let Poppi know?"

Shaun is barely out of the room when Bill, Shelly, and their kids enter through the kitchen door. The children wave to me and then hurry into the living room to join Shaun and Father.

I stand up and hug Bill and his wife.

Over the next ten minutes, the rest of the family streams through the door. Tammy's oldest daughter, along with one of the children who greeted me yesterday. Joe and Tammy-P. And a young woman who no one introduces. In a flurry of activity, they greet me and LuAnn and then help with the final dinner preparations.

"Time to eat," Mother Petrauschke calls out.

Everyone gathers in the kitchen. They look over at LuAnn and I and . . . wait. It takes me a moment to figure out they are expecting us to step up to the front of the chow line. I grab a bowl, a plate, and some silverware and then load up. The meaty smell I noticed earlier is a pot of chili. I want to sample a bit of everything, but the chili temps me beyond my ability to resist, causing me to fill my bowl with meaty goodness.

A square of cornbread goes on my plate, along with a sensible salad. I don't need the family thinking I'm some sort of barbarian who shuns vegetables and other healthy foods.

Father takes a seat at the table next to me. LuAnn, Tammy, and Mother Petrauschke join us. Everyone else situates themselves at the other two tables. A steady buzz of conversation fills the room.

"Save room for dessert," Joe says. "Mom made strawberry shortcake."

"Good," I tell him, "I like strawberry shortcake."

"Mom makes it different from anyone else I've ever met," Joe says.

"If it's anything like her apple pie," I say, "it should be amazing."

I take a bite of the chili. The brightness of the tomatoes in the sauce cuts through the beefiness of the meat, and there is just enough chili seasoning for flavor.

Shaun comes over and stands next to the table. He has a bowl in his hands. "Is the chili spicy enough for you?"

"Do you consider this spicy?" I ask.

"Well . . . a little," he says. "Probably not as spicy as the Mexican food you eat in Arizona."

"What do you know about Mexican food?" I ask. "This is New Jersey."

"We have restaurants that serve authentic Mexican food," Shaun says.

My experience has been that the farther from the border I travel, the more the quality of the Mexican food suffers. Too many meals with friends who grew up in Mexico, or who had mothers who grew up in Mexico, have made me a culinary snob for food from that region. I look up at Shaun and say, "Tell you what. Next time I'm out here, you can take me to this authentic restaurant and we'll find out."

Shaun nods. He finishes chewing the food in his mouth and then says, "Poppi likes Mexican food. He eats jalapeños by themselves. He tells everyone he likes it hot, but I don't believe him."

"Why not?" I ask.

"Because," says Shaun, "the whole time he's eating the stuff his face is red and he's covered with sweat. Then he tells us how good it is, but it's obvious that he's in pain. How can anyone enjoy that? How can that be flavorful? I mean, you can't even taste the food when it's that hot."

I shake my head. Shaun isn't the first person I've met who doesn't get it. My body might react to the heat of the jalapeños, but my tongue is telling me to keep stoking the fires. "If you're not sweating—then it isn't good. You need something hotter."

"That's just crazy," Shaun says. "You're as bad as Poppi if you believe that."

Hearing that I share the same fondness for Mexican food as Father creates a heat in my chest that has nothing to do with the chili. I find myself surprisingly happy to have something else in common with him. I feel another connection.

How strange that I share this love of spicy foods, especially Mexican food, with both my dad and my father. Does that mean anything? I'm sure it does, but I can't figure out what. I file the thought away for later consideration and return to the conversation.

"What do you think about having an extra uncle?" I ask him.

"I think it's cool," Shaun says. His expression is calm. He finishes another bite of chili and then looks at me. "When I was growing up, I used to tease Poppi by asking if he had any kids running around in Arizona."

"It turns out he did." I laugh. "Who knows? Maybe there's more."

All of a sudden, it isn't funny. I remember Mother Petrauschke telling me yesterday that Father said she reminded him of another woman. If that wasn't my mother, then there really is a possibility that another lost sibling is running around in Arizona. No matter how sobering the revelation might be, I can't afford to dwell on it right now. I have fewer than six hours left to visit with my New Jersey family, and I want to make the most of the time that's left to me.

"Yeah, maybe," says Shaun.

The more I talk to Shaun, the more he reminds me of my biological sons. They all have the same calm, easygoing nature. Traits that seem to have mysteriously appeared in my offspring without any indication of where they came from. While I am more sensitive than my Arizona siblings, I am not a calm person. For years, I've wondered why my sons act so differently from me, from their mother, and from our parents. Now I know. They take after my father's side of the family.

I excuse myself to use the restroom and climb the stairs to the second story. The stairway is narrow, barely wide enough for my shoulders. Shallow steps slant to the left. Linoleum covers the bathroom floor. Inside, the room is furnished with a wood cabinet, a wood hutch, a wood bench, and a clothes hamper made out of wood. I check to see if the tub itself is made of wood and am disappointed to find it is not.

A glance at my watch reveals that another two hours have passed. I close my eyes and groan. Where has all the time gone? I want everything to slow down so I can savor this experience, but instead, the hours seem to race past me.

By the time I return to the kitchen, Mother Petrauschke has brought out the strawberry shortcake. This version of the dessert is a sweet biscuit topped with strawberries and a white syrup—like a dessert gravy—instead of whipped cream. She offers me a plate.

Despite Joe's claim about the originality of the shortcake, I find this very similar my mom's version of the dish. I take a bite, and I'm sent back to the past. Warm spring days in our kitchen. Sunlight pouring through the westward-facing windows. My grandmother and her sister sit at the table with my mother and us kids.

"What'd I tell you," says Joe. "No one else makes strawberry shortcake like this."

"It's great," I tell him and then take another bite.

We share a few more stories as the family enjoys the sweet finish to the meal. Mother Petrauschke tells me about Tammy, Bill, and Joe when they were younger. I tell the family about how LuAnn and I started dating at the beginning of summer break and then surprised my oldest son with our wedding announcement when he returned from visiting his mother.

I check my watch. It's already past four. Through the kitchen window, I can see the sun inching toward the horizon. The time is passing too quickly. There's so much more to talk about. There's so much more to learn about my family.

"Why don't we move into the living room," P-Mom suggests.

Father places his hands flat on the table and pushes himself to a standing position. He slowly makes his way to the other room. The rest of the family follows him.

I take a pair of short stairs to the living room. The floor doesn't appear to slant, but where the ceiling meets the wall, the seam meanders up and down like a lazy river. Eventually, I make it over to a sofa and sit down.

The room reminds me of Dad's place back in Arizona. Both rooms are in post-prime condition. Both have the furniture laid out in exactly the same pattern. Two easy-chairs sitting side by side, a visitor's couch at a ninety-degree angle to the parent perches, and a television set along the opposite wall from Father's chair.

Even the decorations are similar. The New Jersey living room is decorated in tans and browns that remind me of the desert back home. A Native American pot sits on a table by the window. A framed collection of arrowheads, a desert landscape, and an image of a Native American brave adorn the walls.

Father hobbles over to a bookcase and returns with a book. He hands it to me. It is a biography on John Wayne's life. Father points at me, smiles, and nods.

Even without him speaking, I can tell Father is excited to have me here. The book is mostly pictures. I read through a few sections that discuss John Wayne's dedication to his sons and how they joined him on the set for several of his movies. If time wasn't an issue, I'd read the whole book, but every minute I spend with the Duke is time lost with my father.

"You certainly are a fan," I tell Father as I hold up the book. "How many John Wayne movies did you say you had?"

"One hundred and . . ." Father pauses. His hand goes to the side of his head. "One hundred . . . I have *Fort Apache*, *The Searchers*, *The Alamo*, and . . ."

Frustration builds in his face as he tries to recall all the movies on his list. It hurts me to watch him struggle to access the information that is so obviously stored inside his head but resists the summons to his accessible memory.

"What about football?" I ask. Maybe he'll have more luck talking about sports. "Are you an Eagles fan?"

"No," says Joe. "He roots for the Cardinals."

"And ASU," says Shaun.

"The Arizona Cardinals?" I ask. "They weren't even a team when he lived out there."

"Bill enjoyed his time in Arizona," says Mother Petrauschke. "He enjoyed his trips back there. He loved the heat. He loved the food. He loved the scenery. That's where he lived when he went to high school. It was an important part of his life before the stroke."

"Arizona is yellow and brown and filled with cactus," I say. "How can anyone who lives in a beautifully green state like New Jersey miss all of that?"

P-Mom shrugs. "Well . . . he does."

Another link with my father. While I love the green grass, fields, and forests of New Jersey I don't want to move here. Nor anyplace else. The desert has a beauty of its own. I love Arizona and don't plan to leave it for an extended length of time.

Father ambles out of the room. He returns after a few minutes, carrying a large picture in a white, wooden frame. He hands it to me. "I played football."

I take the black-and-white picture and find Father's image. He is standing along the back row of the football team, wearing the familiar

PUHS on his uniform. The same designation I wore on my wrestling uniform in high school.

"For you," says Father.

"No, I didn't play football," I tell him.

"He wants you to take the picture home," says Mother Petrauschke. "He's giving the picture to you."

Why would he do that?

"Thank you," I tell him.

What am I going to do with his high school football picture? It seems like an odd gesture. Then it hits me. Father is sharing something with me that was important to him. Something that connects us. He is giving me a trophy of his time in Arizona.

I know it's impossible, but I wonder if secretly . . . or even magically, he loved Arizona because I was there. Could a part of him have sensed my existence?

No! Don't be ridiculous.

The longer I gaze at the picture, the more it means to me. In my mind, it represents the short window in time when Father and I were together in Arizona. It serves as a place marker for the impossibly small moment when the two of us were together as a family. Me in the womb, and him in the real world.

"Honey," says LuAnn, "we have to go."

I check my watch. It's half an hour past the time LuAnn and I had planned to leave. My heart sinks. I don't want to go. I've been here only two days. I want more time with my family. I want a chance to really get to know these amazing people. It isn't fair that we've had so little time together.

LuAnn and I hug each member of the family goodbye. A single thought burns in my mind as we climb into our rental car and drive away. When will I be able to return?

# CHAPTER 17

# POST-FAMILY DEPRESSION

The sun hangs low in the late-afternoon sky. Based on the way its rays are hitting my shoulders, I can tell it's late summer. The rays aren't miserably hot, like the broiler setting of an oven; they're more on the scale of an uncomfortable, stuffed-inside-Satan's-closet sort of hot.

I'm standing in the parking lot of the local grade school. Dad is next to me, wearing his roping outfit: boots, jeans, cowboy shirt, a Stetson, and a rope coiled in his hand. I don't know where we're going, but we're going together.

We stroll through the shadows between the buildings. A gust of wind combines with the cool of the shade to produce a temperature that's as close to pleasant as I dare hope for during this time of year.

A door stands in the central courtyard where the children eat lunch. There's no building attached to it, just a steel door that looks like all the rest at school. A free-standing door that shouldn't be there.

Dad marches over to the portal, turns the handle, and then steps through. I follow him.

The door slams shut and disappears. We're standing in the middle of an apple orchard. A chilly wind blows through the rows of trees. The sun is in the same spot in the sky as it was a moment ago, but it no longer burns my exposed skin. Instead, goosebumps prickle my arm.

Dad reaches up and grabs his face. Fake skin stretches as he pulls off a mask. The face of my biological father stares at me. He smiles at me for a moment and then shuffles through the orchard until we leave the apple trees far behind us. The forests and fields of New Jersey extend for as far as I can see. Green grass, green shrubs, and green trees contrast with the brown landscape I left behind moments ago.

We cross a small country road and enter a field of collard greens. Another door stands in the middle of the ready-to-harvest produce. Again, no building. Just a door.

Father shuffles over to the portal, turns the handle, and then steps through. I follow.

Desert surrounds us. A weird, unnatural desert. A saguaro stands next to me. The cactus is flat, and its color faded. It takes me a moment to notice that the saguaro doesn't have any needles and is bolted to a sand-covered wood floor. We're standing in the middle of a movie set. Bright lights shine down on me, burning my exposed skin.

Father Petrauschke reaches up and grabs his face. Fake skin stretches as he pulls off a mask. The face of John Wayne stares down at me. He smiles and says, "Hello, son."

I wake up. What's John Wayne doing in my dream?

LuAnn is already packing. In fifteen minutes we are ready to leave for the airport. The details of my dream keep replaying in my head. I'm used to bizarre, nonsensical events taking place in my subconscious realm, but this dream feels like it might be a psychological reaction to my family situation.

I decide to worry about it later.

The darkness of very early morning cloaks the streets. With everyone else in New Jersey enjoying the cozy comfort of their beds, we have the roads to ourselves. At least until we reach Philly. Even then the traffic isn't more than a trickle of cars along the freeway.

We return the rental car, take a shuttle to the terminal, and work our way through the security checkpoints. All before the sun rises.

I wait until the last moment to board. That puts us at the back of the plane, where we end up having the three seats on our side of the aisle all to ourselves.

"Aisle or window seat?" asks LuAnn.

"Aisle," I tell her.

She settles in next to the window and is asleep within minutes.

The plane cruises down the runway and then launches itself into the sky. Most of the passengers close their window shades and follow my wife's example. The flight attendants work their way to the front of the cabin, leaving me alone with my thoughts.

How am I going to blend two families together?

I've met the Petrauschkes, and I like them. But it's hard enough for me to keep up with my family in Arizona. What am I supposed to do with a second family located all the way across the country? How am I supposed to split my time and attention between two completely separate families? The only thing both families have in common is . . . me.

That's at least twice as many birthdays to remember.

At least twice as many Christmas gifts to purchase.

At least twice as many possibilities for vacation destinations. All right, that one falls into the benefit category. I guess it's all about how you look at the situation. Now there are twice as many people to wish me a happy birthday and twice as many opportunities to receive packages during the holidays.

The situation still complicates my life, though . . .

"Would you like anything from the refreshment cart?" A flight attendant interrupts my thoughts.

I order a Diet Coke and place it on the tray table in front of me.

My emotions struggle to find a way to structure my life. I now belong to two worlds. Each of those worlds is centered around a man who is my dad/father. It feels as if I have to make a choice between the two, even though I know that isn't the case.

Where do I belong?

Am I allowed to love one of my dads more than the other?

It seems unfair to ask me to even try. One is my blood. The other is my lifelong mentor. One I have a duty to love because of our genetic connection. The other has earned my love through his years of selfless dedication to my welfare. I know it's possible to love both men, but can I ever love them in the same manner? With the same intensity?

The dream returns to my thoughts.

In the movies, characters are often given a chance to see how their lives would have been affected if they'd made a different choice. My dream feels like one of those films, except it's the choice of my parents that determines the outcome of my life.

I grew up with the family in Arizona. But one single choice, one single action, could have dramatically altered the life I experienced. If my mother had attended a different social event or used a different bank to cash her paychecks, she might have met my dad first. Then he would have been my biological father and my life would have stayed the way it had been before I took the DNA test. Or would it? Would I even exist?

A different series of events might have kept Father Petrauschke in my life. Perhaps he wouldn't have returned to New Jersey. I would have grown up with him in Arizona, making trips back East every once in a while to visit the extended family. And my name would have been . . . Petrauschke.

I replay the dream in my head and wonder if any set of choices or actions could have led to John Wayne being my actual biological father. Probably not.

The life I have now includes a man who embodies the spirit of John Wayne films. Dad taught me honor, loyalty, and the value of hard work. I've always wondered if his tougher outlook on life helped balance my overly sensitive nature, allowing me to function better in the world. Without his influence, my emotional sensitivity might have roamed free from one drama-induced disaster to another.

I sit and stare at my drink, watching the beads of sweat trickle down the sides of the plastic tumbler. Our natures set Dad and me apart. We have a fair number of differences in our basic personalities. It seems like that's given me the opportunity to add extra dimensions to my life. I can look at our differences as growth opportunities rather than oddities that distance me from him.

On the other hand, if Father Petrauschke had been a permanent fixture in my life, his calmer nature may have set a different example for me, an example that might have led to me making fewer catastrophic mistakes in my life because I would have thought through before acting on a situation. It might have also meant that I would have relied more on my mother for guidance than I actually did.

There's no doubt that my life would have looked completely different from the one I know. How I act. What I do. Who I know. Where I live. All of it . . . different. I don't know if any of those changes would have made my life better or worse. Or maybe it just would have been different.

I wonder if Father's love for Arizona is a sign that he subconsciously knew I existed. Is that sort of thing even possible? Or does that happen only in movies?

The plane shudders. None of the flight attendants run screaming down the aisles, so I decide not to panic. I watch them for any signs that the few bumps we're experiencing are more than mild turbulence. One of the attendants notices me watching and returns to the back of the plane. "Did you need something?"

"Um . . . sure," I croak in an unsteady voice. "How about another Diet Coke?"

She smiles and returns in a few minutes with my drink.

"Thanks," I tell her and then take a sip.

There's definitely a nature versus nurture thing going on here. Part of who I am was determined by my genes, as is evident from the fact that I share so many traits with a man I didn't know existed until nine months ago. But there are other traits that are a result of the environment in which I grew up. My politics, my habits, and my view on life.

Here I am. A strange mixture of both.

But where does my love of Mexican food fit in?

Dad loves it. Father loves it. I love it. Is it a result of my nature or the manner in which I was nurtured? This kind of thinking is going to drive me nuts if I keep it up.

The pilot announces the landing. I stow away my tray table and hand the attendant my empty cup. In a few minutes, my life will be back to normal.

# CHAPTER 18

# FAMILY FEUD

I soar into the holiday season on the wings of bliss, still high from the tremendous display of affection I've received from my New Jersey family. This should be the best, most joyous, spirit-filled Thanksgiving/ Christmas combo since my youth. Even though it's only mid-October, my nose senses the phantom smell of turkey-yet-to-come.

The final pages of my latest fantasy novel flow from my mind, through my fingers, and onto the computer screen. For the moment, it seems as if everything is going my way, but how long can that possibly last?

Life resembles a war. I fight battles to keep everyone in the family happy. I fight battles to push my career front forward. And I battle to obtain territory in the land of happiness. Seldom do all of those fronts operate on an acceptable level.

My latest book is darker than any of the previous ones, contrasting starkly with my current mood. While the themes and violence of the story might rate only a PG-13 if the book were a movie, I don't want my fans to pick it up thinking it is the lighter, more innocent fare I usually write. I need a pen name.

Petrauschke?

No! Absolutely not! I like the idea of honoring my biological father by using his name, but Petrauschke is a mouthful. And it isn't even the name of his real father. I switch over to Ancestry, locate Tammy's account, and search the family tree.

Lodge. That's the name of P-Dad's biological father. It's short and easy to pronounce. I like the sound of it as well. Now I just have to find a surname that can reasonably pass for a given name.

Not Gaskill.

Not Supplee.

Definitely not Devinney.

Moriarty has possibilities, but I don't want everyone thinking I write detective stories.

Bennet. Bennet Lodge. The name has a nice sound to it. I grab my clipboard and write it a couple of times to see how the name looks on paper. That's the one. I return to my manuscript and change the name on the title page to Bennet Lodge.

I return to the spot in the manuscript where I left off and read the last sentence I wrote.

"Tears rolled down his cheeks as he checked for signs of—"

I hear a knock at the front door. The kids are all at school so it's probably a door-to-door salesperson wanting me to buy a solar-energy package guaranteed to save me thousands of dollars over the life of the product. Why can't it ever be Publisher's Clearinghouse with an oversized check that will allow me to live out the rest of my years in material comfort?

It takes a few moments to stretch my legs, weave a path from my office to the living room, and open the door. Whoever knocked is gone. A plain brown package sits on the porch at my feet. I pick up the box and take it into the kitchen.

Joe and Tammy-P's names are on the mailing label. I don't remember leaving any of my personal possessions behind in New Jersey. The visit itself went well, so I rule out the possibility of them shipping me a bomb. After a few more minutes of trying to guess what's inside the box, I decide to open the package.

Tastykakes.

At least a dozen six-serving packages fill the box. Peanut Butter Kandy Kakes. Butterscotch Krimpets. And Tasty Klair Pies. Joe's sent enough of the treats for everyone in my house to try one of each and still have leftovers. A taste of New Jersey to share with my family.

Joe wasn't kidding when he mentioned he like Tastykakes. He's like the bird who is "cuckoo for Cocoa Puffs." Then it hits me that this is his way of showing how crazy he is for his family. He's sharing food he loves with the people he loves. His emotional generosity stuns me.

Once again, it amazes me how a group of people can take in a stranger and love him with such intensity. I know we're family, but we still barely know one another. Their ability to weave me into the threads of their lives . . . humbles me.

I struggle with the impulse to tear open a box and start sampling the bounty of sugary love Joe has sent us. Instead, I return to my office and open Facebook. It's my turn to express my feelings for them. I look for the picture I snapped of P-Mom's delicious dessert and post it with the caption, "Based solely on the taste of this awesome pie, I am considering a move to New Jersey. Yum!"

Then I check through my social media feeds and find them crowded with posts from the New Jersey clan. The first one I find is from Joe. There's a picture of me with P-Dad and my new set of siblings. Joe posts, "I met my older brother for the first time. What a wonderful gift. What a wonderful man. A great sister-in-law to boot. I love you guys."

Bill responds with, "They were great. I hope we can get together some despite the distance."

Tammy posts, "It was an awesome visit, but way too short."

And one of the family friends posts, "Wait . . . older brother?"

Joe answers the friend with, "They hand them out now at the five-and-ten."

P-Mom answers with, "Yes, a surprise to all of us, but a wonderful surprise."

I slump in my seat and sigh. There are another dozen separate Facebook posts. All of them express similar sentiments. My focus over the last two weeks has been on finishing the latest book rather than keeping in contact with my new family. While writing is important to me personally, maintaining a strong relationship with my family should be higher on my priority list. I should have been exchanging social media posts with the family members in New Jersey every day since I returned.

That's easy enough to fix. All I have to do is post a few substantial messages now, and everything will be all right. I sort the pictures LuAnn took during the trip and find one of me and Father.

I post it with a message, "Apologies to my New Jersey family. I'm not good about posting on social media and even worse when it comes to posting about family. I returned to Phoenix amid a love-storm of well-wishes and declarations of affection and have not returned them as I should. I'm sorry. I love you guys."

That should do it.

I close the internet screen and return to the writing software. My fingers hover over the keyboard, waiting for instructions from my brain. But my brain is busy brawling with a sense of guilt. I remind myself that I responded to them.

Guilt says, "Two lousy messages? Do you really think that's enough?"

"Maybe," I respond to my conscience. "I'm sure they are busy people who have other things to do besides posting on social media all day."

"Come on," says Guilt. "You don't believe that. I expect a better answer from you."

"If I post a truly meaningful message, will you leave me alone?" I ask.

"For a while," Guilt says. "But you're bound to do something stupid later in the day."

I dismiss my inner voice and return to Facebook. A picture of me and Father seems like the best choice for a post that will satisfy my conscience. I write, "Here is the picture many of you have been waiting for—me and my biological father, Bill Petrauschke. This was taken just minutes after meeting him for the first time in my life.

"Stating that as soon as we met, he gave me a hug wouldn't do justice to the event. This man wrapped his arms around me and truly embraced me. I could literally feel the love he has for me flowing through those arms and into my heart. Even though he had never seen me before, I knew right away that he loved me. I had to work hard to keep myself from crying, right there in front of all my new family members."

I wait a few seconds for any lingering doubts to prevent me from going back to work but find my mind silent of incriminations. Confident that I have restored the level of family happiness to where it should be, I marshal my talents to push the boundaries on my career front.

—— ——

Mark calls.

"Hey, what's up?" I ask.

"How was your trip?" he asks.

"It was great. I look forward to telling everyone about it at Christmas. You know, all the juicy details. The short version is it felt wonderful to finally fit in someplace. Not that I felt unloved before, but it's different to be with people who look like me and act like me. It made feel as if I'm not a freak. It felt good."

"I'm glad it worked out well for you." Mark hesitates. I remain silent and give him a chance to find his words. "The economy isn't as strong in New Jersey as it is here. It'd be tougher for you and LuAnn to find work."

"Okay." My mind is spinning in circles, trying to figure out why he's telling me this.

"The real estate market isn't as robust either," he says. "Not to mention, the weather is drastically different from Arizona. I don't think you'd like the snow."

"What are you talking about?" I ask.

"I'm just trying to let you know that moving to New Jersey is a bad idea."

I sit quietly in my office chair. Obviously, my brother has suffered some sort of brain trauma and needs help. Jana would know what to do. As soon as I finish the conversation with Mark, I can call our sister and see what she suggests.

"Got it," I say gently, not wanting to disturb him any further. "Moving to New Jersey is bad. I promise I won't do that bad thing. Is that better?"

"Don't be a jerk," says Mark.

"What do you want me to do? You're the one who called with all this crazy talk about moving to New Jersey. Don't talk crazy, and I won't treat you like a lunatic."

"Hey, I'm just worried about you."

"Probably not as worried as I am about you right now."

"You shouldn't move to New Jersey," he says.

"Why would you think I'm planning to move to Jersey?" I ask.

"You announced it on Facebook," says Mark, his voice in full sarcasm mode. "It was with that picture of a piece of apple pie."

Ding-ding-ding. It finally registers.

"Are you kidding me?" I ask, suddenly annoyed at the suggestion. "Did you think I was really going to move to New Jersey for apple pie? I'm not going to give up my life here for pie. That's just food. You're my family. I'd be a horrible person if I suddenly cared more about dessert than I did the people I grew up with and love."

"So, you're not moving out there?" he asks.

"Give me a break."

"All right . . . good talking with you . . . have a happy Thanksgiving."

"Oh, I will," I tell him. "We're going to have apple pie."

The smell of Turkey Day paradise fills the house. I cruise through the kitchen to check on the preparations. Subtle hints of woodsmoke drift through the air. A dozen boiled eggs lie split on a cutting board, ready for their deviled topping. LuAnn is in the process of placing mini-marshmallows atop a casserole dish filled with heavily sugared yams. Everything seems in order.

This is the second year in a row the family has asked LuAnn and me to host Thanksgiving. All right, I admit it. What that really means is they asked LuAnn to host the event. My duties are limited to setting up all the folding chairs and answering the door when everyone arrives. And if I'm being honest about it, Thanksgiving is better for that arrangement. The farther I am from the food-prep area, the more likely we are to avoid culinary disaster.

I check my social media accounts as I wait. My oldest sister, Carol, has commented on the picture I posted on Facebook. The picture of me and my biological father. She writes, "Oh, my gosh, Randy. You do fit right in. Wow! I'm so happy you had the chance to see and be with your other siblings. But I'm glad you're also my brother. Love you."

Before I have a chance to respond, someone knocks at the door. It's Mom. She usually arrives early to help LuAnn with the meal. She's holding a large container with both hands. I hope it's her potato salad. LuAnn and Mom make the only version of the classic dish I will eat. Even though it isn't traditional Thanksgiving fare, whenever Mom asks what she should bring, I always tell her potato salad.

"Happy Thanksgiving," Mom cheerfully chimes.

"Let me carry that for you, Mom." I take the container and escort her into the kitchen.

She gives me a hug and a kiss, then wanders over to see how she can help LuAnn. I take a quick peek into the container to verify that it's potato salad. Score! I sneak out of the kitchen while the two of them talk about whatever it is they talk about when they're in the kitchen. I'm pretty sure they're not talking football.

There will be plenty of time for me to visit with Mom later. I return to my office, intending to dash off a quick response to Carol, but before I can even sit down, there's another knock on the door.

It's Dad and Judy. I let them in. Judy takes a bowl covered with aluminum foil into the kitchen and starts talking with LuAnn and Mom. They mention something about cooking, and I immediately tune them out.

"Happy Thanksgiving, Dad."

He sits on the love seat, and I take a spot on the couch. The Thanksgiving parade is on the television. Dad sneers at the show and then turns to face me. "How was the trip?"

"Good." How much do I tell him? I don't want to mention how awesome it was to meet everyone out there because I don't want to hurt Dad's feelings. Sure, I felt comfortable with the Petrauschke clan, but it also feels natural for me to sit in a room with Dad and talk about whatever's been happening in my life. Especially if it has to do with my writing.

I tell him about Florida. About the miserable heat and humidity. The amazingly beautiful granddaughter. About how wonderful it was to see my daughter Alex. And how I look like my siblings in New Jersey.

He leans forward and fixes his good eye on me.

Uh-oh. Dad must have something serious on his mind if I'm getting his full attention. I briefly consider changing the channel to distract him and thus avoid the possibility of a surprising, or otherwise uncomfortable, discussion, but decide I better listen.

"What's your father like?" he asks.

The question takes me by surprise. Why does he want to know that? This is the same man who laughed last year when I told him he might have a secret brother the family didn't know about. This is the man who thought it was a hoot that I really was the milkman's son. He hasn't been fazed by any of the events over the last year. Why does he care about this?

I mean, if I were in his position, I would want to know about the other father figure in my child's life. I would want to be comforted in the knowledge that my child is loved, nurtured, guided, and protected by the other father. But that's me, and this is one of the ways where I'm different from Dad. The emotional stuff seems to roll off him like bad whiskey poured over a duck's back. Dad just shrugs and keeps doing what needs to be done.

"He's your age," I tell Dad. "About the same height as you. He had a stroke in his early twenties, so he doesn't talk much. Oh yeah. He is a big John Wayne fan. He might be an even bigger fan than you."

"Is he a good man?" Dad asks.

All of a sudden, I understand what he wants to know. He's not worried about me loving Father Petrauschke more than him. Dad is calculating whether I would have been better off if I had been raised with my biological father.

"He is a good man," I tell Dad. "And if he had raised me, I have no doubt that I would have been sufficiently provided for and felt loved. The funny thing about the situation is the ways in which I'm different from Mark and Jana and Carol are the same traits I share with my siblings in New Jersey."

Dad nods but says nothing.

"Meeting the family in New Jersey answered a lot of questions I had about myself. Questions that have been lurking in my mind since I was little. Now I know why I don't look like the rest of the Lindsay kids. I know why I have a more sensitive nature than Mark, Jana, and Carol. I know where my interests in dinosaurs, aliens from space, and monsters come from. And knowing all of that has brought a great deal of peace to my soul."

I take a breath, hoping I've said the right thing. Dad will understand that even though I've embraced my new family, I still love him as much as I ever have. In fact, I love him even more because of what I've learned.

"Well, good," Dad says. "When's dinner going to be ready?"

On Christmas afternoon, LuAnn loads two large casserole dishes into the back of my van. The dishes contain her famous and much-demanded corn pudding. I load the children, a task that requires me to stand at the front door and holler, "Get in the van!"

At first glance, my task looks easier. All I have to do is tell the children it's time to leave. But the corn pudding doesn't roll its eyes at me, hide out in the bathroom for ten minutes while everyone else is waiting, or run back inside the house twenty times because it forgot something. After telling my youngest, for the fifth time, to get into the van, I'm wondering why we had children.

Music full of jingling bells plays on the radio all the way over to my sister's house. We arrive early and let ourselves in. Jana is running around her kitchen like an insane monkey, trying to put the finishing touches on her part of the meal—two large roasters filled with brisket. I know from past experience she's been up all night getting ready for the events of the day.

The rest of the family trickles in and deposits their contributions to the feast, lining them up along the breakfast counter.

As soon as Dad and Judy arrive, they make a quick circuit through the room to hug the family and then make their way through the food line. It doesn't matter if everyone has arrived or not. There's food, and they plan to eat.

Jana announces, "Mark is on his way."

Several members of the younger generation have grabbed plates and joined Dad and Judy. Jana looks at the food line and sighs. "I guess everyone might as well eat. You never can tell how long it will take Mark to get here."

The first container of corn pudding vanishes within minutes. All that is left of LuAnn's tasty offering is the casserole dish, the serving spoon, and a few scattered crumbs. I decide Mark can fend for himself, and I dive into the second casserole dish before all the pudding is gone.

Things settle down after lunch. The children go outside to play. Dad finds a spot in front of the television. I grab a spot between Jana and LuAnn. Mom, Judy, and Carol take the other side of the table. Along with Mark and his wife, this is the usual Christmas Day discussion group. We visit for hours. Most of the conversation is inconsequential, but there is plenty of finding out what everyone else has been doing since our last gathering.

Mom doesn't do much talking when there's a crowd. She sits at the table and follows the discussion everyone else is having. I'm not sure if it's a matter of her not being able to hear people talk when there's so much noise or if she would just rather listen to what's going on in her children's lives.

Jana gives us an update on her grown children. I listen to the long list of current events, happy just to be with my family no matter the topic being discussed. Problems shared with family feel more like life being lived to me. I ask questions to keep her talking. Each story fills me in on another chunk of my sister's life. A section of life I missed while I was too focused on my writing to pay attention to anyone else.

Despite the bleak nature of some of the events Jana describes, I enjoy the process of reconnecting. I always do. I never feel as complete as when I'm with my family. Just like every other Christmas, I wish this day could go on forever.

"Randy," Jana says.

It takes me a moment to realize she's stopped telling stories and is asking me a question.

"Yes," I respond with only a slight hesitation.

"How's your family in New Jersey?" she asks.

Looks like it's my turn to share. I recount all the details of the trip out East. This has to be the fiftieth time I've told the story since I returned from New Jersey. I explain how the crazy parts of my life finally made sense once I met my Petrauschke siblings. How amazing it felt to look like part of a family for the first time in my life. And how even though I know I'm loved here, I feel as if I fit in with the Jersey crew.

As I'm scouring my brain for any details I might have left out, Jana asks another question. "So what's up with all the social media posts the New Jersey folks make?"

"What?" I have no idea what she's talking about.

"You know," she says as if it should be obvious to anyone who hasn't suffered severe brain trauma. "All the mushy, lovey-dovey stuff. Do they really need to go on and on about how much they love you and can't wait for you to go back there?"

Is she putting me on?

I look for some sign that she's kidding around with me, but I can tell she isn't. Besides, the Lindsays aren't big on practical jokes. We prefer to employ biting sarcasm as our weapon of humorous choice. She actually seems upset over the public displays of verbal affection. Which is strange since she was the first member of my immediate family to suggest I embrace the Jersey clan.

Apparently, there's a limit to how much I am allowed to be loved.

"What's wrong with them expressing their feelings?" I ask.

"They can," she says, "but they don't need to go overboard with all the posts."

"I don't think they have," I say.

"Well, they have." There's no hint of a smile or anything to indicate she's kidding. She isn't angry, but she sure isn't happy about the situation. "You're our brother. Not theirs."

I want to tell her that I'm a brother to all of them. It doesn't seem fair, after everything I've gone through on this journey, to have my baby sister claim me for the Lindsays. As if they have some exclusive right to be my brother. Then I stop to think about it. Maybe instead of letting it bother me, I should be grateful she and Mark have been resistant to my efforts to insert myself into another family. It makes me feel loved.

"Take a moment and put it into perspective," I say, hoping to quiet her concerns over the matter.

She arches an eyebrow, daring me to continue.

"You, Mark, and Carol can see me anytime you want. All you have to do is call me on the phone and we can arrange to have lunch together. During the holidays, like today, we sit until late in the evening and share our lives with one another. We see each other at family birthdays, weddings, and funerals. Those things have already created a special bond that I may never have with people who are as equally related to me as you are."

Jana folds her arms and turns her head away. She looks less upset.

"Social media is the only way my New Jersey family has to love me. It's the only medium I have to connect with them. Maybe they have been overly expressive of their feelings during the last couple of months. And maybe I have too. So what?"

I pause, searching for the words to express my thoughts. "As good as the Jersey folks have been to me, I think a little Facebook loving is the least I can do for them. They didn't have to accept me. They didn't have to love me. But they did. Come on . . . you have me. Let them have my social media specter."

To drive my point home, I lean over and give Jana a hug. "Isn't this better than swapping Facebook posts? I don't know about you, but it sure feels better to me."

"Okay," Jana says. Her shoulders relax. "Point taken. Let's have dessert."

"Do you have apple pie?" I ask.

"Oh, shut up," she says.

I smile as I watch her head over to the prep counter and start slicing pies. A sigh of relief escapes my lips. Catastrophe averted . . . at least for the moment. Jana's outburst leaves me wondering how much family drama still lies ahead of me.

# CHAPTER 19

# THE DREADED CALL

The holiday season is over, and the first blooms of spring are only a few weeks away. Birds sing outside my office window. The cat is on the back porch, curled against the night's chill in her fuzzy pet bed. I spend a couple of minutes enjoying the morning before I start on the mountain of author chores needing my attention.

My cell phone rings. It's Joe. A good night's sleep and the ideal weather outside has me feeling pretty good. I decide to answer the phone and surprise Joe.

"Dude, how many times do I have to tell you, the peanut butter Tastykakes are superior to all other flavors?"

"Dad's in the hospital," says Joe. "He had a stroke."

My heart drops into a dark pit of fear and doubt. Strokes, even minor ones, could be deadly to Father at his age. I just met the man. It isn't fair to take him away so soon. A small part of my brain whispers, "At least you had the chance to meet him," but I don't care about that right now. I want to see him again. I have to see him again.

"What did the doctors say?" I ask.

"They don't know yet." Joe's voice has the same gruff sound as it always does, making the news all the more ominous in this situation. "Dad's still unconscious. I'm going to stay with him at the hospital. I'll call you when I find out more."

"Let me know as soon as anything changes," I tell Joe.

"Later." Joe disconnects the call.

I'm not sure what to do. If any of my family in Arizona were in the hospital, I'd put on my shoes and drive over and stay with them. Even if the person was unconscious, I'd still be with the rest of the family, lending our loved one emotional support with our presence. At least, I would feel like I was doing something to help. But in this situation, all I can do is wait and worry . . . by myself.

A little over a year ago, I found out P-Dad was my father. I didn't want to believe it. I didn't want it to be true. In those fourteen months, I've had a chance to find out what kind of man he is and how much his genetic legacy has affected who I am as a person. I don't want the news of his stroke to be true. I don't want to believe it. I don't want him to die.

Minutes pass as I brood over the news. I have to do something. I can't just sit here. A quick glance at my computer gives me an idea. I log in to Facebook and post a request for those who know me to keep my father in their thoughts. Maybe the combined will of many people can make a difference in whether my father recovers.

I post the message. Then I close my eyes and focus all of my thoughts on healing Father, imagining that I am there, at his side.

— —

Early the next morning, Jana calls me. She sounds worried. "Are you all right?"

"Yeah, I'm fine. My biological father is in the hospital with a stroke."

"I'm sorry to hear that," she says, but her voice has lost the tension of a moment ago. "I called as soon as I read your Facebook post. Next time, say something about what's going on so I don't think you're in trouble."

"Well, I am in trouble," I tell her. "One of my parents is barely clinging to life."

"I get that," she says. "And I'm sorry you're hurting. I feel bad that someone you love is in trouble. Is there anything I can do to help you?"

"Just keep my father in mind over the next few days."

"I will," she says. "Give my love to LuAnn and the kids. Call me if you need anything."

"Later," I say.

"Later, gator," she says, then disconnects the call.

Thanks, Jana. I feel better knowing she's worried about me. Even though she doesn't know the man, my pain is her pain. Our bond is strong, and I marvel at how we rally together in times of need. We share our burdens. We share our triumphs. That's what family is about. All right, maybe not just that, but it's one of the things family is about.

An hour later, Mark calls. "How you doing?"

"I'm guessing Jana called you."

"Yep. She said your other dad is in the hospital. Have you had any updates on him?"

"Not yet," I tell him. "It could still go either way."

"How are you taking the news?" Mark asks.

"I'm tremendously worried. Isn't that weird? A little over a year ago, I didn't know the man existed. How can I be this upset about a person I know so little about?"

"He's still your dad," says Mark. "You should be worried about him. How's the rest of the family? The kids keeping you busy?"

We spend the next twenty minutes catching up with the events in our lives. It's the same thing we do when a member of the Arizona family is in the hospital.

—➤ ◄—

My cell phone rings, and I snatch it up. Joe is on the line.

"Dad's awake," Joe says. He sounds tired but not worried. "And he's responding to questions. The doctor asked him how many children he had, and he said four. When the doctor asked him to name his kids, Dad said, 'Tammy, Joe, and Randy.' At least he hasn't forgotten about you."

Relief floods through me. I hadn't considered the possibility of the stroke wiping away the sections of Father's memory where I reside. And if he can remember me, then he should be able to recover. I close my eyes and mumble a silent thank-you.

"That's funny he didn't name Bill." I laugh. "The middle child is the one that's always left out. Does Bill know?"

"No," Joe says. "Mom didn't think we should tell him. It might hurt Bill's feelings."

"What else did the doctors say?"

"They think Dad will recover most of his functions. He's going to stay a couple more days in the hospital, and then the doctors will transfer him to a rehab center for a week."

"I am so relieved," I tell him. "Thanks for calling and letting me know."

"That's what family is about."

"You got that right," I say. "Anything else on your mind?"

"Yeah. Everyone knows the Kandy Kakes are the best."

◆—◆

I check with Joe and Tammy every week to make sure Father continues making good progress on his recovery. The thought keeps haunting me that I have to return to New Jersey for another visit, a longer visit where I can really get to know everyone. A trip long enough that I won't feel I missed my chance to bond with Father.

Just knowing I plan to go back to New Jersey lightens my mood. It occurs to me that I've actually missed them. The intensity of my feelings surprises me. How can I miss a group of near strangers this much? And, how could I not have known I would miss the Jersey clan this much?

Despite the mental boggarts hiding in the dark edges of my mind that have me worried about dividing my heart between two families, I want to embrace the feelings I have for the Petrauschkes. I allow my affection for them to bubble up from where they've been hiding, deep in my heart. It feels warm and comforting and good.

Content with the progress my father is making and my relationship with the Jersey crew, I return to my writing. I stroll into my office and start on a brand-new chapter. Thoughts of family fade away as I search for some insightful lesson to teach Pounce in his story. Something to do with a riddle of fire.

—•—

It's spring. I drive through my neighborhood with the windows down. The smell of citrus blossoms fills the neighborhood, and I thrill at the touch of the night air as it chills my exposed skin. This is my favorite time of the year. This is heaven on earth for me.

Thoughts of my biological father cross my mind. What would my life be like if I had grown up in New Jersey? As far as I know, they don't have citrus trees. I wouldn't be able to enjoy this moment if I lived there. Instead, Jersey has snow. Cold. Slippery. Snow. A lousy substitute for citrus trees. Snow scares me. Not the actual fluffy white flakes that float through the sky, but snow that turns to ice on the road and sends cars careening out of control.

What would my favorite time of year be if I had lived in New Jersey? Would I like the snow? Would I cheer for the Eagles? Would I be a total wimp who doesn't like spicy Mexican food? So many questions pass through my mind as I drive. Most of them focus on what differences might be in my life if I had grown up with the Petrauschkes. Not that it matters. I can't change the past . . . even if I want to.

I park the van in our driveway, then stroll inside. LuAnn is sitting on the couch, crocheting while she watches some sappy romantic comedy. I sit next to her and say, "What do you think about me making another trip to New Jersey?"

"I think you should," she says without taking her eyes off the needles and thread in her hands. "The anniversary trip drained our spare cash; you'll have to take the money out of your business account."

You have got to be kidding.

A small coal of anger rises from my chest, threatening to inflame my thoughts. We take six or seven trips a year to see LuAnn's mother. Even though those are in-state trips, if you add up the cost of gas for all of them, the total approaches the cost of a round-trip ticket to New Jersey. Then there's the annual family reunion for her side of the family. That alone costs more than my one trip back East. And let's not even start on the vacations she insists we take to see the grandchildren. Why is it all right to spend money to see her family, but not to see mine?

Or is it just the Petrauschke family that has to take a back seat when it comes to decisions about how to spend the family funds?

Rather than start an argument, I rise and march into my office to check how much money I have in my business account. It isn't enough to cover travel expenses for the trip. It barely covers my upcoming author expenses. I need to find another way to get the money.

I cruise through my social media outlets as I think. My eyes catch a crowdfunding project on Facebook. Is my story compelling enough to convince a host of friends and acquaintances to donate a few dollars to my cause? Is it even appropriate for me to ask them?

My cell phone rings. It's Joe.

I cross my fingers, hoping Father hasn't had a relapse. "Hey, bro."

"Pop's back in the hospital," Joe says. "He fell in the kitchen. The doctors are going to x-ray him to make sure he hasn't broken any bones."

The words catch in my throat. What do I say? What's appropriate? My head is telling me a fall like this could be a sign that Father's health is getting worse. That he may have a limited number of days left to him.

But I don't want to say that to Joe, even though he is probably thinking the same thing.

I settle for saying, "That's not good."

No kidding! Is that the best I can do? I'm not at a loss for words when I talk with Jana or Mark about our parents' health issues. Why should this be any different?

"Do the doctors think he'll be all right?" I ask.

"They haven't said anything, but Pop is responding to their questions."

I close my eyes and mentally sigh. Maybe he just tripped.

"Keep me updated, please," I tell Joe and then disconnect the call.

That does it. I have to find a way to pay for a trip to New Jersey. I'm not willing to take my chances that Father will remain healthy long enough for me to collect enough royalties to get out there. I send off an email to my friend Deb. She knows more about crowdfunding than I do. Hopefully, she can give me some advice on raising the money.

The news keeps playing through my mind. I go for a walk through the neighborhood. Gone is my appreciation for the cool night air or the scent of citrus blossoms. All I sense is the darkness around me. For the first time, I wish I had taken the DNA test sooner rather than wishing I had remained in blissful ignorance of my father's existence.

Eventually I grow too tired to storm through the neighborhood any more. I return home and then go to bed. Concern about my father keeps me awake most of the night. I need him to stay alive until I can travel out there and see him again. Is that thought, that desire, selfish?

I don't know. I don't care.

In the morning, I check my emails and find a message from Tammy. She writes, "Update on Dad. They didn't find anything wrong with his pacemaker. They said it didn't record any incident, so I'm not sure why he fell. Could be from the virus he's currently fighting."

I check my cell phone. There's a text from Joe. "They released Dad.

He wasn't hurt from the fall, and the doctors can't find anything wrong with him."

The crisis seems to have passed. I can breathe now.

"Guess that means I can uncross my fingers," I text. "Thanks for the update."

There's also a message from Deb, advising me on how to crowdfund a personal trip. She recommends a website, and I immediately switch programs to start the process. It takes all morning to put together a project that explains my situation and solicit help in purchasing a plane ticket to New Jersey. I launch the funding campaign and then lean back in my chair.

An uneasy feeling settles in my stomach. I think about canceling the crowdfunding campaign. It's not that I'm above accepting help from my friends—nobody is. That's just a part of life—helping others and accepting help when you need it. But I can't think of another way to raise the money as quickly as I need it. This method at least isn't putting anyone on the spot. If they see my request, they can ignore it. I'm not standing in front of them looking all pathetic. There's no pressure.

The first donation hits my campaign within the hour. One of my aunts. If the response continues like this, I should have enough funds to purchase a plane ticket by the end of the week. But it doesn't. A week passes. Two weeks pass. Eventually, a friend in the neighborhood drops off a generous donation one morning.

It's amazing how an act of charity can change the way you view a person. My friend is a kind and wonderful person. It doesn't surprise me she offered to help. It only deepens my respect for her and gives me greater insight into her inner beauty.

My mother-in-law sends me a check, and another friend donates through the crowdfunding site. And while my heart overflows with gratitude for each and every act of kindness these people show me, the total amount of the funds falls far short of my need. A second trip remains out of my reach. Maybe a return visit just isn't a part of my destiny. I can wait until the end of the week, and then I'm out of time.

The next day, Mom calls and wants to have lunch. Her apartment is too small for me to bring the children to, so our visits there are normally just the two of us. I haven't been out to see her in a few months. And I never say no to a visit with either of my parents . . . or a free meal. I agree to pick her up at noon and then disconnect the call.

I spend what's left of the day writing. If that's what you call sitting at my desk, hands carefully poised over the keyboard, and staring at the screen. I type a sentence. Look at it. Then delete the words. At the end of the day, it isn't so much a matter of having written anything entertaining as it is a robust session on how not to write the current scene. After reworking the scene for the twelfth time, I give up and play video games.

— —

Mother is waiting for me when I arrive. I lean over and give her a hug. She kisses me on the cheek. Then we do the usual where-are-we-going-to-eat ritual. It's hard to find food I don't like, and Mom is pretty broad in her culinary tastes. I suggest Cracker Barrel. It's Mom's favorite place to eat, and it provides a cozy environment for a quaint chat.

I open the passenger door for Mom and help her inside the van. Then we drive to the restaurant. Mom asks about LuAnn, the children, and me. I give her the usual response, "The same as always. LuAnn works too hard, the children fight all the time, and I'm busy writing my next book."

"How's Carol?" I ask, knowing Mom will spend the rest of the drive to the restaurant talking about my sister and the latest calamity in her life. Mom talks. I drive. We reach Cracker Barrel, and I hurry to the other side of the vehicle and open the door for her.

Mom continues to give me a blow-by-blow account of Carol's life as we walk inside and take our seats. Carol needs a lot of parental help, and Mom seems committed to never allowing my sister to experience adulthood on her own. Twenty minutes later, Mom has run out of stories about Carol, the waitress has brought us our food, and I am ready to eat.

"The other day, I noticed you were trying to raise money on Facebook for another trip to New Jersey," Mom says. "How's that going?"

I shrug. "Not very good."

"Hasn't anyone donated money?" she asks.

"A few," I mumble with a mouth full of food. "Just not enough."

"That's a shame, honey," Mom says, using the same tone of voice she used whenever I injured myself as a child. Or had nightmares because I stayed up all night watching monster movies by myself. "I want you to be able to see your father again."

"Me too," I say as I pour maple syrup over my grits. "I want to make a million dollars on my next book, but what are the odds of that happening?"

"I don't know about the book, but you can go to New Jersey."

"How?" I ask.

"Me," she says. Mom looks over her glasses at the ham steak on her plate, intensely studying the slab of meat. Then she pokes it with her fork. "I will give you the rest of the money you need to go visit your father. It's a real shame you didn't have a chance to meet him until last year. You need to go out there before he has another stroke."

My mouth hangs open. I feel as if an angel of mercy has landed across from me, swooping down to perform a miracle. Then again, Mother has always been there for me. Sometimes as an angel of comfort, at other times as an angel of healing, and when needed, as an angel of conscience. I don't want to cry in this restaurant, in front of all these strangers, but this token of Mom's love brings me to the brink of tears.

"Thank you, Mom," is all I can manage to say.

Now I just have to worry about Father Petrauschke staying healthy until then.

# CHAPTER 20

# RETURNING HOME

My oldest son, Roger, decides he wants to go with me to New Jersey. He's an adult and can pay his own way. We book a red-eye for the first week of November. I can stay up all night, making it easier for me to fall asleep at bedtime the next day. The first twelve hours in New Jersey will be rough, but then I'll have adjusted to the local sleeping schedule for the rest of the trip.

The weather in Arizona is unseasonably warm. I bring a jacket in the likely event that it's much cooler in Jersey. Because we purchased our tickets separately, Roger and I have assigned seats in different rows. An airline attendant announces that the flight has entered the boarding phase. I make my way through the line and then wedge myself into the middle seat.

As soon as the plane takes off, the rest of the passengers settle in and fall right to sleep. Lucky them. My overhead light is a beacon amidst a sea of darkness. I worry that the light will disturb my neighbors, but a snore from the guy to my right tells me that isn't really a concern.

"Anything to drink?" asks a flight attendant.

"A Diet Coke, please."

I pull out a brand-new book from my computer case. This should keep my mind occupied until I reach Philadelphia. The back cover promises a tale of conflict between a fallen angel and the heavenly host who seek to eliminate the taint he represents to their esteemed race. Just my kind of story.

I speed through the first few chapters. By the time I finish the drink, my enthusiasm for the story has faded. Another hour of a whiney angel complaining about the rigors of high school is all I can take. I leave the book on my lap, turn off my overhead light, and stare into the darkness.

Eventually, my thoughts move away from the angel story and focus on the week ahead. My first trip to Jersey was about meeting the Petrauschkes, but this time it's about fitting in. About mentally cementing myself into the family. Rather than thinking of them as my new family or my East Coast family, I want them to just . . . be . . . family.

We arrive in Philly, and it's almost cold enough for a jacket. Roger and I stand outside while we wait for our ride. Tammy's son, Shaun, pulls up to the curb and helps us load our bags into the trunk of his car. I introduce Roger to his cousin. The two of them nod to one another, and then we climb into the car and are on our way to Jersey.

"What do you have planned for this trip?" Shaun asks.

"Nothing," I tell him. This isn't a vacation. I want to spend time with my family and gain a feel for what their everyday life is like. I want to watch some television, go to the grocery store, take a walk through the neighborhood. I know it doesn't sound exciting, but I'm not here to be thrilled or entertained. I'm here to absorb as much of what it means to be a part of this family as I can.

"What's there to see and do?" asks Roger.

"The Jersey Shore," Shaun answers. "Except I think it's closed this time of year."

"Then that should be fun," I say dryly. "Maybe we can try that authentic Mexican food you talked about last time I was here?"

"Yeah, yeah, yeah," Shaun says. "The one in Clayton is good. There's another in Vineland, but I haven't tried it."

The sun peeks over the horizon. I stare out the car window as we cross the Delaware River. City gives way to rural landscape. This is not the New Jersey I remember. The trees are no longer green. Instead, they display their bright fall colors of red, orange, and yellow. Like the muted colors of a flame but without the heat. A sprinkling of leaves adorns the ground at the base of each tree.

All things have their season. The trees act as a reminder, a sign, that Father Petrauschke approaches the fall of his life. One more stroke could send him into the cold depths of winter, from whence no man returns.

"I'm taking you to Joe's, right?" Shaun asks.

"Yep. He offered to let us stay with him."

"You could have stayed with anyone," Shaun says. "My place is open, so is Poppa's, and my mom would love to have you stay with her, but her place is kind of small."

"Maybe next time."

Joe's sitting on the front steps of his house as we pull onto the property. He has a coffee cup in his hands and is wearing a T-shirt. Apparently, it isn't cold enough to bother him either. His efforts to stand are stiff and awkward, but there's a smile on his face.

That he's waiting for me outside feels like a warmer welcome than any words could convey. Even better than a hug. Joe's expression is stern most of the time. It's the little acts of kindness, or in this case excitement, that give him away.

In that way he's like me. Family and friends have no trouble reading my emotions, but strangers often find my standard, everyday expression intimidating or gruff. Maybe that's why it's so easy for me to connect with Joe. We are as much alike as I am different from my siblings in Arizona.

I give Joe a hug. "Good to see you, bro."

"Yeah," Joe says, in a raspy voice. "Same here."

Joe gives us a tour of the house. Roger and I will stay in the upstairs bedroom where Joe's granddaughter sleeps whenever she stays with them. We leave our bags in the room and head to the kitchen. Tammy-P sticks her head out from one of the other bedrooms. "Oh, good. Glad youse both made it. Joe stayed up all night waiting. Welcome, welcome."

She pulls her head back into the bedroom and closes the door.

We continue downstairs. Joe points out where everything is located in the kitchen, including a tube-shaped package of pork rolls. "Now it's your fault if you starve. We have plenty of food, but I'm not your maid, or your cook, or your chauffeur. You can make your own food. You're family, which means this is your home too."

"Thanks." I feel at home. With a smirk on my face, I point to the fridge and ask, "Does that mean you aren't going to make pork rolls for breakfast? I mean, it is breakfast time, and I thought every self-respecting Jersey native swore by the state food."

Joe grunts. "All right. I'll make them this morning, but you need to pay attention so you can make your own from now on."

"Absolutely." I watch the process and hope Roger has better culinary instincts than I do.

Joe serves up the sandwiches. They're better than I remember. How is that even possible? I close my eyes as I enjoy the first mouthful of heaven-sent breakfast meat. My mind is already working on how to convince Joe to make another round of sandwiches tomorrow morning . . . and every morning during my stay. I'm willing to give it a try, but why mess with perfection when Joe has clearly perfected the method of crafting highly addictive breakfast sandwiches.

"You like it?" Joe asks.

I nod my head, unwilling to stop eating in order to answer him.

"Good. You can make your own tomorrow." Joe walks stiffly into the living room and grabs the remote. He spends a few minutes showing us how to operate the television and then heads upstairs. "I'm tired. Relax, watch some television, or do whatever it is you normally do at home. See you when I get back up."

Then he walks upstairs, leaving us alone in the kitchen. He really wasn't kidding about this being our home. Except for the part where they leave us by ourselves, this is the sort of everyday experience I've wanted. What surprises me is how comfortable I feel sitting around in my brother's house without him or Tammy-P attending us. Roger and I watch television for a couple of hours before my lack of sleep catches up with me. I call it a morning and take a short nap.

— —

Two hours of sleep refreshes me enough to function for the rest of the day. I amble downstairs and find Roger talking with Tammy-P. "I can see the two of you have met."

Tammy-P offers me a smile. It's been more than a year since my last visit, and I had almost forgotten the magical brilliance of those smiles. The whole room seems to glow from her radiance. "We've been getting to know one another while youse slept. I can't believe how much the two of youse look alike."

"I'm glad someone in Arizona looks like me," I tell her. "After I found out the results of my DNA test, I tried to convince Roger to take one . . . to make sure I was really his dad. But he doesn't seem to think that's necessary."

"I keep telling you, Dad," says Roger. "It's the lips. The lips don't lie." We all laugh.

"Are you ready to go?" Tammy-P asks.

It takes me a moment to figure out what she's talking about. Today is Sunday. That's the day Mother Petrauschke has everyone over for dinner. I'm still tired, but I don't want to miss the family event. I nod my head, trying to infuse as much enthusiasm into the action as my jet-lagged body can manage.

"Tammy decided to let you use her car to get around this week," Joe says. "Pay attention to the directions I give you on the way over there because, after tonight, you'll be on your own."

A micro panic attack surges through my chest. I mentally picture Roger and me navigating the roads of rural New Jersey in the dark, growing more lost with each passing moment. What if the car breaks down while we are lost . . . and it snows?

"Don't worry," Joe says. "Dad's place is easy to find. You only have to make about six turns to get there from here. I'll make sure you know how to find your way back."

"And youse can always call us if you get lost," says Tammy-P.

Tammy-P gives me her keys, and we follow Joe over to Father's house. We barely crawl out of the car when Mother Petrauschke hurries outside to greet us. She gives me a quick hug and then says, "This must be Roger."

"Hello, Grandmother," Roger says as he hugs her.

P-Mom leans in close to me and says, "Just so you know, Dad doesn't talk as much as he used to, and he was never much of a talker. He's in the living room if you want to go visit him."

I don't know. I'm not sure I'm ready to meet Father again. What am I going to find when I walk into the room with him? How is he going to respond? Fortunately, Roger and I are here all week, giving me plenty of time to reconnect with him.

"Make sure you duck your head when you walk inside," P-Mom tells Roger. "The structure of the house is suited for short people. Which means it's never been a problem for me, but your grandfather had to learn to walk around the house with a slight bend."

She turns to me and asks, "Did you warn Roger about what to expect from us?"

Actually, I hadn't. I hadn't seen any need to let my son know he'd be meeting a wonderful group of people. Roger is a gentle soul and tends to get along with everyone—much like the Petrauschkes. I know he will be all right with them. I only hope he will love them as much I do.

"You are a wild bunch," I tell P-Mom. "I thought I would let him discover that for himself. Besides, if I told him about everyone before we boarded the plane, he might not have agreed to come with me."

"Good thinking," she says as we walk inside the house.

Tammy is sitting at the kitchen table. My heart does a double pump of joy as soon as I see her. It continues to amaze me how comfortable I feel whenever we are together. What a shame we didn't have the chance to grow up in the same household. Imagine the storehouse of fond memories we could have built together.

But no matter how good that life might have been, I'm not willing to trade it for the one I shared with my Arizona parents and siblings. I might as well wish I had lived twice.

Joe heads into the living room to join Father, while Roger and I sit at the table with Tammy. P-Mom scurries over to the kitchen counter. She picks up a pie and says, "I'm afraid I have bad news. I made an apple pie for you but left it in the oven too long."

This pie looks darker than the one I remember from my first trip. Not too dark, though. I think it might still be pretty good. "I'm willing to risk a slice . . . or two."

"I made a cherry pie too," she says as she puts the pie back on the counter and returns to working on Sunday dinner. "You might want to try that one instead."

How bad can it be? As far as I'm concerned, extra-brown crust tastes even better.

Tammy opens a manila folder that's sitting on the table. "I thought you might want to add this to your family research files. It's a map from Ancestry showing the regions where the Petrauschkes originated. The file also has copies of a few emails John Lodge sent me."

I take the folder and look at the map. Some of the ancestral regions don't match mine. Then again, they shouldn't. We have different mothers, and half the highlighted areas on the map come from the maternal DNA.

The first email John sent Tammy is on top of the stack. I pick up the message and read it: "So far, Randy is not entertaining the idea that W. P. is his father."

"He was right," I tell Tammy. "I was not entertaining the idea at all. I was convinced you guys were not family. When you told me the same thing, I called you the Crazy Lady. The Crazy Lady who thinks she's my sister."

"I am crazy," says Tammy.

"No, you're not," I say. "Let me tell you something. You made it very easy for me. I received your emails and felt a connection right away. I would tell myself, 'I like Tammy. I don't know why I like her. This isn't someone I know. We've never met, but I like her.'"

Tammy offers a shy smile, and I can tell from her expression that she appreciates my comment. It's the least I can do for someone who's made this whole experience less stressful than it could have been.

"The initial DNA results were weird," Tammy says. "At first, I couldn't figure out what the 'Close Family Relationship' meant. Nope. No clue. Then I went back and started clicking on stuff. That opened a page which said you were a half brother. I was shocked. I have a brother. It took two weeks for me to contact you after I figured all that out. I went through a lot of emotions. I didn't think I would react that way, but I kind of cried a little bit. Then I'd be thinking, wow, I have another brother. A sister would have been nice, but another brother is all right. And he's older. I always wanted an older brother. Then I just went back and forth with the emotions, figuring out how I was going to tell you."

"Were you nervous?" Roger asks.

"I was worried how the family here was going to react, because I was pretty sure Dad didn't know. I was, like, what is this going to do to him at his age? I realized that I was the one who had to tell everybody and didn't know how they would react."

P-Mom nods her head. "I told Tammy, 'You're going to get into this DNA stuff, and who knows what you're going to find.'"

"She was right," Tammy says. "I was up and down, trying to figure out what I was going to say to you. I ran it through my head so many times and . . . ahh, no, that's stupid. Nope. Nope. I wrote that the wrong way. Then I finally decided I just had to do it. I had to make the effort and write something."

"I think it was beautiful," I tell her.

"Mom was fine when I told her," Tammy says. "And Dad was just kind of in disbelief. He told us he didn't have any kids in Arizona, but then we had him take the DNA test. Joe was all right with it from the start. He told me, 'Cool. I have another brother.'"

"The thing is," P-Mom says, "you didn't even know. If you're adopted, you know you have other parents. You can go looking for them if you want to. But in this situation, you had no clue that another family existed."

Father waddles in and sits down next to me.

"Anything you want to say about this, Dad?" Tammy asks Father.

"About what?" Father asks.

"About finding out you had an extra son," Tammy says.

Father hesitates. He starts and stops a couple of times before the first words come out of his mouth. "Well . . . well . . . I knew I got an extra son."

"While he was in rehab," P-Mom says, "the doctors asked him how many children he had, and Dad told them seven instead of five. But he remembered to include Randy."

"There must be another one out there, Dad," Tammy jokes.

Father laughs. I can tell he wants to say something but doesn't. Maybe he wants to tell us one surprise is enough. Or that the rest of us will just have to wait and see who shows up next. Whatever it is, I feel robbed of the chance to find out. I want to know how he thinks and the sorts of things that go through his mind during these table-side discussions. I want to be able to fully interact with him, but I realize that will never happen.

The back door opens, and Tammy's oldest daughter, Jessica, enters with her family. A few minutes later, Shaun and his family arrive. Then Tammy's youngest daughter, Tara. I introduce them to Roger as they enter, and then we sit down to eat.

Pork roast, beef roast, sweet corn, and mashed potatoes with creamy, homemade gravy. This is pretty close to the same menu I had during my last visit. It's probably the same meal they have every Sunday, and I'm all right with that. I only wish I was a regular part of the tradition.

But the food is secondary to the company. The parents, the siblings, the nieces, and the nephews all treat me and Roger like cherished members of the family. I sit quietly, savoring the meal almost as much as I relish the warm environment this family provides.

After dinner, P-Mom slices up two pies. I insist on apple. The crust is slightly burnt, as is the top layer of apples. But as far as I'm concerned, that's all for the better. For some reason, I like slightly burned desserts.

"I warned you about the pie," P-Mom says.

"You can make pies like this for me anytime," I tell her. "I like them well-done."

"Dad does too," Tammy says.

I look up and notice Father is eating apple pie. He says, "I . . . like it."

Maybe I'm not as weird as I thought. This is another trait I have in common with my biological father. Of course, I've never heard of DNA that results in people liking burnt food, but I suppose it could exist. Maybe there's one for liking cherry-flavored taffy rather than the more superior banana flavor. That would explain why everyone doesn't agree with me on the topic.

"What's your schedule for the rest of the trip?" P-Mom asks.

A schedule? Now, that they mention it, I probably should have made some sort of plan for how to spend my time out here. "I don't have one."

"Tammy and I were talking earlier," P-Mom says. "We want to have Thanksgiving on Saturday."

I love Thanksgiving! The food. The football. The family all gathered in one place, or as many of the family members as you can convince to show up. Then a thought pushes its way to the front of my mind. This is an attempt by Mother Petrauschke to include me in their family holiday. An important ritual for most families and one I've never had the chance to share with this portion of my family.

My nose and eyes sting from the tears welling up inside me. What a thoughtful expression of their love for me. On Saturday, I'm going to celebrate Thanksgiving with the Petrauschkes.

— —

I spend Monday with Joe and Tammy-P. Despite his warning to the contrary, Joe makes breakfast for Roger and me. Pork rolls. Just as good as the last batch. This could definitely become a food addiction.

Breakfast gives me my first chance to meet everyone in the household as they prepare for the workweek. In addition to Joe and Tammy-P, two of their adult children, a young woman named Alice, and ten formerly stray cats all live in the house.

The young woman fixes breakfast and then leaves for the day.

"Who's that?" I ask Joe.

"That's Alice. She's Johnny's ex-girlfriend."

Ex . . . girlfriend? Shouldn't that make this her ex-home? I wonder what happens when the two of them run into one another in the hall, or at the tiny breakfast table? This just doesn't sound right.

"If she's an ex-girlfriend, then why does she still live here?" I ask.

"She's going to school," Joe says.

Tammy-P straightens up in her chair. "Youse can't expect us to kick Alice out of here just because her and Johnny aren't together anymore. Her family is in Michigan. She doesn't have anywhere else to go."

Then it clicks. Joe might have a gruff exterior, but he apparently has a soft spot for people and animals who need a home. I watch him as he hobbles over to the kitchen door and talks to the meowing cat that's sitting there.

"You can't go outside, kitty," Joe tells the cat. "It's raining and you'll catch a cold."

What a softie!

I spend the rest of the day visiting with Joe and Tammy-P. All right, mostly Tammy-P. Joe tends to wander a lot and say little. The vast majority of Joe's comments are meant to tease, but I'm on to him now. All of the jokes, all of the sarcasm, are to cover up the gentle nature inside him. I imagine he has a reputation to maintain. Or, at least, he thinks he does.

— —

It rains for most of the week. Roger wakes up on Tuesday with a cold and spends all day in bed. Even though he's over thirty and my size, I still feel bad for the little guy. He decides to hang out in the bedroom rather than risk getting everyone else sick. I drive to the nearest pharmacy and buy him medicine, then go over to Father's house by myself.

I visit with Mother Petrauschke until I generate the courage to go into the living room, where Father is watching television. The room looks different from my last trip. Two air mattresses occupy the bulk of space.

"Dad sleeps on that," P-Mom says, pointing to the larger of the two mattresses. "I use the other mattress because he doesn't like to sleep alone."

The reality of the stroke sinks in for me. Both of my Petrauschke parents have had their lives radically changed since my last visit. Father's easy chair is only a few feet away from the mattress. Other than trips into the kitchen at mealtime, his world is limited to this room.

And while P-Mom has more freedom to move about, it can't be comfortable for her to sleep on the small mattress that close to the floor. The sacrifice this arrangement represents speaks to the love and dedication she has for Father. Not the flowery, giddy love I see in romantic movies but a real, powerful love that comes from selfless action and sacrifice.

Good for you, Mother Petrauschke. Good for you.

I spend a few awkward moments trying to figure out what to say to Father. He seems more interested in the television than visiting with me. Then I remember that he likes the Cardinals, and I decide to talk about football with him. "What do you think of Arizona's new quarterback?"

His expression brightens. He motions with his hands. "They . . . they need a good quarterback."

Father struggles to find what he wants to say. Still, he ends up talking to me more than he did during the first trip. P-Mom has already mentioned that most of the time they just sit next to each other and don't say anything at all, so this must be a wild talking streak for him. This is Father, showing how excited he is to see me.

Wednesday night, I spend the early part of the day on my laptop, writing a presentation I'm scheduled to give at the library next month. I visit with Tammy-P in the afternoon. Drew, my sister's kinda-sorta son-in-law, stops in with cheesesteaks from a place in North Philly. "This place is the best," he tells me. "Thought you should try an authentic cheesesteak rather than that made-for-tourist stuff you had last time."

Drew has a heavy Philly accent. He spends an hour asking about my DNA story and what it was like to find out one day that my life wasn't totally what I thought it was. Here's another member of the family I immediately like.

"That's crazy," he says. "It really has to mess with your mind to find out at your age that you have more family."

"You don't know the half of it," I tell him. "Thanks for the cheesesteaks. I can't believe how good they are."

"Hey, no problem," he says in that thick Philly accent. Then he leaves.

The cheesesteak is incredible. As much as I enjoyed the sandwiches I had last time, they are second-rate compared to this meaty-cheese version of El Dorado. Now I understand why the inhabitants of the City of Brotherly Love are so crazy about their cheesesteaks. If I had a mountain of money, I'd fly out for one of these cheesesteaks every week.

So, yeah. It's good.

I spend Thursday at Father's house. He watches television while Tammy, P-Mom, and I talk about all the years that were lost because we didn't know we had more family. A situation that wouldn't have existed if someone would have told me the truth. A situation that wouldn't have existed for my father if someone had told him the truth.

But all of that has changed. No one can expect to keep these type of secrets hidden anymore. DNA testing is now shining the light of science into skeleton-filled family closets all over the world.

I head back to Joe's. Roger is still hiding out but seems to be feeling better. I eat and visit some more. Joe orders four varieties of strombolis: cheesesteak, pepperoni and cheese, spinach, and Italian. All of them are good, but the cheesesteak is the best.

Saturday finally arrives.

This is my chance to experience the holiday with the trees full of fall colors. This is Thanksgiving the way I see it on television and the way it's depicted on paper plates, napkins, and all the other items the stores sell for the big meal.

But it's much more than that. Tammy and P-Mom have made a special effort to share the holiday with Roger and me, giving our connection to the family an official stamp of approval. Perhaps not so much in their mind, but definitely in mine.

The celebration doesn't look all that different from the Thanksgivings we have in Arizona. Turkey, dressing, potatoes and gravy, sweet-potato pie, and green-bean casserole. The corn pudding is a little stiffer than LuAnn's, and P-Mom mixes strawberries in with the cranberries, but otherwise, the food looks and tastes about the same. Only the colors of fall make the holiday feel any different.

Billy, Shelly, and their boys arrive, triggering a round of teasing between my siblings.

"Randy is my favorite brother," Bill says. "Because we get two Thanksgivings now."

Two Thanksgivings. That's something to be thankful for.

"Randy is my favorite brother," Joe tells Bill. "Because now I have another brother beside you."

Ouch.

Tammy steps up to the other two brothers, hands on her hips, and says, "Randy is my favorite brother because he didn't tease me as a child. And also, because I'm not the oldest anymore."

We all laugh at the comment, including Father.

Everyone fills their plate with Turkey Day bounty and finds a spot to sit. Father takes his food into the living room so he can eat while he watches television. Tammy, Tammy-P, Bill, Shelly, Roger, and I all crowd around the kitchen table.

A conversation starts about Thanksgivings past. Which leads to a discussion about our favorite and least favorite foods.

We talk briefly about the surprising number of people who reveal they have a story of their own when they find out I took a DNA test and discovered my dad wasn't my dad.

Bill's wife, Shelly, says, "I guess there are more families than you thought who have been blended together in one way or another. And since we're on the topic, I have a story too. My mother was adopted."

# CHAPTER 21

# SHELLY'S STORY

I have a secret DNA story, and because of that, all of the Petrauschkes have one too. Tammy-P has a secret DNA story. Apparently, Shelly also has a hidden-family story that was revealed only through a DNA test. Was there anyone who didn't have a story involving a hidden family and a DNA test?

"All right," I tell Shelly, "let's hear it. What happened to your mother?"

Shelly leans back in her chair, crosses one leg over the other, and then puts her hands on her knee. "My mother was an only child. Or that's what she thought. Her parents were very strict, and she felt they didn't love her. When she was twelve, my mother found a box in the attic and went through it. The box held her adoption papers."

"Surprise," I yell.

"They had never mentioned that she was adopted," Shelly continues. "She never told them she found the papers. Her parents passed away without any of them telling the other what each of them knew.

"A few years ago, my mother purchased a DNA test from 23andMe. She used the family connections the test revealed to find her sisters. They agreed to meet at Applebee's. Her two living sisters and two nieces showed up at the restaurant. And now they get together as often as they can. One of the sisters has passed away, and my mother talked about how glad she was that they had the opportunity to meet one another before she died."

"That's neat," I say. "It feels like instant family."

Shelly nods her head but sighs. "My grandmother held on to the adoption secret her whole life, afraid to tell anyone because she didn't want to betray my mother's parents. Mom didn't know why she was adopted. She was the oldest of the siblings."

"There must be a heck of a story behind that choice," I tell Shelly. My author instincts want to pursue the tale of how only the oldest child is given up for adoption. In a way, it reminds me of my own story. Being the oldest served as my personal proof that I wasn't adopted, even though I looked nothing like my siblings or the rest of the Lindsays.

Then my mind switches gears. "You mentioned that your mother didn't feel loved because her parents were strict."

"Y-e-e-e-e-s." Confusion shows in Shelly's eyes.

"That doesn't make sense," I tell her. "I mean, it doesn't make sense that your grandparents didn't love your mother. She was their only child. They went through all that trouble to adopt her. Why do that if they didn't want a child? Or didn't plan to love her?"

"What does it mean, then?" Shelly asks.

"I think it's a matter of nature versus nurture," I tell her. "Your mother thought her parents' strictness meant they didn't love her. But what if they just expressed their love in a different way? I read a book a few years ago by Gary Chapman called *The Five Love Languages*. He describes five ways people express their love. The five ways people understand love. I think these emotional centers could be passed down genetically."

The look of confusion fades from Shelly's face as she realizes what my idea means.

"If our emotional centers are part of our nature," I continue, "then your mother would inherit the way she perceives love from her biological parents. The odds are good that her adopted parents operated under a completely different method of expressing love. Which means every action your grandparents took could have been an expression of love, and your mother would not have seen it that way."

How tragic.

Sometimes my mouth moves faster than my brain. This is one of those times. I sit for a moment to let what I just said sink into my head. How many millions of adoptive families struggle because parents and children have different emotional centers? For that matter, how many traditional families suffer from the same problem?

Certain situations may make it seem as if the parents love a child less, when they actually love the child to the best of their ability. But how do you teach families that it isn't a matter of not being loved, only that we are being loved differently than what feels right to us?

My heart goes out to Shelly's mother and her parents. It goes out to all the families I don't know, and will never know, who could have benefitted from the knowledge of the different ways people show their love. How many family rifts could have been avoided if they knew what to look for when asking themselves, "Do my parents/children love me?"

P-Mom makes room on the table for two pies she baked earlier. Unfortunately, neither of them is apple.

The rest of the day passes quickly. It feels as if one moment I'm taking my first whiff of roasted turkey and the next I'm hugging everyone and telling them goodbye. My week of life-with-the-Petrauschkes has nearly come to an end. It doesn't make up for a lifetime apart . . . a lifetime of lost moments together, but it has put their memories firmly in my head.

"You can stay with us next time," P-Mom says.

"Or Miranda and me," Shaun says.

"No way," Joe grumbles. "He's staying with me."

I'm not even gone, and they are already arguing over where I'm going to stay. It feels nice to be wanted, but I'm ready to go home. I miss LuAnn and the kids. A week is apparently the limit for how long I can stay away from my family . . . and from Arizona.

Roger and I climb into the car and head back to Joe's place. It's too dark outside to watch the scenery as I drive, leaving my mind to drift over the events of the day. My thoughts return to the adoption story Shelly told me.

Of course, she isn't the only one in the family with an adoption story. My two youngest children are adopted. The difference is the boys know their story. I haven't tried to hide it from them, and they were too old when they came to live with us for that to have worked anyway.

The boys still have plenty of questions about their biological parents. Some of those questions I can answer. Some of them I can't. Fortunately, they still see their father at Christmas every year. Any questions I can't answer, they can ask him.

I hear stories all the time from people who thought they were done having children and then found out there was another one on the way. Well, surprise, surprise. LuAnn and I had not one but two unexpected additions to the family at the same time.

Memories of the adoption run through my mind as I drive.

Until 2008, the housing boom had treated us pretty good for a while. Then the market burst, and we were financially devastated. We lost our home and our rental properties. LuAnn lost her job a couple of months later, and we were forced to move into a small rental house that was uncomfortable and hot most of the time.

One afternoon, the phone rang. A representative from Child Protection Services told us they would be bringing two children to stay with us. The children would arrive within twenty minutes.

"Great," I told her. "Do we know these children?"

"They belong to your nephew."

Only one of my nephews had more than one child. It was no surprise that he'd had them taken away by the state. Wasn't even a surprise that they decided to leave them with me. My nephew had lived with me for a couple of years, during his troubled teens. I had seen the boys a few times, but they weren't going to recognize me.

The welfare worker dropped the boys off with a bag of clothes for each of them. Nick, the older of the two, clutched a man-purse to his chest as if afraid someone would take it from him. I could tell that the contents of that bag represented the only constant in his life. Whatever toys or mementos the bag carried were the only source of comfort and mental security the boy had. The younger boy, Patrick, stood behind Nick. Even though he didn't look scared, he appeared determined not to be separated from his brother

My heart broke at the sight. I would make sure these two boys had the best home, the best life I could provide for them for as long as they stayed with us. They deserved that much of a break after the years of neglect they had suffered.

Two years later, the boys became legal members of the family, never again to worry about their next meal or where they would sleep at night. Nick held on to his bag for most of that time before he felt secure enough in his home, in his family, to leave it behind.

It'd be a lie if I said I immediately loved the boys as much as I did the children who were born into the family. It took time to reach that stage. It took shared family experiences to bring us together. In order to make the boys feel as loved as the rest of the children, I told them a sort of story. I told them that LuAnn and I had married one another a little later in life than perhaps we should have. Too late to have as many children together as we would have liked. I told the boys I thought they had been given to us because we couldn't have any more children of our own.

The funny thing is, the more I told them that story, the more I believed it myself.

I don't know if Nick and Pat share the same emotional center as their biological parents. Nick is easy for me to love because his emotional center drives him to seek acceptance through acts of service and he responds well to being told he is loved. He and I both thrive on hugs, and that means I know how to reach him in a way that is meaningful to me as well.

Pat is more difficult to love at times. His emotional center seems to be tied to things. Gifts. Money. Treats. I do my best to translate the way that I love into actions that appeal to his emotional center, but I fail as often as I succeed. Even though he still beams at me when I tell him I love him or give him a hug, I wonder if it's enough. Will he grow up like Shelly's mother, thinking his parents were too stern and didn't love him?

I hope not. And I have to believe that Shelly's parents had the same wish in their hearts.

"You ready to go back home?" Roger asks. His question breaks the silence and brings me out of my melancholy reflections. I turn into Joe's yard and park the car. It's time to pack for the trip back to Arizona.

# CHAPTER 22

# SURPRISE, SURPRISE

It's my anniversary.

The weather couldn't be any more perfect for a celebration. A few fluffy, white clouds drift across the sky. A cool breeze blows across my face and arms. The rain from last week has left the air smelling fresh. It's the kind of day that makes me want to drive out to the desert and stroll through the mesquite and juniper in order to enjoy the sensory pleasures of nature.

If only I can figure out what I should do for this kind of celebration. I mean, it's not a traditional anniversary—the kind where you bring your wife roses, go out to eat, and then maybe see some yucky romantic movie. It's the kind of anniversary where you mark the point when your life has been changed forever.

How do I celebrate that kind of event in my life? Definitely not with a movie. Since food seems to be a part of all important celebrations, going out to lunch or dinner might be appropriate. Especially if I try something new each year. Something I've never eaten before. Maybe a dish from my previously secret genetic heritage.

What do I even call this sort of anniversary? DNA Discovery Day? Who's Your Poppa Day? Hide-and-Go-Seek-the-Skeleton-in-Your-Closet Day? The last one has a nice ring to it, but I don't see it being put on a greeting card anytime soon.

My phone beeps with a text alert, interrupting the debate with myself.

Joe texts, "Hey bro, how are you? Just thinking of you."

I text back, "Super busy. How are you and Tammy? I've been thinking of you as well."

Joe texts, "We are doing good. Every day we wake up is a good day."

A life lesson from my little brother. Not what I expected today.

"Yes, it is." I wait for a response, but that's it from Joe.

There are too many things going through my mind to write today. I slip the cell phone into my pants pocket and take the Bush Highway out to the desert. The Salt River runs to my left. I see a picnic ramada positioned next to the river and pull into the parking lot. This time of year, I have the area all to myself.

I find a bare patch of ground along the bank and watch the river flow past me. Maybe my thoughts will drift away with the current. Then I can focus on something more important than whether I should celebrate the discovery of my other family.

For fifty-seven years, I was safely cocooned within my limited view of what it meant to be a normal family. I knew of no family-destroying dramas like the ones depicted on television. I knew of no skeletons lurking in our family closet. Or, at least, none I was willing to admit existed. I had thought we were just the typical, nuclear family.

Obviously, I was wrong.

I've opened the Pandora's Box of the DNA generation and cannot put back what I have personally let loose. Perhaps my problem was I held on too tightly to what I thought a family should be instead of realizing that it changes. Births, deaths, marriages, and adoptions all bring change to families, so why not DNA testing?

During the last two years, I've talked with people who have had to deal with all kinds of life-changing surprises. It seems as if almost everyone has some sort of surprise happen to them, their family, or a friend. The more I talk to people about their experiences, the more amazing stories I hear about how these events brought them together to live as families. Good, functional families where a hole had existed in their lives before.

I pick up a stone and skip it across the river. It travels halfway across before sinking into the water. I watch the ripples blend with the natural disturbance of the current.

Even if I could undo the decision to test my DNA, I doubt I would. In exchange for several uncomfortable months where my emotions were smacked around like a handball, I put to rest a lifetime of self-doubt. I no longer feel like an outsider in my own family. Either one of them. I look and act like one set of siblings . . . and they love me. I look and act different from my other set of siblings . . . and they love me too.

It took two years, but I'm finally at peace with the situation. I don't have to choose one family over the other. I belong to both. And that makes me happy.

With that final thought, my head clears.

I could go back and write, but it's my anniversary. That just doesn't seem appropriate. A celebration like this calls for something family related. Something that embraces discovery. An activity that shows I am no longer afraid of any skeletons that might still be hiding in my closet. I can think of only one thing that fits all those criteria.

Family history research.

I take my time driving home, stopping at Dairy Queen for some ice cream. After all, it is supposed to be a celebration. I understand that most anniversaries don't involve ice cream, but that's just stupid.

—•—

Once again, William "The Immigrant" taunts me. I can hear him say, "You'll never find me, lad. We Lindsays are a clever bunch. Much too clever for the likes of you."

"I've got news for you, William," I tell him . . . suddenly glad no one is in the house to hear me talking to myself. "You've met your match, because I'm going to find you."

A quick search of my usual genealogy sites doesn't reveal that any new records have been added that would help me find William. My best bet still seems to be an out-of-print book about the Lindsays of Lisnacrieve. Published in 1885, it might contain some mention of William or the Crawford family he married into.

I log in to Amazon. They still don't have a hard copy of the book I can buy. I switch over to Google and conduct a search. It produces the same results from the last time I tried to find the book.

Hold on . . .

One of the search results takes me to a web page that offers an electronic version of the book. I hadn't wanted to take a risk on the site before, but it appears to be my only chance to read the information inside.

I order the ebook.

It takes a couple of days, but it finally arrives in my email. I pump my fist in the air and shout, "Yes! This could be it."

Then I open the file and read it. The book tells about the arrival of James Lindsay to the town of Derry, Ireland. In 1689, his four sons fought in the Siege of Derry. One of the sons was killed, but the oldest moved away and built Lisnacrieve. The records for the Lindsays in the area surrounding Fintona seem to be his descendants.

However, the book mentions two other brothers by name and indicates the majority of their children moved to America between 1772 and 1810. If these are my Lindsays, then I've been looking for them in the wrong place. I need to look for them here, in America.

I jot down some notes on the few names and places mentioned for the brothers Robert and David. Then I sit back and contemplate my next move. William seems further out of my grasp than ever before. The only way I can find any of his siblings in North America is to try and track them down through Dad's DNA results.

Why hadn't I thought of that before?

It isn't going to be easy, but I can search through DNA matches to find Lindsays who are part of our family line. Search and compare. Search and compare. Do that enough times and I should be able to place more Lindsays onto our family tree. And they will lead me to William.

The Great Lindsay Quest is on again.

# CHAPTER 23

# MY DAD IS STILL MY DAD

The holidays are finally over. I load the children in the van and drive over to see Dad. Only the three youngest children travel with me, Merlin is eighteen now, and visiting the grandparents no longer interests him. The others climb into the van with their headphones on and immediately stick their noses in their books. They don't say a word all the way there. Whatever stories they are reading have them too absorbed to chat with me.

At least they're reading.

The air is cold. Not Alaskan, freeze-your-face-solid kind of cold. Just the Arizona variety. Chilly enough to make me regret not wearing a jacket but not cold enough to make me go back inside the house and get one. The yard is still wet from recent rain, and the scent of woodsmoke drifts on the air from a nearby fireplace.

I turn on the radio. Christmas music is blissfully absent from the channels. A month and a half of "Jingle Bells" is more than I can handle. I check one station after another for something peppy but don't find anything that suits my mood. Instead, I let my thoughts drift on the waves of post-holiday remembrances.

Dad missed celebrating Christmas with the rest of the family. My stepmother had a cold, and he isn't steady enough to drive himself anymore. I'm sure one of the grandchildren could have driven out and brought him over, but he isn't the kind of man to leave his wife alone on Christmas Day. At least that hasn't changed.

The last two years have brought a tidal wave of unwelcome change. Dad plays golf instead of competing at the local Friday-night rodeos. He uses a cane to walk. And I found out that he isn't my biological father.

None of which seems to bother Dad. In that regard, he remains the same bastion of strength he's always been to me.

I pull onto the dirt road on his property. The corrals are empty. The trees are bare, giving the place an abandoned look. A car is parked in the barn, but there's no sign of a truck. It takes me a moment to remember that Dad doesn't drive anymore. They don't need a truck. They don't need a corral either. They don't even need a barn. The place doesn't feel right to me. This is no longer the kind of horse property where Dad belongs. I don't care how old he is, he deserves horses, and trucks, and a pack of barking dogs.

The children and I march up to the glass door on his porch. I knock, but no one answers. I slide open the door and call out, "We're here."

I can hear the television playing in the living room. Something about the invasion of Normandy. I hurry inside, wondering if Dad is all right. It isn't like him to not answer the door. A pair of quick steps takes me into view of him. He is sleeping in his easy chair. So is his dog.

"Hey, Dad," I call out loudly.

Dad jerks awake. He recognizes me right away and then struggles to rise from his chair. Once he reaches his feet, he stumbles forward. Fortunately, I'm there to catch him. I wrap my arms around him and give him a big squeeze. Not the kind that breaks ribs or crushes the breath out of a person, but a hug that is meant to tell the man just how much I love him.

"I must have fallen asleep," he says. "There's Popsicles in the fridge on the porch. I think they are banana-and-fudge flavor. Help yourself."

The kids each take a turn giving Dad a hug and then head for the goodies. Then they return and sit on the visitors' couch.

"How are the kids doing?" Dad asks.

I give a report on the four still living at home. Each comment I make triggers at least one story from Dad. It takes the most of an hour to update him on how the children are doing, but I don't mind. I love his stories. I always have.

A smile spreads across my face as I sit and listen to him. He masterfully weaves nuggets of wisdom into the tales of his personal experience and seasons them with a bit of humor. The skills I've learned as an author allow me to appreciate his stories on a whole different level from when I was a child sitting at his knee. I literally could sit here all day and listen to his stories.

"Dad," I say, "why don't you record all the stories you tell me?"

"A couple of people have suggested the same thing," he says, "but I told them no."

Dad shakes his head. "Who wants to hear an old man talk about his life? I haven't done anything important. I'm sure as hell not interesting."

They may be his words, but it's my voice I hear speaking them. My life is boring. I can't imagine anyone wanting to read about what I've done, but Dad is a character and has led an incredible life. All right, maybe I'm biased—a little. That doesn't mean I'm wrong, though. I know what makes for a good story, and Dad's life is full of rich, entertaining moments I could weave into an impressive tale.

"I want to write your story as my next project," I tell him.

"You promised me you were going to finish book four," he says.

"Okay. I'll finish that book first."

"What kind of pizza do you guys like?" Dad asks.

The children respond with, "Pepperoni."

"Do you like thin crust?" Dad asks.

The children shrug, obviously not enthused with the suggestion. All right. So they're not the most adventurous eaters in the world. Regular crust. Pepperoni. Extra cheese is acceptable, but that's as far as they are willing to go on their culinary adventure.

I convince the children to go with their grandmother and help her with the pizza. That leaves Dad and me alone. He launches into storytelling mode. One of the stories, I've never heard before. He tells me about a vision he had when I was a child and how it has served as a symbol of faith ever since. I wonder how many more wonderful tales remain unheard inside his head.

He talks about ships and being overseas. I can tell from his comments that there is more to his tale than what he is sharing with me. Stories that are, perhaps, too personal for even family. Or too painful. I can't tell which.

All I know is that I want to hear his stories. I would love to tell them to the world. This is where I belong—the son of a storyteller. It can be no mistake that this man raised me.

Blood doesn't define family. My experiences over the last two years have taught me that. It's about accepting the people who are in my life, despite their faults. Not just accepting them but loving them as well. Embracing my siblings, half-siblings, marriage siblings, children, stepchildren, and adopted children regardless of how much or how little they look like me. To find joy in the ways we are alike and marvel in the diversity of our differences.

It doesn't matter how it happens. People make mistakes. All of us have flaws. What matters is that we are family . . . and family rocks.

It is the love we share that makes us family.